BEN JONSON

English Literature

—————

Editor

JOHN LAWLOR
Professor of English Language and Literature
in the University of Keele

BEN JONSON

J. B. Bamborough
Principal of Linacre College, Oxford

HUTCHINSON UNIVERSITY LIBRARY
LONDON

94531

HUTCHINSON & CO (*Publishers*) LTD
178–202 Great Portland Street, London W1

London Melbourne Sydney
Auckland Johannesburg
Cape Town

First published 1970

*This book has been set in Fournier, printed in Great Britain
on Smooth Wove paper by Anchor Press, and
bound by Wm. Brendon, both of Tiptree, Essex*

ISBN 0 09 101690 8 (cased)
0 09 101691 6 (paper)

CONTENTS

	Preface	7
1	The early comedies	9
2	Jonson's tragedies and masques	50
3	The great comedies	82
4	The last plays	113
5	Jonson's poetry, prose and criticism	151
	Notes	177
	Bibliography	185
	Index	187

PREFACE

There is a considerable mass of scholarly and critical material concerning Jonson, and in writing a book intended primarily for those approaching him for the first time there is a difficult course to be steered between glossing too lightly over points of uncertainty and argument and overweighting a small book with too much detailed reference. Chapter and verse cannot be given for every assertion, and—more regrettably—every debt to others cannot be acknowledged, nor full justice be done to views with which disagreement is expressed. No one who works on Jonson, however, can fail to record his debt to the editors of the great Clarendon Press edition, the basis on which everyone builds.

My thanks are due to Mrs Jill Ratcliff for producing comprehensibility from the chaos of my drafts.

J.B.B.

I

THE EARLY COMEDIES

I

A useful point of departure for the study of Jonson's drama is provided by the Elizabethan critic Willam Webbe. To his *A Discourse of Englishe Poetrie* (1586) Webbe appended 'the Cannons or generall cautions of Poetry, prescribed by Horace', of which the fiftieth runs:

Poets are either such as desire to be liked of on stages, as Commedie and Tragedie wryters, or such as woulde bee regestered in Libraries. Those on stages have speciall respect to the motions of the minde, that they may stirre both the eyes and eares of their beholders. But the other, which seeks to please privately within the walles, take good advisement in their workes, that they may satisfy the exact judgments of learned men in their studies.[1]

Webbe's distinction is between dramatic and non-dramatic poets, but throughout Jonson's lifetime the same line could be drawn between 'popular' and 'closet' dramatists, of whom the first wrote primarily with the idea of performance in mind, apparently often having no further interest in their plays once they had delivered them into the hands of the actors, and the second wrote 'dramatic poems', rarely expecting their works to be performed, and concentrating their efforts on 'satisfying the exact judgments of learned men in their studies'. Much of what is most characteristic in Jonson's work is explained by the fact that all his life he was trying to be both

[1] Superior figures refer to the *Notes*, arranged by chapter, on pp. 177–85.

of these kinds of writer at once, and to produce plays which would successfully 'stir both the eyes and ears' of the theatre audience, but which would also be worthy of being 'registered in libraries'.

It may be that if circumstances had been different Jonson would never have become a dramatist at all. We know little about his early life, but it seems that he was born about 1572, the posthumous child of a clergyman. It is usually assumed that he was born in London, though no record survives. Fuller says:

Benjamin Johnson was born in this City. Though I cannot with all my industrious inquiry *find him* in his *cradle*, I can *fetch him* from his *long coats*. When a *little child*, he lived in *Harts-horn-lane* near *Charing-cross*, where his Mother married a *Bricklayer* for her Second husband;[2]

and there is other evidence to support most of this. Whether he was born in London or not, Jonson spent nearly all his life there, and much of it in the Westminster area. The description of his stepfather as 'a bricklayer' may suggest to us that his early life was more straitened than it actually need have been: a man could be a very substantial builder and still be correctly styled 'citizen and bricklayer' by virtue of his membership of the Bricklayers' and Tilers' Company. Everything suggests, however, that Jonson's background was circumscribed, and that like so many others he depended for his start in life on his brains and his education.

Fuller says 'he was first bred in a private school in Saint *Martin*'s church'—presumably one conducted by the parish clerk of St Martin-in-the-Fields—and 'then at *Westminster* school'. In fact Jonson's name does not appear in the rolls of Westminster, but it is very likely that he did attend the great school so near his home, particularly since he frequently paid tribute to the friendship and guidance of the great scholar and antiquary William Camden—

> CAMDEN, most reverend head, to whom I owe
> All that I am in arts, all that I know. . . ;[3]

when Jonson was young Camden was the Second Master at Westminster.

Camden certainly saw to it that Jonson got a sound classical education. The range of Jonson's scholarship has perhaps always been rather exaggerated by his admirers. Even in the eighteenth century Pope noted, in the preface to his edition of Shakespeare, that the attractive neatness of the antithesis had led critics to emphasise the greatness of Jonson's learning and unjustly minimise Shakespeare's; modern scholarship has shown that he was right, and that Shakespeare's 'wood-notes' are less 'wild' than the eighteenth- and nineteenth-century critics thought they were, while Jonson's displays of massive erudition are not always completely genuine— at least, it can be shown that he frequently depended for his learned references and his citations on encyclopedias, *florilegia* (collections of useful quotations), and other Renaissance short-cuts to learning. In his own day there was nothing shameful about this; our modern insistence on going back to primary sources was unknown. But there is no doubt that Jonson was a good, though not an impeccable, Latin scholar, and if his Greek was less good, it was still very respectable at a time when Greek was often regarded simply as an aid to the study of Latin.[4] He was perhaps not so widely read as Donne (and certainly not as learned as Milton), but even allowing for his use of secondary sources, his range of knowledge was considerable, and the number of his books to survive today is remarkable—especially since he told the Scots poet William Drummond that 'Sundry tymes he heth devoured his bookes [that is], sold them all for Necessity'[5] and that there was a fire in his lodgings in 1623 which must have destroyed many more. He was obviously properly equipped to appeal to 'learned men in their studies', and indeed he mixed freely, and from choice, with the great scholars of the day, men like Raleigh, Selden, and Sir Robert Cotton.

More important than what he actually learned from Camden, however, is the fact that Jonson acquired the scholarly habit of mind. This was not simply a matter of anxious and scrupulous attention to accuracy in matters of detail or of meticulousness in the citing of sources and authorities, though Jonson evidences both. Fundamental to his cast of mind seems to have been a passion for order, logic and consistency, for leaving no loose ends and for bringing everything within a systematic and coherent framework. No doubt this was ultimately a matter of temperament. Indeed, it is possible to see in Jonson the type of Jung's 'introverted artist', whose creative activity is dominated by the need to impose pattern on experience, and by constructing a controlled simulacrum of life to defend himself against the chaos of reality; he takes his place here with Milton and Joyce, with both of whom he has similarities. A desire for order, however, may turn a man into a pedagogue or a policeman as well as into a writer. There was something of the former in Jonson, if not the latter, and we may owe it to Camden that it was to literature that he eventually devoted his talents.

Not everything which Camden taught him may seem to us to

have been beneficial. Late in life Jonson boasted of his retentive memory:

I my selfe could, in my youth, have repeated all, that ever I had made; and so continued, till I was past fortie: Since, it is much decay'd in me. Yet I can repeate whole books that I have read, and *Poems*, of some selected friends, which I have lik'd to charge my memory with.[6]

This was a gift which would have been strengthened at West-minster, for learning by rote and repetition played a large part in the Elizabethan grammar-school system. We might be inclined to wonder whether the ability to recall other people's work is really an advantage to a creative writer, and whether Camden was doing Jonson a service by encouraging him to memorise so much. Our concept of Art, however, is in this respect still dominated by the Romantic insistence on the importance of originality. Jonson's contemporaries did not despise originality, but they certainly did not think it a supreme virtue. Indeed, 'imitation' of other authors was to them not dishonest plagiary, but a positive literary merit, provided always (and the proviso was important) that the borrowed material was not simply copied, but fully adapted and assimilated into one's own work. Boys were taught at school to imitate and 'vary' their set authors; in *Discoveries* Jonson emphasises the need for a novice writer to study and imitate the best models, and notes that it is a requisite for the poet 'to bee able to convert the sub-stance, or Riches of an other *Poet*, to his owne use'.[7] It was sup-posed to be part of the reader's pleasure to recognise the use that had been made of earlier authors and to admire the skilful way in which their writings had been adapted to modern times; this is a delight which few of us nowadays can expect to receive without prompting, although the devoted labours of the commentators have left us in no doubt as to the extent of Jonson's debt to others. Yet, although Dryden's famous phrase describing Jonson's borrowings from the ancients—'you track him everywhere in their snow'[8]—is often quoted, it may still come as a shock to realise that 'Drink to me only with thine eyes' is put together out of pieces from the epistles of Philostratus, or to find Jonson expressing his critical opinion of Shakespeare in *Discoveries* by adapting Seneca's account of a remark made by the Emperor Augustus about a minor Roman rhetorician.

Westminster—or Camden—left a lasting mark on Jonson. We cannot of course say what kind of writer he would have been if he had been educated in a different tradition; what we can see is that he most firmly and consistently embraced the dominant ideas of his time about the nature of literature and the proper methods of authorship, and it does not seem that they were uncongenial to him. Perhaps he was the more ready to demonstrate his allegiance to them because of fear that he might not be regarded as wholly qualified to follow the career of a scholar-writer. We do not know when he left school, though it could not, under the statutes of Westminster, have been long after his eighteenth birthday. Despite some legends, there is no record of his having gone on to a university, as it might have been expected he would. He may have been prevented by his religion, if he was a Roman Catholic at this time, as he certainly was later; more probably his family simply could not afford to support him and he failed to find the rich patron on whom many poor boys relied for their university career. Instead he was apprenticed to his stepfather and worked as a bricklayer when, says Fuller, 'having a *trowell* in his hand, he had a *book* in his pocket'.[9] Not surprisingly he disliked this life, and enlisted as a soldier; this was probably in the early 1590's, and he presumably joined the English forces fighting the Spanish in the Netherlands. He was afterwards very proud of his military service, and refers to it several times, though never to his earlier trade; his enemies, naturally, never let him forget that he had been 'a morter-treader', and 'whoreson poore lyme- and hayre-rascal'; as late as 1601, by which time he was well known as a writer, he could still be referred to as 'the wittiest fellow of a Bricklayer in England'.[10]

How long Jonson served as a soldier is uncertain; in 1597, when we begin to get more definite information about him, he is already connected with the theatre. References to his taking 'mad Jeroni-moes part, to get service among the Mimickes' (i.e. playing the lead in Kyd's *The Spanish Tragedy*), and 'ambling in a leather pilch by a playwagon, in the highway',[11] suggest that he started by joining a touring company; later he appears to have been one of Lord Pembroke's men. Traditionally he was not a good per-former; Aubrey records that, unlike Shakespeare who 'did act exceedingly well', 'B. Jonson was never a good actor, but an excellent instructor'.[12] He may not have continued very long as an actor, although it was no doubt important that, like so many great dramatists, he had had actual practical experience of the theatre in his early life. By the summer of 1597 he had definitely begun his career as a playwright and, very characteristically, had got himself into trouble. The details are obscure, but the play involved was a satirical comedy called *The Isle of Dogs*, of which the original version or the original idea was Thomas Nashe's. According to

Nashe's own account, he himself wrote only the Introduction and the first Act: the rest was completed by someone else, presumably Jonson, and this was the part which gave offence. Since the play is lost we cannot know why it caused such a furore, but the Privy Council took it sufficiently seriously to close all the theatres, to arrest some of the actors, Jonson among them, and to have them interrogated by a special commission. The excitement seems to have subsided fairly quickly: the prisoners were released early in October and the theatres were reopened shortly afterwards. Some of Pembroke's men who were involved went over to Henslowe, and from this time onwards Jonson appears regularly in Henslowe's *Diary* as a writer of plays. Nothing he wrote for Henslowe has survived except the famous 'Additions' to *The Spanish Tragedy*, if indeed they are his.[13] By the autumn of 1598, however, he was well enough known for Francis Meres to include him in *Palladis Tamia* as among 'our best for Tragedie', along with Marlowe, Kyd, Shakespeare, and some others, and by the end of 1598, when he was about twenty-six, the success of *Every Man in his Humour*, played by the Lord Chamberlain's men, firmly established him as a playwright.

So far there is nothing unusual about Jonson's career; the drift of impoverished intellectuals into the theatre was a commonplace of Elizabethan life. It seems very unlikely, however, that it is what Jonson would have chosen for himself. By temperament and training he was better fitted for the life of a scholar, and when he could he associated with scholars and men of learning. Playwriting was certainly a way of earning money (though the financial rewards were not very great), but it was not a highly esteemed profession, and it put him on a footing with other writers for whose learning and style, as well as for whose morals, he could only feel contempt. Indeed, Jonson more than once expresses his regret that he was forced into the theatre. In the 'Apologetical Dialogue' which he published with *Poetaster*, he refers to the charge made by his enemies that he wrote slowly, producing only one play a year, and adds:

> 'Tis true.
> I would, they could not say that I did that,
> There's all the joy I take i'their trade,
> Unless such Scribes as they might be proscrib'd
> The'abused theaters . . .   (194–8)

He made an even franker reference to his distaste for his profession in 1605, when he was in prison once again, this time for giving offence to the Scots in *Eastward Ho!*, a play he wrote in collaboration with Chapman and Marston. Writing to Lord Salisbury to ask for help, he explains the cause of his imprisonment:

The Cause (would I could name some worthier . . . is, a (the word yrkes mee, that our Fortune hath necessitated us to so despised a Course) a Play, my Lord . . .[14]

This need not imply that Jonson never took pleasure in writing his plays, still less that his genius was not for the theatre at all. No one could write with the energy and zest which Jonson displays without rejoicing in the exercise of his creative power; nor are his plays at all like those of later writers—the Romantic poets, for example—who had no talent for drama and wrote plays only because they felt they should. Jonson was a born man of the theatre; he had a natural flair for the creation of dramatic illusion and excitement. Nevertheless it cannot be without significance that in the decade 1616–26, when he had a steady income from his work as a writer of Court masques—a more noble and refined form of dramatic art—he was prepared to give up the public theatre altogether. Popular playwriting was not a fit occupation for a scholar, and it must have irked him beyond endurance when his enemies sanctimoniously forgave him the badness of his plays because he was driven to write them by his poverty. Just as, lacking the stamp of a university education, he had constantly to demonstrate his learning and his understanding of the best literary doctrines, so it was vitally necessary for him to demonstrate that the writing of plays could be a worthy vocation, and that he was no less deserving of the respect of the learned for having embraced it. The challenge offered him was a severe one, and his response to it was vigorous and sustained.

He lost no opportunity to defend Poetry against all its enemies, and by 'poetry' he understood all forms of creative writing (he always referred to his own plays as 'poems'). One of his earliest defences is also one of his best. In the first version of *Every Man in his Humour* Lorenzo junior bursts out, in answer to his father's observation that Poetry is abjectly ranked in the World's opinion:

Opinion, O God let grosse opinion
Sinck & be damnd as deepe as *Barathrum*.
If it may stand with your most wisht content,
I can refell opinion, and approve

> The state of poesie, such as it is,
> Blessed, aeternall, and most true devine:
> Indeede if you will looke on Poesie,
> As she appeares in many, poore and lame,
> Patcht vp in remnants and olde worne ragges,
> Halfe starvd for want of her peculiar foode,
> Sacred invention, then I must conferme,
> Both your conceite and censure of her merrite.
> But view her in her glorious ornaments,
> Attired in the majestie of arte,
> Set high in spirite with the precious taste
> Of sweete philosophie, and which is most,
> Crownd with the rich traditions of a soule,
> That hates to have her dignitie prophand,
> With any relish of an earthly thought:
> Oh then how proud a presence doth she beare.
> Then is she like her selfe, fit to be seene
> Of none but grave and consecrated eyes: (V.iii.312–33)

The argument is the same as Sidney's in his *Apologie for Poetrie*; it may be true that poetry is despised, but this is because many so-called poets are unworthy of the name—'leane, ignorant and blasted wits', Lorenzo calls them. True poets are rare, for good poetry can only be written by good men, men who are both intellectually and morally superior to ordinary mortals. If the world will look upon the work of these men, it will see Poetry as it really should be, and cannot fail to value it at its true worth.

It was the function of the true poet both to write well himself and to attack and destroy bad writing; Jonson speaks in the Dedication to *Volpone* of his ambition to

> raise the despis'd head of *poetrie* againe, and stripping her out of those rotten and base rags, wherwith the Times have adulterated her form, restore her to her primitive habit, feature, and majesty, and render her worthy to be imbraced, and kist, of all the great and master-*spirits* of our world.[15]

However great the element of personal vanity in this—and obviously in raising the status of his art Jonson was dignifying his own position—it was no unworthy aim, and he set about achieving it manfully. The insistence that his plays should be regarded as 'poems'—that is, as serious works of literature—was a move in his campaign, as was the care which he took in printing and publishing them. Many dramatists were, like Marston, ready to admit that their plays were only printed because it was customary,[16], but Jonson prepared his texts meticulously and made each quarto almost a showpiece; his master-stroke was the publication of his *Works* in Folio in 1616. If it now seems ridiculous to us that plays were once not considered to be literature, this is because of a shift in the position of the playwright which Jonson more than anyone else initiated.

Publishing his plays in this way was obviously to challenge the attention of Webbe's 'learned men in their studies'. It does not follow that Jonson was not interested in popular success. He could be scornful enough of the applause of the ordinary theatre-goer— 'fomie praise, that drops from common jawes', he calls it in the Prologue to *Cynthia's Revels*—and the story how he,

> (having composed a Play of excellent worth, but not of equal applause), fell downe upon his knees, and gave thankes, that he had transcended the capacity of vulgar,[17]

may be apocryphal, but is certainly not out of character. But his most savage attacks on popular taste tended to come after one of his plays had failed—by no means an uncommon thing with writers—and at times he was ready to be almost humble in his appeal for the favour of his audience. Financially, of course, he needed success, nor should we let ourselves be too readily deceived by the mask of bluff independence he habitually assumed; very few writers indeed have been truly indifferent to success or failure. What Jonson would not allow himself to do was to pander to the vices of popular taste, or to reproduce the faults of his fellow-playwrights.

He saw very clearly what those faults were, and throughout his life he maintained a consistent attack upon them. His major charge against contemporary drama was that it was immoral, or at best frequently failed to be positively and obviously moral—the same charge that Dr Johnson was later to make against Shakespeare; many popular plays were full of 'ribaldry, profanation, all licence of offence to God, and man'. This was something of which he could claim that he himself was guiltless, or almost completely so: there is hardly ever any moral ambiguity in his plays, and he is remarkably free from the obscene jokes and double meanings which his comtemporaries seem almost to a man to have been quite unable to resist. To Jonson, again, the subject-matter of many contemporary plays was trivial and conventional, and their plots repetitive and absurd;

there was too much reliance on violent and noisy action—battles, sea-fights, tempests, and so on—and (as Sidney also complained) a wanton disregard of probability and verisimilitude, together with startling and unnecessary jumps in space and time. More generally, Jonson objected to the failure to keep the separate *genres* of drama apart, so that instead of 'correct' tragedies and true comedies, the public was offered a Polonius-like hotch-potch of 'Pastoral-Comical, Historical-Pastoral, Tragical-Historical, Tragical-Comical-Historical-Pastoral' absurdities. Lastly, and by no means least disastrously, the drama he saw around him contained so much bad writing: many solecisms, much bombast and nonsense, and a welter of stale and feeble jests. With all this there could be no compromise.

Publicly attacking these errors was a necessary part of Jonson's struggle to 'raise the despis'd head of *poetrie* again', but only a part. He had also to demonstrate *how* comedy and tragedy should be written, and on what principles, for it was a basic assumption of Renaissance critical theory that every literary 'kind' had its own rules of form and style which the correct writer had to know and observe. Much effort had already gone, in France and Italy, into arguments about the proper forms of drama, but there was hardly an agreed body of rules for him to follow. Jonson was not in any case ready to accept uncritically rules formulated by others. He subcribed in general terms to the literary precepts of his age, but he reserved his right to work out the details of his own Art, making use of whatever insights were available from classical and modern writers and critics. Very little thinking of this kind had been done in England, and Jonson was quite ready to assume the role of the first law-giver of the English stage. Not very long before he died he wrote some verses to be prefixed to *The Northern Lass*, a comedy by Richard Brome, his friend and former servant; in them he refers rather patronisingly to the 'good applause' which Brome has justly gained from the Stage

> By observation of those Comick Lawes
>   Which I, your *Master*, first did teache the Age;[18]

he may not have been wholly serious in this, but the claim was not unjustified.

In starting to construct his own dramatic rules, Jonson was faced among other problems with the necessity of achieving a harmonious combination of the native and the classical traditions in the theatre. Renaissance scholarship had made classical drama (and especially comedy) much more available, so that in a way it seemed more modern and exciting than what still survived of the medieval vernacular tradition. No dramatist, unless he were content to appeal to only the lowest and least cultivated play-goers, could afford to seem ignorant of the lessons to be learned from the classical writers and their modern imitators. On the other hand popular taste still demanded the kind of satisfactions provided by native drama, and only the closet dramatist could afford to ignore this demand completely. Jonson depended on popular favour for his livelihood, but even if this had not been so he might not have abandoned the English traditions; certainly he was very much steeped in earlier native drama and constantly made use of it in his own work.

The two traditions were not totally incompatible, but while the neo-classical tended towards intensiveness, exclusion of irrelevance, verisimilitude, and unity of tone, survival of the medieval tradition in native drama made for discursiveness, variety, a kaleidoscopic alternation of mood, and a carelessness about probability and consistency. Their essential qualities can be summed up as control on the one hand, and exuberance on the other, and the combination of the two is the most marked characteristic of Jonson's work. Nor does there seem to be the struggle between the two which we might expect. The impression Jonson gives is not one of wildness struggling against restraint; it is rather of a very carefully and precisely ordered framework to which is added lavish (and sometimes excessive) ornamentation. The best image for this is the kind of Jacobean design of which the title-pages of the different plays in his own Folio are an example, in which a symmetrical, more or less 'classical' framework is filled with a rich intermixture of classical motifs and traditional symbols. It is for this reason also that the rather old-fashioned debate as to whether Jonson should properly be called a 'classical' or a 'native' writer is rather beside the point. He was both: we normally approach him after reading Shakespeare and Marlowe, and in comparison with them he is bound to seem severe and disciplined; to a foreign critic, such as his French biographer Maurice Castelain, brought up on the formalities of Racine and Corneille, he is more likely to seem irregular and self-indulgent. It is true also that as it progressed through the seventeenth century the neo-classical movement grew stricter, to the point where the Ancients themselves were criticised for not being classical enough. Jonson came nearly at the beginning of this movement in England, and his neo-classicism was of a very English kind.

We cannot in any case see the classical drama as the critics of the Renaissance saw it: they read it differently and for different reasons. Study of 'literary influence' always shows that what one country or age borrows from the literature of another may not be a very prominent feature of the original—indeed it may be something that is not really there at all; but it is always something that the borrowers admire, and find lacking in their own literature. What the Renaissance saw in the classical dramatists seems to have been above all sophistication and skill—sophistication in tone and style, skill in construction. Construction in particular was a problem to the Elizabethan playwrights, for they had inherited very little notion of dramatic form. The Middle Ages, indeed, apparently regarded drama only as a special kind of narrative or chronicle and, even after Jonson had been writing for some time, less scholarly dramatists than he were producing History plays of which the only constructional principle was that of the King of Hearts—'begin at the beginning and go on till you come to the end: then stop'. Jonson devoted especial attention to the articulation of his plays, working out his own principles and experimenting freely, and his superb skill in plotting and the manipulation of action distinguishes him from his contemporaries more perhaps than any other of his strengths. There are never any loose ends or unexplained incidents in his plays, nor any faltering of his control over his material, and there is no other Elizabethan or Jacobean dramatist of whom this could be said.

The learned drama began in Italy with the adaptation of the plots of classical comedies to modern circumstances, and the putting together of bits from separate classical plays to form new wholes. *The Case is Altered* seems to show Jonson starting in the second way, although since it may not be wholly his (and almost certainly contains more than one layer of composition), it would be dangerous to deduce too much from it. It happens that the two plays by Plautus on which it is based—*Captivi* and *Aulularia*—are very good examples of the 'romance' elements in classical comedy: they involve, that is, much play with mistaken identity, young lovers at cross-purposes, and even the restoration of a long-lost child. The result is very unlike the kind of play we expect from Jonson, and indeed it is a good deal nearer to Shakespearean comedy than he ever came again. Parts of *The Case is Altered* are reminiscent of *The Two Gentlemen of Verona* and *The Merchant of Venice*, and its two heroines are quite like Beatrice and Hero in *Much Ado*. The high-life characters are motivated by ideals of love and friendship in a way only elsewhere found in *The New Inn*, although they are surrounded by a large group of low-class comic figures who are much closer to the types we expect to find in Jonsonian comedy. There is in fact a distinct gap between the two levels and a sense of strain in the tone of the play which would be unremarkable in another Elizabethan dramatist, but which Jonson usually succeeded in avoiding.

Obviously he was not satisfied with *The Case is Altered*, since he did not print it in his *Works*. *Every Man in his Humour* is a much better attempt at naturalising classical forms (though it should be said that the earlier play would be thought very creditable for many of Jonson's contemporaries). *Every Man in* is modelled on the comedies of Terence: that is, it is concerned with a conflict between generations ending with victory by the gay and lively younger age-group over the older, and the mainsprings of its action are the demands of love and the machinations of an intriguing servant. There are modifications of the typical pattern, however, which accord with Jonson's own views about the proper nature of comedy. The father is severe, and perhaps even priggish, but he is neither tyrannical nor absurd—certainly nothing like the pantaloon he would have been in an Italian comedy of this *genre*; the son is quick and witty, but he is not in the least vicious or immoral, as the young men sometimes are in this kind of play. More obviously still, the love-story is pushed right out of the centre of the picture; the lover is not the son, who is the nearest thing to the 'hero' of the play, but his friend, and the affair occupies very little stage-time at all. We are so used to this off-hand treatment of romantic love in Jonson—only in *The New Inn*, of all his plays, does it play a central role in the action—that we need to remind ourselves how extraordinary it was to suppress this essential element of Roman comedy. Instead Jonson concentrates our attention on a large group of comic characters, and particularly on Mosco, the servant, and Bobadilla, the braggart soldier. Both of these were stereotypes of neo-classical comedy, but Jonson succeeded not merely in 'englishing' them (even in the earlier, Italianate version of the play), but in giving them much more roundness and depth than they would ever have in an Italian *commedia erudita*. Bobadilla, overcome by confusion at being discovered by Matheo in his poverty-stricken lodging and begging Matheo not to tell people where he lives because he 'would not be so popular and generall, as some be', and Mosco, in his disguise as an old soldier, offering to sell his sword to Lorenzo and Stephano—'you seeme to be gentlemen well-affected to martiall men, els I should rather die with silence, than live with shame'—have the genuine note of a kind of human

experience we could all share. In the same way, though not quite
to the same extent, Jonson rounds out the characters of Thorello
('the suspicious man') and Giuliano ('the irascible man'), and
succeeds in making these type-characters mingle easily with the
more native 'gulls' Matheo and Stephano, and the very traditional
English clown Cob and Tib his wife (Jonson never bothered even
in the early version of *Every Man in* to italianise their names).

It is this that must have impressed the Elizabethan audience:
almost for the first time it had a dramatist combining, with what
seemed effortless ease, the constructive ability and sophistication
of the classics with indigenous comic figures and native humour, a
dramatist capable of pleasing both 'the judicious' and 'the vulgar'.
But the success of *Every Man in his Humour* depended also on
something else; it was one of those plays, like Coward's *The
Vortex* or Osborne's *Look Back in Anger*, that exactly hit the taste
of the time. The last years of the sixteenth century were marked by
a sudden burst of satirical writing distinguishable in kind from
earlier English satire. In the early 1590's the work of Nashe, Green
and the other prose pamphleteers was often satirically outspoken,
but although it could be sharp and homiletic, it was frequently
quite jovial and relaxed. The verse satire of the last half of the
decade, though it took over many of the themes and topics of the
prose satirists, was altogether harsher and more bitter in tone:
adjectives such as 'biting', 'snarling' and 'whipping' were used to
describe the new collections of poems and epigrams, and the
satirists were apt to represent themselves as surgeons lancing the
foul sores of Society or 'probing' the country's ulcers 'to the
quick'. Many causes have been suggested for this shift of mood:
disillusion with the ageing Queen and her sycophantic Court;
economic distress coupled with open corruption; growing luxury
accompanied by moral laxity; religious doubt and the undermining
of accepted standards; over-education and the consequent unem-
ployment of intellectuals; even the spread of venereal disease. Any
or all of these causes may have been operative, but in large measure
it was a question of a shift in literary taste. The work of scholars
on the Continent had brought new classical authors into prominence
and made them more available for study and imitation. In prose the
change was from the orotund polish and balance of Cicero to the
terse, aphoristic, 'pointed' style of Seneca, Tacitus and the Roman
moralists and historians; in verse the models became, instead of
Ovid and Petrarch, the Roman satirists, Persius, Juvenal, Martial
and (to a lesser degree) Horace. Stylistically it was a move away
from what Ezra Pound called the 'upholstered' Elizabethan manner

and towards a more direct and down-to-earth, though witty and 'conceited', tone; it is familiar to us in the contrast between Spenser and Donne. Donne, too, is an example of the new type of intellectual who wrote and enjoyed this kind of poetry; neither a high priest of literature like Spenser, endeavouring to 'fashion a gentleman or noble person in vertuous and gentle discipline' nor a politically and morally suspect Bohemian like Marlowe, but a writer gay yet learned, witty but fundamentally serious, and, even to us, very 'modern'. Jonson knew Donne as a friend and admired much of his work; he also had many friends like Donne, educated in the Inns of Court, and it was to them he dedicated *Every Man out of his Humour*.

The out-spokenness and not infrequent obscenity of the verse epigrams and satires led in 1599 to a ban on their publication, and it has been suggested that Jonson at this point consciously decided to transfer the topics and some of the style of this type of writing to the stage.[19] As a theory this is a little too neat, and will not quite cover the facts—verse satire continued to be written, for instance, after 1599, and 'satirical comedy' of a kind had been seen on the stage before that. It is more likely that in producing his English version of Terentian comedy Jonson was quite naturally influenced by the fashionable satirical tone of the day, and found that the amalgan produced in *Every Man in his Humour* was a very success-ful one. It is what he did then that is so characteristic—and more truly original than a simple decision to transfer the satirical mode to the stage. The standing temptation for a writer who has scored a success with a novel or play is to try and repeat it—and some writers go on doing this very successfully all their lives. Jonson did not simply set out to capitalise on the success of *Every Man in his Humour* by repeating its effects in a second 'Humour' play. Instead he seems to have set himself to consider seriously what the proper form of Comedy was, what its role, and how it related to Satire; as a result *Every Man out of his Humour* despite the simi-larity of title, is quite a different sort of play from its predecessor.

II

In considering the true nature of Comedy, Jonson could not lean much on the classics. Little of what the Ancients had written on the subject survived, and what remained was not altogether satisfactory. Not only did they rank it below Tragedy and Epic, as might have been expected; they tended to speak of it as a rather suspect form of Art. Laughter, to them, was a not wholly reputable emotion, in

that it tended too much towards the sardonic—that is, it was an
expression of pleasure in which there was mixed a good deal of envy,
hate and bitterness. Thus, while it was useful to the orator to be
able to discredit an opponent by making him appear ridiculous,
anyone who aimed consistently to make people laugh at others
could not be a wholly good man. In this there may have been, as
some modern scholars have thought, a survival of the fear of the
spiteful jester in primitive societies, where a man may literally die of
shame if mocked; and certainly some of the ancient Greek writers
had the reputation of having brought men to their death by the
virulence of their poetic attacks. But without harking back to the
traumas of pre-history, we can all recognise in ourselves a certain
anxiety in the company of someone who continually makes fun
of everybody; it is amusing as long as he is talking about other
people, but we can never be sure he won't start on us. Classical
writers habitually made a distinction between 'liberal' and 'illiberal'
jesting—between, that is, the sort of jokes a decent, well-bred man
may make without causing offence to anyone, and the coarse,
offensive mockery of the *scurra* or buffoon—and it was very
important to Jonson to maintain that he always carefully kept on
the right side of that line, and that his 'manners', as he put it in the
Dedication of *Every Man in his Humour*, would not make his
'most learned and honoured friend' Camden blush. This was
doubly important because the reputation of native comedy was
also not high; Jonson could not fail to be aware of the equivocal
position of the comic writer whom, Sidney said, 'naughtie Play-
makers and Stage-keepers have justly made odious',[20] and it was a
handicap that the Ancients had not praised Comedy more warmly.

There was some help to be got, however, from the classical and
Renaissance theorists, and more from other playwrights, and
Jonson was prepared to avail himself of it, though neither then nor
later was he prepared to be a slavish follower of other men's ideas.
He prepared *Every Man out of his Humour* as a demonstration piece,
and when he published it in 1600 he surrounded the text with a
commentary by a two-man Chorus whose duty it is to explain his
principles to the reader and to defend them where necessary. At
the end of Act III, scene vi, Mitis, who fills the role of Innocent
Enquirer, raises the question of what a Comedy really is, and
Cordatus ('the author's friend') produces the definition which was
attributed to Cicero, that it should be *Imitatio vitae, Speculum
consuetudinis, Imago veritatis*; he adds that it should be 'a thing
throughout pleasant, and ridiculous, and accommodated to the
correction of manners'. The last part of this may be a direct quota-

tion from Plautus, but it is more generally in the spirit of the tag
from Horace which Jonson quotes more often than any other
critical dictum:

> Aut prodesse volunt, aut delectare Poetae
> Aut simul et jocunda et idonea dicere vitae,

or in his own translation,

> Poets must either profit, or delight,
> Or mixing sweet, and fit, teach life the right.[21]

The principle that literature should instruct was as basic to Renaissance theory as the principle that it should obey the proper rules—
or perhaps we might take 'to be conducive to the moral good of
the public' as the first and more important of the Rules. Cordatus'
conjunction of the two insights from Cicero and Horace immediately sharply defines the kind of comedy that Jonson was proposing
to write. If it was to be an Imitation of Life, 'the glass of custom'
and an image of the Truth, then it was clearly to be realistic, in
some sense of that notoriously ambiguous critical term. And if we
take Realism to mean faithfulness to the audible and visible sur-
faces of life, then Jonson is always realistic, as he is, too, if we
equate 'realism' with 'credibility'; not all his characters and incidents
are equally acceptable, but he never demands from us the unwilling
suspension of disbelief. But the required element of didacticism at
once restricts the area of his realism—for in real life events do not
always neatly illustrate moral principles—and so also do some
other of the classical principles which he accepted. Aristotle, for
example, had laid it down that while Tragedy represented people as
better than they are in real life, Comedy showed them as worse. It
was also generally agreed among literary theoreticians that comic
characters should not be of more than middling social status, so
that people who were noble either in birth or in character (and there
are some in real life) were excluded from the comic playwrights'
purview. Another generally agreed precept was that it was 'illiberal'
to make jokes about serious or painful matters, and from this it
followed that Comedy should deal only with comparatively trivial
accidents and embarrassments, or as Jonson himself put it in the
prologue to *Every Man in his Humour*, should 'sport with human
follies, not with crimes'; this was yet another sharp constraint.

In view of this last rule it is even more astonishing that Jonson
should have been prepared almost totally to abandon the love-story

as a motivating force in his comedy. To the writers of the classical 'New Comedy' Love had been the most useful of the emotions, for if could bring about misunderstanding, confusion, and all kinds of extravagant and ridiculous actions without ever causing serious distress or unresolvable complications; and in this of course they have been followed by countless modern novelists and dramatists. Just before Cordatus utters his definition of Comedy, Mitis asks why the 'argument' of *Every Man out of his Humour* could not have been of another kind:

> as of a duke to be in love with a countesse, and that countesse to bee in love with the dukes sonne, and the sonne to love the ladies waiting maid: some such crosse wooing, with a clown to their servingman, better then to be thus neere, and familiarly allied to the time.
>
> (III.vi.196–201)

Many have thought that Jonson was glancing here at *Twelfth Night*, or at Shakespearean comedy in general. In fact he was dismissing some three-quarters of the comic plots of the world, and accepting the most radical limitation that can be imagined on his range as a comic writer. Exactly why he was prepared to do this we cannot know. Perhaps he felt Love to be not sufficiently serious and weighty a matter for his genius; certainly he appears to have recognised (correctly) that it was not a subject about which he wrote easily. Whatever the reason, this was the most truly original thing he ever did.

If Jonsonian comedy was to be moral, realistic, and 'familiarly allied to the time'—or, as we might say now, 'of contemporary relevance'—and if it was to work as comedy in the theatre by the simple test of provoking laughter, then it was almost inevitable that it should be satirical. This would have been so even if satire had not been agreeable to contemporary taste and also, one may suspect, in line with Jonson's own attitude to life. There was, moreover, an established historical connection between satire and comedy, since it was generally accepted in the Renaissance that comedy had its origins in the Ancient Greek 'satyr plays', rough, rustic farces in which it was supposed that the dramatists

presented the lives of Satyers, so that they might wisely, under the abuse of that name, discover the follies of many theyr foolish fellow citesens.[22]

This proto-comedy was believed to have developed in time into the 'Old Comedy' of Aristophanes, which had a more direct moral intent and ridiculed named offenders against the canons of Society,

and this in turn became the 'New Comedy' in which actual persons
were no longer represented on the stage but general follies were
attacked in their typical guises. This genealogy was helped by
semantic confusion of the words 'satyr' and 'satire' (which have
quite different philological origins), and Jonson could thus rely on
any educated person understanding what he was after when he
called *Every Man out of his Humour* a 'comicall satyre'. In the first
Chorus he made his intention even plainer by making Cordatus
refer to the play as 'of a particular kind by itself, somewhat like
Vetus Comœdia'. Exactly what Jonson understood in his various
references to the *Vetus Comœdia* or 'Old Comedy' is not always
clear, but here he seems definitely to be referring to the sort of
Comedy that Aristophanes wrote, as he did again when he referred
in the 'Apologeticall Dialogue' after *Poetaster* to 'the salt'—that is,
the wit and sharpness—'in the old *comedy*'. He was serving notice,
in fact, that he was not going to repeat the more urbane Plautine
or Terentian modes of *The Case is Altered* and *Every Man in his
Humour*, but was going to intensify the satirical element in both
and aim at a style of comedy at once more savage, more moral and
more intellectual.

This was a dangerous proclamation to make. It was the fierce
and outspoken indignation of Juvenal's work, sometimes described
as 'tragical satire' because of its intensity and its use of the high
style, which struck the imagination of the later Elizabethans, and
many writers had found the pose of the savage, high-minded
flayer of the evils of Society a very satisfying one to adopt. This
type of satirist had become a stock figure in literature and on the
stage: in fact a secondary *genre* of 'satire-of-satire' had sprung up.
It was easy to attack the satirist by saying he was just as bad as
everyone else and only wrote out of envy (this is the gambit the
Duke uses against Jaques in *As You Like It*); possible even to
represent him as a sinister figure who could easily slip over into the
role of the 'politician' or Machiavellian intriguer. To guard himself
against this kind of attack Jonson adopted an elaborate strategy. At
the beginning of *Every Man out* he introduces Asper (the name
means 'sharp', and the adjective was frequently used to describe
Roman satire), who is said to be 'of an ingenious and free spirit,
eager and constant in reproofe, without fear controuling the world's
abuses'—that is, the archetype of the fearless moralist. Asper
begins very much in the High Style in the Induction:

> Who is so patient of this impious world,
> That he can checke his spirit, or reine his tongue?

Or who hath such a dead unfeeling sense,
That heavens horrid thunders cannot wake?
To see the earth, crackt with the weight of sinne,
Hell gaping under us, and o're our heads
Blacke rav'nous ruine, with her saile-stretcht wings,
Ready to sinke us downe, and cover us.
Who can behold such prodigies as these,
And have his lips seal'd up? not I: my language
Was never ground into such oyly colours,
To flatter vice and daube iniquitie:
But (with an armed, and resolved hand)
Ile strip the ragged follies of the time,
Naked, as at their birth . . .
          . . . and with a whip of steele,
Print wounding lashes in their yron ribs.
I feare no mood stampt in a private brow,
When I am pleas'd t'unmaske a publicke vice.
I feare no strumpets drugs, nor ruffians stab,
Should I detect their hatefull luxuries:
No brokers, usurers, or lawyers gripe,
Were I dispos'd to say, they're all corrupt . . .   (5–15,19–26)

Cordatus and Mitis try to calm him down, and when he espies the
spectators round him he modifies his tone considerably:

Gracious, and kind spectators, you are welcome,
APOLLO, and the MUSES feast your eyes
With gracefull objects, and may our MINERVA
Answere your hopes. . . .   (52–5)

He is quick to add, however, that he is not speaking them fair out
of any servile wish to win their favour or because he doubts his
own merit; indeed he welcomes criticism:

Let me be censur'd, by th'austerest brow,
Where I was arte, or judgment, taxe me freely . . .   (60–1)

This is a fair statement of the position Jonson always took up, a
confident offering of his work to the consideration of the 'judicious'.
For 'attentive auditors', Asper later says (201–4):

Such as will join their profit with their pleasure,
And come to feed their understanding parts:
For these I'll prodigally spend myself. . . ;

throughout his life Jonson consistently claimed that he was ready to devote every effort to please those who really tried to understand what he was trying to do, and to accept their judgment willingly.

Cordatus and Mitis remind Asper of the dangers he is running, and warn him of the offence that will be taken by those who apply his strictures to their own lives, and he answers with a return to his grandest manner:

> If any, here, chance to behond himselfe,
> Let him not challenge me of wrong,
> For, if he shame to have his follies knowne,
> First he should shame to act'hem: my strict hand
> Was made to seaze on vice, and with a gripe
> Squeeze out the humour of such spongie natures,
> As lick up every idle vanity.   (140–6)

In fact, 'if the cap fits, let them wear it'—the stock defence of the satirist. Jonson many times complains about the 'application' of his satirical portraits to particular people, attributing it either to ignorant misunderstanding of his purpose or to deliberate and malicious twisting of his meaning. This was undoubtedly disingenuous, as most disclaimers of this sort are: he may very probably have been portraying some real persons in *Every Man out of his Humour* and he certainly did so in *Poetaster* and some others of his plays; but he always maintains his innocence with such fervour that we are almost convinced that he believed in it. Perhaps he regarded this kind of self-defence as a conventional part of the satirist's role, as well as having at least some value as an insurance against trouble.

Cordatus tries to protect Asper, by commenting on this last speech

> Why, this is right *Furor Poeticus*,

and asking the audience to bear with him:

> Kind gentlemen, we hope your patience
> Will yet conceive the best, or entertaine,
> This supposition, that a mad-man speakes,   (147–50)

the suggestion being that Asper has been carried away by a combination of moral and poetical fervour. When the play proper begins, Asper plays the part of Macilente, the Envious Man, who maliciously attacks those around him because he is 'violently impatient of any opposite happiness in others'. He thus fills the role of intriguer and discomforter of others, and as such he is capable of really mean actions. Jonson has, however, doubly safeguarded himself against attack on this count: Macilente is not Asper, but only a part played by Asper, and like the other characters he is cured of his envious 'humour' at the end of the play; Asper is not Jonson, or if he is, he is Jonson carried away by moral fervour and 'poetical fury', and not at all actuated by envy or spleen. To avoid another kind of charge, Jonson included the character of Carlo Buffone, who may be based on a real person, but is in any case the typical *scurra*, an illiberal jester who mocks everyone without regard to tact, or truth, or loyalty ('Friend! is there any such foolish thing in the world?'). He too is finally shaken 'out of his humour', and we are meant to see that Jonson was as much against this type of satire as anyone else.

Jonson had thus defined his new kind of drama and made clear his stance: he had also to specify what he regarded as the proper objects of his satire. He had voluntarily discarded the lover as a subject, and had accepted rules which prevented him from dealing with criminals, or anyone who deviated seriously from the norm of human behaviour. In the *Induction* to *Every Man out of his Humour* he states the kind of person he regards as appropriate for his attack, and in so doing defines the 'Comedy of Humours'. It is the innocent Mitis as usual who initiates this passage by casually using the word 'humour'. Asper asks him what he means by this, and Mitis, not unexpectedly, is unable to answer. Asper then expounds the true meaning of the word, saying, correctly, that it is properly a medical term referring to one of the substances, choler (or 'yellow bile'), melancholy (or 'black bile'), phlegm and blood, which were supposed to circulate in the body, and to give a man his distinctive 'temperament' or physical and psychological character; an excess of choler in the blood made a man quick and irascible, an excess of phlegm, slow and lethargic, and so on; we still use the humoral terminology freely today. Strictly speaking there could only be four Humour types—choleric, phlegmatic, sanguine and melancholic—although the list could be extended to six by including the man of perfect temper, in whom the humours were in exactly equal proportion, and the 'mercurial man', in whose constitution the preponderant humour changed frequently, so that he could be choleric at one moment, melancholic the next, and so on. If Jonson had been proclaiming his intention to limit himself to characters who were 'Humorous' in this strict sense, as has sometimes been said,

he would thus have had a very restricted cast indeed. He does have
some characters who are perfect examples of this kind of 'humour':
Waspe, the testy servant in *Bartholomew Fair*, is a pure choleric,
and Cokes, his foolish master, may be regarded as having the
typical feebleness of wit of the phlegmatic; Crites in *Cynthia's
Revels* is described as being of the 'perfect temperament', in which
all the humours are equally balanced. Comparatively few of
Jonson's characters will yield to this analysis, however, and his
range is obviously very much wider.

Asper goes on to say that by an allowable extension of meaning
one can use 'humour' in the sense of 'master passion' or *idée fixe*:

> As when some one peculiar quality
> Doth so possess a man, that it doth draw
> All his affects, his spirits and his powers,
> In their confluctions, all to runne one way . . .   (105–8)

There are many characters in Jonsonian comedy who have a humour
in this sense—Morose, for example, with his passionate hatred of
noise, or Mammon, who is dominated by his greed and sensuality.
Asper then proceeds to speak of another use of 'humour', and this
time one of which he thoroughly disapproves—the loose colloquial sense in which the unfortunate Mitis has just used the word. In
the 1590's 'humour' had come to be used as a cant word rather as
'complex' is used today; an Elizabethan might say that it was 'his
humour' to dislike cats, much as we might say that we have a
complex (or 'a thing') about them. It could be applied to the most
trivial things:

> Ask *Humors* why a feather he doth weare?
> It is his humor (by the Lord) he'll swear![23]

Usually, however, one's 'humour' was something on which one
prided oneself, because it was something which marked one out
from the common run of mankind, a singularity which indicated
one's superiority of character or class.

It is this cant use that Asper attacks:

> But that a rooke, in wearing a pyed feather,
> The cable hat-band, or the three-pild ruffe,
> A yard of shooetye, or the *Switzers* knot
> On his *French* garters, should affect a Humour!
> O, 'tis more then most ridiculous,   (110–4)

and he goes on

> Well I will scourge those apes;
> And to these courteous eyes oppose a mirror,
> As large as is the stage whereon we act;
> Where they shall see the times deformitie
> Anatomiz'd in every nerve, and sinnew . . .   (117–22)

This is a clear declaration of intent. In the play which is about to
be played before the 'courteous eyes' of the audience, Jonson is
going to provide an *imago veritatis* by 'holding the mirror up to
nature'—that is, reproducing on the stage the faults and follies of
the audience itself, and especially those affectations which were
dignified with the name of 'humours'. This is to be the way in
which Jonson will combine 'profit' with 'delight', for by illustrating
and ridiculing these absurdities of conduct he will disgust the
spectators with their own failings, and so discharge the moral duty
of the comic poet who, Sidney had said, should present 'the common errors of our life'

> in the most ridiculous and scornefull sort that may be; so that is impossible
> that any beholder can be content to be such a one.[24]

This represents a codification of what Jonson had actually done
in *The Case is Altered* and *Every Man in his Humour*, and a pro-
gramme for all his future work. It also explains why a lot of ink
has been spilled to little purpose in the effort to distinguish between
'the comedy of humours' and 'the comedy of manners'. Essentially
there is no real difference, as Jonson himself makes plain. He made
an interesting clarification when he was revising *Every Man in his
Humour* for publication in the 1616 Folio. In the Quarto version
a 'humour' is defined as 'a monster bred in a man by self love, and
affectation, and fed by folly' (III.i.157–8); in the Folio this becomes
'It is a *gentleman-like* monster, bred, *in the speciall gallantrie of our
time*, by affectation; and fed by folly' (III.iv.20–2), which points up
both the snobbish quality in the cult of the 'humour', and the
importance of topicality in this kind of comedy. In the prologue
to *The Alchemist*, where he is primarily interested in justifying
himself for setting a play in contemporary London, he brings
'humours' and manners even closer together:

> Our *Scene* is *London*, 'cause we would make knowne,
> No countries mirth is better then our owne.

No clime breeds better matter, for your whore,
   Bawd, squire, impostor, many persons more,
Whose manners, now call'd humours, feed the stage. . . ;   (5–9)

and towards the end of his life, in *The Magnetic Lady*, when he was trying to link up his later with his earlier work and remind the audience of his past successes, he spoke of himself as 'beginning his studies of this kind, with *Every Man in his Humour*' and 'continuing in all his *Playes* . . . some recent humours still, or manners of men, that went along with the times. . . '. The differences between Jonson's comedy and Wycherley's have more to do with changes in society and its moral tone, and more still with changes in literary style, than with the exploitation of different comic material or a shift in the comic vision.

Jonson's new kind of comedy required, or at least implied, a new style of comic acting; the old-style, jovial, rustic, knock-about 'clown' was replaced in his work by up-to-the-minute, sharp, realistic portraits, chiefly of city types. Jonson may have been anticipated in this by others—for example, by Chapman with *An Humorous Day's Mirth*—but he stamped his own mark on the new style, and it profoundly affected others, as we can see by comparing the treatment of Bottom and the mechanicals in *A Midsummer Night's Dream* with that of Bardolph, Pistol and Nym in *Henry V*. Hamlet's adjuration to the players—'and let not those that play your clowns, speak more than is set down for them'—reflects another aspect of the change: there was no place in Jonson's controlled comic world for the ad-libbing comedian. Compared with a great deal that had gone before it, Jonson's new comedy seems both more modern and more professional.

This was the practice rather than the theory of comedy, but behind it lay, as usual with Jonson, a considered theoretical position. Much of what has been attributed to a theory of 'Humour Comedy' is, in fact, the result of Jonson's observance of an already established critical precept, the principle of Decorum. Decorum laid it down that characters in a drama should always act and speak 'in character': that is, they should behave as one would expect persons in their time of life and social positions to behave; as George Whetstone put it:

to worke a Commedie kindly [*that is, according to its nature or 'kind'*], grave old men should instruct, yonge men should show the imperfections of youth, Strumpets should be lascivious, Boyes unhappy, and Clownes should speake disorderlye. . . .[25]

B

This was restrictive enough, but there was a further limitation summed up in a tag from Horace which Cordatus actually quotes in *Every Man out* (V.v. 57–8): *Servetur ad imum, qualis ab incepto processerit, et sibi constet.* In effect this meant that a dramatist had to establish his characters on or before their first entrance, and then see to it that they never subsequently did or said anything that contradicted their original presentation. Behind all this was a concept of personality as something fixed and unalterable, of character as a kind of bundle of traits assembled to certain established patterns, which was dominant in the Renaissance. At the time Jonson was writing his first Humour plays this way of looking at human beings had been given a new impetus by the revival of interest in character-writing: this was a development of an old rhetorical exercise (*ethologia*) much practised in schools, but the rediscovery of Theophrastus had given it a new sharpness and wit. The Theophrastan 'character' was a short, epigrammatic, highly stylised sketch of a type: Jonson uses the *genre* both to describe his *dramatis personae* before *Every Man out* begins, and within the play itself, as when Cordatus describes Buffone:

> He is one, the Author calls him CARLO BUFFONE, an impudent common jester, a violent rayler, and an incomprehensible *Epicure*; one, whose company is desir'd of all men, but belov'd of none; hee will sooner lose his soule then a jest, and prophane even the most holy things, to excite laughter . . .   (*Induction* 356–61)

This neat and tightly contained way of looking at and presenting character was inescapably limiting to Jonson. The principle of Decorum left no room for untypical behaviour, inconsistency in action, mixture of motive, or development of character—most, in fact, of what makes human beings interesting. It is very largely because Jonson was ready to accept this limitation and Shakespeare was not that Jonson inevitably loses in the traditional comparison. Bobadil, to take the most obvious example, is a vivid and real-seeming person, but he never does anything unexpected; Falstaff is a mixture of characteristics—a 'bolting-hutch of humours', Hal calls him—and in every sense a far from decorous character, and he engages our sympathy and imaginative response all the more for that. There can be no answer to the objections Strindberg raises in the preface to *Miss Julie* to this kind of rigid characterisation: people simply do not come equipped with a neat bundle of qualities which can only be assembled in certain ways. Moreover, by accepting that characters must stay the same throughout the play,

Jonson was radically limiting the kinds of plot he could use; since they cannot modify their natures or change their mode of behaviour, all his characters can do is to batter each other about according to their individual natures until they are in some way stopped or, as in *Every Man out of his Humour*, shocked or startled into a new character-configuration. It is this persistence in set patterns of behaviour which justifies Coleridge's remark that Jonson's characters seem sometimes to be 'the hopeless Patients of a Mad-doctor'.[26]

This having been said, it must be added that his resolve to portray the humours or manners of his age and to observe faithfully the dictates of Decorum was not only a hindrance to Jonson. If he never equalled Shakespeare in his portrayal of human beings—and how many writers have?—he was at least guarded against the absurd inconsistencies and psychological impossibilities of many of his contemporaries; no one ever 'leans against the wall and repents' in order to bring about the denouement of one of Jonson's plays. Again, although they are types, his characters are not without idiosyncrasy; they are constructed, as it were, from bits of real people, not *a priori* from some abstract and ideal pattern. It is said that when Sir Thomas Lawrence was commissioned to paint a portrait of a Society beauty he would begin by putting on canvas an actual likeness, and would then alter this gradually towards the ideal of beauty current at the time, stopping at the point where his sitter considered he had achieved the perfect likeness (a point, no doubt, always nearer the ideal than the actual). Jonson gives the impression of having worked something like this: he was a sharp observer of the quirks and oddities of behaviour, but habitually related them to underlying laws of human nature: as a result his characters have both vividness and an intellectual consistency. Nor, although many of them can be parallelled elsewhere in Elizabethan and Jacobean drama, is he any the less original as a creator. Bobadil is not just a copy of Falstaff: he is a different man, although of the same general type; similarly Lafoole in *Epicoene* is like, but not the same as, Sir Andrew Aguecheek. Questions of priority are always difficult to settle in the drama of the period, since so many dates are uncertain, but there is always so much sharpness of observation and richness of detail in Jonson that he never appears anything but a fresh and independent imaginative force.

The actual 'humours' of *Every Man out of his Humour*, like those of its predecessor, are a rather mixed bag, combining in different degrees typical and local characteristics. Macilente approaches nearest to the concept of the 'master-passion'; he is given a touch of the 'melancholy' or discontent of the poor scholar and traveller, but is essentially the Envious or Spiteful Man. Similarly Sordido, although he is represented as a grain-hoarder and speculator of a very real contemporary type, is pretty much the 'Avaricious Man', even to the extent of complaining of the extravagance of the countrymen who have saved him from hanging himself because his speculations have gone wrong by cutting the rope:

> You thred-bare horse-bread-eating rascals, if you would needes have been meddling, could you not have untied it, but you must cut it? and in the midst too!   (III.viii.22–4)

At the other extreme, Sogliardo the 'essential clown' who wants to be a gentleman, Brisk the overdressed and extravagant courtier, Fungoso the lawyer's clerk whose sole ambition is to be dressed like Brisk, and Puntarvolo the vain-glorious knight who is determined to be singular and 'sticke to his owne particular phrase, and gesture', can all be seen as examples of perennial types of fool, but are very much specimens of 'the special gallantrie' of Jonson's own time. (Sogliardo and Shift, the pimp who pretends to be an old soldier and whom Sogliardo takes as his mentor in gentlemanly behaviour, are also both given to the fashionable and virtually meaningless use of the word 'humour'.) The most vivid character besides Macilente is Buffone, the back-biting, greedy scrounger (Jonson calls him 'a good Feast-hound or Banquet-Beagle'); he is undoubtedly a version of the classical parasite who 'sang for his supper' by making maliciously witty jests, but Jonson, perhaps with a living model before him, brought him very much up-to-date and 'Englished' him perfectly. All that the characters in *Every Man out* really have in common, however, is that by the end of the play they have by various means been shaken out of their humour, and in this Jonson is forcibly—and, one must add, rather crudely—asserting the overt didactic purpose of his comedy. As Sidney required, the audience were to be disgusted with the follies of the characters and to approve of the punishment meted out to them, and so to transfer the lessons they had learnt to their own lives. Whether in fact anybody in the original audience ever gave up hoarding grain or dressing too expensively after seeing *Every Man out* seems excessively doubtful, but Jonson's position was covered: if the spectators fail to profit from his plays, the fault is their own.

The machinery of the play, the means whereby the characters are made to interact with each other and their final discomfiture is prepared, is something to which Jonson gave particular consideration and took especial pains to justify. Before the play begins Mitis enquires anxiously 'Does he observe all the lawes of *Comedie* in it?', and when asked 'what laws?', answers

> Why, the equall division of it into *Acts*, and *Scenes*, according to the *Terentian* manner, his true number of Actors: the furnishing of the *Scene* with GREX or CHORUS, and that the whole Argument fall within compass of a daye's businesse. (*Induction* 237–41)

For his reward he gets a lecture on the history of the development of Comedy, which Cordatus gives in order to make the point that, since successive classical writers had altered the comic form,

> I see not then, but we should enjoy the same licence, or free power, to illustrate and heighten our invention as they did; and not bee tyed to those strict and regular formes, which the niceness of a few (who are nothing but forme) would thrust upon us.
> (*Induction*, 266–70)

By this statement Jonson dissociated himself firmly from the academic purists who would not accept anything as 'authentic' (to use Mitis' word) which was not sanctioned by the authority of the Ancients, and declared that he was attempting his own original solution to the problem of shaping a comedy. In fact *Every Man out of his Humour* is truly 'somewhat like *Vetus Comedia*' in that in form as in tone it is closer to the Aristophanic than to any other classical model. It has a very loose structure indeed, very different from the Terentian neatness of its predecessor, and it would be difficult to defend it from the charge of being episodic. Simply as a vehicle for the presentation of a group of assorted eccentrics and *poseurs* it was effective enough, but it probably disappointed those who came to it expecting another *Every Man in his Humour*. Although it has some good scenes it has never found much favour with critics and readers, and it represents an experiment which Jonson seems to have made very deliberately and consciously, but which he realised had not fully succeeded.

In his next play he attempted something different again, and took his starting point from a very different kind of drama. *Cynthia's Revels* was his first play for the boy actors, and the first written with the idea of Court performance in mind, and he took as a model the plays of the great Court writer of an earlier generation, John Lyly. Lyly had faced the same problems that Jonson was facing in the attempt to write comedy that was at once topical enough for the fashionable, serious enough for the intellectuals, and robust enough for the vulgar, and had managed (especially in his *Mother Bombie*) to combine homeliness, raciness and vigour with the most polished and rigorous artistic control. By the time Jonson wrote *Cynthia's Revels* Lyly was out of favour and his style had become a stock subject for parody. Jonson makes no attempt to reproduce the mannered artifices of Euphuism, but he does imitate one of Lyly's most striking qualities, the almost mathematical symmetry and balance of the characters and plots of his plays. The whole idea of writing a play for presentation before Queen Elizabeth of which the subject is the preparation and the performance of a masque before the goddess Cynthia is very Lylyan, as is the mixture of mythological, allegorical and real-life figures.

The play opens with a meeting between Mercury and Cupid, who have come to Court for different reasons—Cupid to see if he can win over any of Cynthia/Diana's chaste maids of honour, and Mercury on an errand from Jupiter—and have disguised themselves as the impudent pages so typical of Lyly's comedies. Most of the action is concerned with the activities of eight courtiers, four men and four women, who represent the kind of follies and vices that were (at least in Jonson's eyes) most prominent at Court—Self-Love, Frivolity, Voluptuousness, Impudence, Extravagance, and so on. The plot is slight. Near the beginning of the play the courtier Amorphus, a boastful traveller who has 'lost his shape' in aping foreign customs and manners, finds the Fountain of Self-Love, the same fountain in which Narcissus had drowned himself for love of his own image. He tells of this discovery at Court, and in Act II the pages are sent off with bottles to collect some of the water. They do not return until half-way through Act IV, and the interim is filled with a prolonged display of the follies of the courtiers, with instruction by Amorphus in proper court behaviour, and with court pastimes (which bear an interesting resemblance to modern television panel games). In Act V comes the masque, devised by the noble poet Crites, in which the eight Courtly vices appear in disguise as their complementary virtues—Self-Love, for instance, appears as 'allowable pride in oneself', and Extravagance as Simplicity. In the presence of Cynthia, however, they are unmasked, and are handed over for sentence to Crites; it was to bring about this purging of the court that Mercury had been sent down by Jove.

The moral purpose of all this is clear enough, and modern scholarship has disentangled the complex symbolism which underlies *Cynthia's Revels*.[27] The central theme of the play is Vanity or Self-

Love and the Presumption which is the product of this. Jonson connects the Fountain of Self-Love in the play with the destruction of Actaeon by Cynthia's hounds—Actaeon, who spied upon the naked Goddess, being a type of presumption. By the fountain stands a statue of Niobe, who in her vanity and pride in her children presumed to set herself above Latona, the mother of Apollo and Artemis, and in consequence was turned to stone. Echo, the nymph of the fountain, was often taken to represent babbling small-talk, of which all the courtiers in *Cynthia's Revels* are certainly guilty, and also rumour and common gossip, which we are told was unfavourable to Cynthia after Actaeon's death. It is after drinking the water from the Fountain of Self-Love that Amorphus and the other courtiers are emboldened to appear before Cynthia disguised as Virtues: this is at once Vanity, Presumption and Hypocrisy. As a penance they are sent on a pilgrimage to drink the waters of Helicon, the well of Truth; since this is also the fountain sacred to the Muses, Jonson is able to reinforce the connection between Poetry, Truth and Goodness which has already been demonstrated in the play in the close friendship between Crites and Cynthia's hand-maiden Arete (or Virtue); furthermore the supervision of this penance is entrusted to Mercury, the God of Letters, and patron and friend of Crites. All this very much resembles the kind of intellectual foundation Jonson later gave to his masques, and in *Cynthia's Revels* we can see anticipated many of the devices he was afterwards to use in his Court productions, including the antimasque.

He seems to have been trying out the kind of structure which he thought appropriate to a well-born and well-educated audience; in the Prologue he says of his Muse

> She shunnes the print of any beaten path;
> And proves new wayes to come to learned eares ...　　(10–11)

Unfortunately he does not seem to have had the success he expected. Apparently the reference to Cynthia/Diana's treatment of Actaeon gave offence: whether he meant it or not, he was taken to be referring to the recent disgrace of the Earl of Essex (*Cynthia's Revels* falls in between the abrupt return of Essex from Ireland and his futile attempt to start a revolution). Apart from this, *Cynthia's Revels* might well have been sub-titled *Every Courtier out of his Humour*, and Jonson was hardly being realistic if he expected this application of the satirical techniques of the earlier 'humour plays' to a higher social level to win him favour among the dispensers of patronage.

Theoretically the lesson of the play is that even in an ideal Court folly and vice may enter and be received with favour for a while, but once they are brought into contact with the real virtue and nobility which dwell there their falseness and insufficiency must stand revealed; this may have been too subtle for the courtiers, who only saw that their manners were being ridiculed and their morals disparaged. A more genuinely literary objection to the play is that the allegorical/didactic passages do not marry well with the realistic/satirical, and that altogether too much time is spent on the demonstration of the ludicrousness of court behaviour. Much was no doubt cut in performance (the Quarto edition is a lot shorter than the Folio version), but even so, Jonson failed in this play to solve the difficult technical problem of reproducing tiresome and trivial social behaviour on the stage without actually boring and irritating the audience.

He had also given a handle to his enemies by his portrait of Crites, the 'creature of a most perfect and divine temper', who 'strives rather to bee that which men call judicious, than to be thought so; and is so truly learned, that he affects not to show it'. Jonson may not have intended this to be a self-portrait,[28] just as he may not have intended to bring himself to the Queen's notice when Arete presents Crites to Cynthia:

> Loe, here the man, who not of usuall earth,
> But of that nobler, and more precious mould,
> Which *Phœbus* selfe doth temper, is comp os'd. . . ,   (V.viii.21–3)

but it was easy enough to believe that he had. In any case Queen Elizabeth was not the sort of monarch to appreciate the demonstration Jonson gave in *Cynthia's Revels* of the proper way for a Queen to receive a poet:

> With no lesse pleasure, then we have beheld
> This precious christall, worke of rarest wit,
> Our eye doth reade thee (now enstil'd) our CRITES;
> Whom learning, virtue, and our favour last,
> Exempteth from the gloomy multitude.
> 'With common eye the supreme should not see';
> Henceforth be ours, the more thy selfe to be.   (V.viii.29–35)

Jonson had been asking for trouble for some time by his assumption of the role of the stern moral critic of his age, the superior and scornful observer of folly, and here he carried his apparent arrogance even further. Other writers must have envied his early successes, just as they resented his other scornful references to themselves; he was to have cause to remember Bacon's dictum:

Certainly, he that hath a satirical vein, as he maketh others afraid of his wit, so he had need be afraid of others' memory.[29]

He was not daunted by the failure of *Cynthia's Revels*, however, and published it in 1601 with an Epilogue which ends with the famous line:

By God 'tis good, and if you like't, you may!

—no doubt a fair expression of his own opinion. *Every Man in his Humour* was published in the same year, and both plays have on their title-pages two lines from Juvenal's Seventh Satire: *Quod non dant Proceres, dabit Histrio* ('what the rich and powerful do not give, the Actor will'), and *Haud tamen invideas vati, quem pulpita pascunt* ('you will hardly grudge the poet the living he makes from the stage'). The meaning was clear: 'You cannot blame me for descending to write for the stage', he told his rich and powerful friends, 'for without your help I must earn my living as I can.' The attack he had to face, however, came not from annoyed patrons but from his fellow-dramatists.

III

The *Poetomachia* or Poet's War is a subject of literary-historical rather than critical interest, and indeed it has had a great deal of attention, particularly because Shakespeare was apparently involved in it at one stage.[30] The main opponents, however, were undoubtedly Jonson on the one hand and Marston and Dekker on the other: what is not so certain is the exact course of the battle. Apparently Marston and Dekker, apart from their general objections to Jonson's self-righteousness and arrogance, believed that he had satirised them on the stage, either in *Cynthia's Revels* or possibly earlier in *Every Man out of his Humour* (they may in fact be Clove and Orange, the 'two mere strangers to the scope' who make a brief appearance in that play). One or other of them may also have brought out a satirical portrait of Jonson, and scholars have combed Marston's plays in particular for a character who may be he, the great difficulty being that all satirical portraits of satirists

bear a family resemblance, and there is nothing sufficiently definite
to show that Jonson was being aimed at in person in any one play.
At all events, in the spring or summer of 1601 Jonson got wind of a
rumour that one of the companies of adult players had commissioned Marston and Dekker to write a play in which he was to be
'untrussed'—the modern equivalent would be 'taken down a peg'.
Working with unusual speed—he boasts that it was written in
fifteen weeks—he set out to forestall them, and got his blow in first
with *Poetaster*, played by the Children of the Chapel probably at
the beginning of the autumn playing season.

The main plot of *Poetaster* is concerned with Ovid's love for
Julia, the daughter of the Emperor Augustus, and his subsequent
banishment. The part relevant to the 'War' is the sub-plot,
which deals with the attacks made on Horace, who represents
Jonson, by the poetaster Crispinus and his friend Demetrius
Fannius. Crispinus is Marston, who is ridiculed chiefly for his
inflated and bombastic style: 'he pens high, loftie, in a new stalking
straine; bigger than half the rimers i' the towne, againe . . .'; the
justice of this can be seen by a glance of Marston's *Scourge of
Villainie*, a satirical work of turgid obscurity as well as remarkable
obscenity. Demetrius is a much more humble figure: Jonson did
not forget that Marston, however misguided, was at least a scholar
and a gentleman, whereas Dekker was 'a very simple honest
fellow . . . a dresser of playes about the towne . . .' (a 'dekker' is one
who dresses or decks). Between them Crispinus, Demetrius and
some of the other characters repeat all the charges against Horace
which Jonson knew or suspected might be levelled against himself—
arrogance, impudence, 'railing' or spiteful attack, stealing from
classical authors ('filching by translation'), and so on. In the end
the two would-be 'untrussers' are brought before Augustus, who
makes Virgil their judge; he finds them guilty, pointing out that
the good opinion which Horace entertains of himself is only the
calm self-confidence of the truly virtuous man, and that translation
or imitation had always been accounted

> a worke of as much palme
> In clearest judgements, as t'invent, or make.   (V.iii.366–7)

As for Horace's asperity, 'that is most excusable/As being forc'd out
of a suffering vertue' (V.iii. 368–9). Demetrius is put into a fool's
coat and cap, and Crispinus is given a purge of hellebore, which
makes him vomit up choice specimens of Marston's inflated
vocabulary:

Crispinus	O, I am sick—
Horace	A bason, a bason, quickly; our physick works. Faint not, man.
Crisp.	O—*retrograde—reciprocall—incubus.*
Caesar	What's that, HORACE?
Horace	*Retrograde, reciprocall,* and *Incubus* are come up.
Gallus	Thanks be to JUPITER.
Crisp.	O—*glibbery—lubricall—defunct*—O . . . (V.iii.465–72)

Finally both pretenders to Poetry are made to swear never to attack
Horace again.

The sub-plot, although no doubt it had the greatest appeal to the
immediate audience of *Poetaster*, is only its negative aspect. Jonson
did not merely devote his energies to attacking his enemies, but,
consistently with his general policy of dignifying his art, restated
in the main plot his positive views of the nature of true Poetry.
Some confusion has arisen over his exact meaning because the
initial defence of Poetry is put in the mouth of Ovid:

> O sacred *poesie*, thou spirit of artes,
> The soule of science, and the queene of soules,
> What prophane violence, almost sacriledge,
> Hath here beene offerd thy divinities! . . .
> When, would men learne but to distinguish spirits,
> And set true difference twixt those jaded wits
> That runne a broke pase for common hire,
> And the high raptures of a happy *Muse*,
> Borne on the wings of her immortall thought,
> That kickes at earth with a disdainefulle heele,
> And beats at heaven gates with her bright hooves;
> They would not then with such distorted faces,
> And desp'rate censures stab at *poesie*.   (I.ii. 231–4,240–8)

In the end, however, Ovid is disgraced and banished by the
Emperor, and Jonson seems to accept this as just. This looks
puzzling, but the difficulty is removed if we accept that Jonson was
postulating an order of merit among poets. Ovid was undoubtedly
a true poet, with a genuine devotion to his arduous craft, but his
subject was love—a comparatively trivial theme, and one that he
did not always treat in a strictly moral fashion. Thus, although
Ovid as an artist is manifestly superior to a poetaster such as
Crispinus, he is equally obviously to be ranked below Horace, who,
like Crites, is an unswervingly virtuous and moral writer. Jonson
permits himself a scene (IV.ix) in which Ovid and Julia part after

his sentence has been pronounced. If we can dismiss *Romeo and Juliet* from our minds it may strike us as finely if frigidly written, but even here Jonson is careful to show how limited are Ovid's horizons; he grieves at his banishment from the Court because he regards it, mistakenly, as the centre of life, and his love for Julia, although undoubtedly real, is shown as physical desire rather than spiritual or intellectual in nature. (Jonson would have been false to his own principles, of course, if he had made this scene too moving, since he was renouncing the whole genre of Ovidian erotic poetry of which *Venus and Adonis* and *Hero and Leander* are the supreme examples.)

Horace was the obvious writer for Jonson to identify himself with: moderate, urbane and impersonal, the master of the 'middle style', he was free from the bitterness of early Roman satire, and from the harshness of Juvenal, the obscenity of Martial and the obscurity of Persius. The posture of the good-natured man driven into Satire by the intolerable vexation of fools was an attractive one, and in *Poetaster* (III.i) Jonson actually dramatises the famous satire (I.ix) in which Horace represents himself as tortured beyond endurance by a bore. Pope later took up the same pose, and it probably had about as much relation to reality in Jonson's case as it did in Pope's, or for that matter in Horace's; satire is not written by good-natured and imperturbable men. For Jonson the equation with Horace was another way of defending himself from the charges of arrogance and personal spite, and of indicating how he wanted his 'comicall satires' to be taken—as the dramatic equivalents of Horace's *sermones*, amusing and entertaining, yet earnest and moral. But there was yet a higher level of poetry to which Jonson was ready to admit he had not yet aspired, and that was the Epic, Virgil's level. Where Love poetry is imaginative, and moral poetry realistic, Epic (and Tragedy) are idealistic, inspiring men to great thoughts and high endeavours. Not only Horace but Augustus himself defers to Virgil, who is represented as reading part of Book IV of the *Aeneid* (in Jonson's translation). Caesar in fact has a truly remarkable respect for poets, and even accepts a reproof from Horace with chastened grace:

> Thankes, HORACE, for thy free, and wholesome sharpnesse;
> Which pleaseth CAESAR more, then servile fawnes.   (V.i.94–5)

As in *Cynthia's Revels*, Jonson did not miss the chance to demonstrate the proper relationship between Prince and Poet.

No contemporary writer but Jonson would have taken so much

trouble over what was, initially at least, a move in a personal quarrel—but then no one but Jonson felt so keenly the need to justify his art: an attack, even from writers he professed to despise, necessitated a re-statement of his position and another attempt to 'raise the despis'd head of Poetry'. Taken as a Defence of Poetry *Poetaster* has considerable merit, stating clearly Jonson's views of the different 'kinds' in poetry, their relative importance, and the value each had for humanity; it can hardly claim to have permanent theatrical value, but this was not to be expected. Jonson may well have been proud of it, but in the event it proved something of a disaster for him. It did not, in the first place, deflect or silence Marston and Dekker: in the same autumn season *Satiromastix*, which seems to be mainly Dekker's work, was staged both by Shakespeare's company and by the Children of St Paul's. As would be expected, it is a far less polished piece of work. Even stripped of its topical interest *Poetaster* is still a perfectly consistent, logical and well-made play; *Satiromastix or The Untrussing of the Humorous Poet* is nothing of the sort. The main plot is a romantic love-intrigue set in the reign of William Rufus, into which Horace and various other characters from Augustan Rome irrupt with a cheerful lack of concern for chronology or relevance. Jonson/ Horace is accused again, and this time convicted, of arrogance, vanity, insolence and boastfulness, and also of malice, toadying to the great, back-biting and cowardice. At the end of the play he is stripped of his satyr's hairy coat ('untrussed'), and is made to con-fess his various crimes, such as offering to hang himself if anyone could write plays as good as his, boasting of his gentlemanly friends, saying that his plays are out of the Courtiers' element, and so on. The real value of *Satiromastix* to us lies in the picture it gives us of Jonson. Naturally the portrait drawn is not a flattering one: Jonson is lean, 'a hollow-cheeked scrag'; his face is ugly, swarthy and pock-marked ('full of eyelet holes like the cover of a warming-pan'); he has a loud voice—'a good rouncivall voice to cry Lanthorne and Candle-light' (like a nightwatchman); he is poverty-stricken, famished and badly dressed. There is a good scene (I.ii) in which he is revealed actually composing a poem, and an even more vivid description of how he makes a spectacle of himself in the theatre in order to be noticed:

> Moreover, you shall not sit in a Gallery, when your Comedies and Enterludes have entred their Actions, and there make vile and bad faces at everie lyne, to make Gentlemen have an eye to you, and to make Players afraid to take your part . . . Besides, you must for-

sweare to venter on the stage, when your Play is ended, and
to exchange curtesies, and complements with Gallants in the
Lordes roomes, to make all the house rise up in Armes, and to cry
that's *Horace*, that's he, that's he, that's he, that pennes and purges
Humours and diseases.   (V.ii.298–307)

Satiromastix is not really a very savage lampoon, and Dekker
seems to have taken the whole affair less seriously than Jonson:
his epilogue even suggests that he regarded it as something of a
stunt to attract the attention of the public, and was expecting Jonson
to carry on the sham battle. What was far more serious for Jonson
was the number of other enemies *Poetaster* had aroused. It had contained an incidental, but vicious and unpleasant attack on the men
players, who had after all originally made Jonson's reputation; old
soldiers had been offended by the portrait of Tucca, the time-
serving, scurrilous and dishonest Captain; more seriously still he
had offended his friends at the Inns of Court by Ovid's contempt
for the study of law—they could hardly be expected to relish lines
like 'A simple scholar or none at all may be a lawyer'. One of
his lawyer friends—Richard Martin, later to be Recorder of the
City of London—had to come to his assistance to rescue him from
some serious difficulty of which we do not know the details, and
Jonson later dedicated *Poetaster* to him in gratitude. All in all
Jonson found it safest to retreat for a time from the public stage.
Poetaster was acted once more with the addition at the end of an
'Apologeticall Dialogue' between Horace and two friends, in
which Jonson, with distinctly uncomfortable dignity, explains that
his motives throughout have been of the highest, and that he really
feels nothing but pity for his enemies. Even this he was forced to
omit when *Poetaster* was printed in 1602, but he still managed to
put a defiant tag from Martial on the title page to show that he felt
he had nothing to be ashamed of (*Et mihi de nullo fama rubere
placet*). In February 1603 John Manningham the diarist noted that
'Ben Jonson the poet lives upon one Townshend, and scorns
the world',[31], and it seems that Jonson was fulfilling his
intention, announced at the end of the 'Apologetical Dialogue', to
devote himself to art of a higher order than comedy, and sing
something

> high, and aloofe,
> Safe from the wolves black jaw, and the dull asses hoofe.

The first movement of his career was over.

IV

In the last analysis, the position that Jonson had tried to maintain was untenable. He could strike the Horatian pose, but his own social position was far too weak to sustain it; in the eyes of the world he was only an upstart journeyman with ideas above his station, and he had no Maecenas to support and protect him. As Asper he might proclaim his intention to 'strip the ragged follies of the time Naked as at their birth', but in practice he was very restricted in the targets he could choose for attack if he was to avoid bringing down more trouble on himself than he could risk; throughout his early life he was in frequent difficulty with the authorities. He could not count on much support from his fellow writers, who had had to endure his scornful account of their failings and mocking parodies of their style. Yet although in 1603 he appeared to have been defeated and silenced, he had in fact gone a long way towards achieving his main objectives. He had demonstrated his ability to adapt to the English stage three different kinds of classical comedy, Plautine in *The Case is Altered*, Terentian in *Every Man in his Humour*, and Aristophanic in *Every Man out of his Humour* and (especially) *Poetaster*; in addition he had produced a 'modernised' version of Lylyan Court Comedy. No one had combined learning, moral fervour, and realism in so thorough and impressive a way before, and he had established himself as a serious playwright while, initially at least, achieving considerable popular success.

The plays he wrote during this period have not all survived equally well. *Every Man in his Humour*, although it is seldom put on the stage, is a perfectly viable play, and, with some pruning, *The Case is Altered* would repay production. The three 'comicall satyres' are not likely ever to be staged again, except for purely antiquarian reasons. *Cynthia's Revels* is the least satisfactory, and illustrates most clearly the danger inherent in being 'nearly allied to the times'. As Wilde put it, 'the trouble with being up-to-date is that you grow old-fashioned quite suddenly', and the tedious reproduction of the amusements of Elizabeth's Court can only be of interest now to the social historian. This was a trap into which Jonson was liable to fall throughout his career. *Every Man out of his Humour* and *Poetaster* suffer from the same fault, although both have some good scenes and good characters; Captain Tucca in *Poetaster* in particular is a very good part for an actor (although he is hardly central to the play):

What's he, that stalkes by, there? boy, PYRGVS, you were best let him passe, sirrah; doe, ferret, let him passe, doe.

Pyrg. 'Tis a player, sir.

Tucc. A Player? Call him, call the lowsie slave hither: what, will he saile by, and not once strike, or vaile to a *Man of warre?* ha? do you heare? you, player, rogue, stalker, come backe here: no respect to men of worship, you slave? What, you are proud, you rascall, are you proud? ha? you grow rich, doe you? and purchase, you two-penny teare-mouth? you haue *fortune*, and the good yeere on your side, you stinkard? you have? you have?

Histrio. Nay, sweet Captaine, be confin'd to some reason; I protest I saw you not, sir.

Tucc. You did not? where was your sight, OEDIPUS? you walke with hares eies, doe you? I'le ha' 'hem glas'd, rogue; and you say the word, they shall be glaz'd for you: come, we must have you turne fiddler againe, slave, get a base violin at your backe, and march in a tawnie coate, with one sleeve, to Goose-faire, and then you'll know us; you'll see us then; you will, gulch, you will?

(III.iv.116–36)

It can be said against Tucca, however, that he is a little too remin-iscent at times both of Buffone and of Bobadilla, and it does seem that Jonson was having difficulty in stocking the Comedy of Humours: there is a close resemblance, for instance, between the doting citizens, their spoiled wives and their wives' affected lovers in all the plays of this group. It is difficult to see how Jonson could have avoided this. There is not an infinite number of social types at once distinctive, interesting, and funny enough to be worth putting on the stage, and the more fashionable an affectation is, the more people copy it. It is really rather more remarkable how much variety Jonson got into his early version of the Comedy of Humours, given its nature and scope, but he was undoubtedly right to break off with it and modify his ideas of the proper form of Comedy. In the years 1598–1601 he has thought out and executed some major dramatic experiments, and he was to go on to investigate the possibilities of other dramatic forms with the same thoroughness and the same independence of mind. *Every Man out of his Humour* had not quite come off, and *Poetaster* was something of a dead end; oddly enough it was *Cynthia's Revels*, insofar as it prefigured some of the techniques of the masque, which offered most promise of development. From all of these plays, however, he had no doubt learned something, but perhaps the most cogent achievement of these years was that he had firmly established himself as a figure on the literary scene. If he had never written another comedy, the plays of his early period would still be interesting and important in the history of the drama, although, as it is, their value to us is mainly as prefigurings of the directions Jonson was later to take.

2

JONSON'S TRAGEDIES AND MASQUES

I

In the 'Apologetical Dialogue' after *Poetaster* Jonson had announced his intention of testing himself in a different field of drama:

> And since the *Comick* MUSĖ
> Hath prov'd so ominous to me, I will trie
> If *Tragædie* have a more kind aspect . . .   (222–4)

Sejanus was accordingly produced at Court in the winter of 1603, and again at the Globe in the spring of the following year. In this original version Jonson has a collaborator. Who this was we do not know, nor how big his share was in the play, for when Jonson printed the Quarto version in 1605 he replaced the other writer's work by his own, in order, as he courteously put it, not 'to defraud so happy a *Genius* of his right, by my lothed usurpation'. If the collaborator was Shakespeare, as it is very tempting to think it may have been, we have every reason to regret Jonson's punctiliousness.

Sejanus was not a success, partly for political reasons; apparently Jonson was brought before the Privy Council and accused of Popery and treason. At this time Jonson was a Catholic, but it is difficult to see any trace of this in the play, or any evidence of seditious intent. Whatever the charge was Jonson seems to have cleared himself of it, but he did not attempt tragedy again until 1611, when *Catiline* was produced. Once again he failed: according to his own account the Globe audience endured the first two acts but lost patience with the long orations of Cicero. Jonson followed his usual practice in the face of disaster and published the play in the same year with a battery of commendatory verses by his friends, and a dedication to the Earl of Pembroke in which he refers scornfully to the 'thick and dark' ignorance of the 'Jig-given times'. He never again tempted Fate in this way, although an unfinished tragedy on the downfall of the Earl of Mortimer was found among his papers at his death.

Apart from a brief vogue enjoyed by *Catiline* at the time of the Restoration, Jonson's two tragedies have never had any stage success. The judgment of critics has almost uniformly been against them, although Hazlitt committed himself to the remarkable opinion that they are better than his comedies.[1] The objections to them in his own day and our own may, however, be slightly different. The popular audience at the Globe was simply bored: Leonard Digges, praising Shakespeare's plays at Jonson's expense, says that *Catiline* was found 'tedious (though well laboured)', and that '*Sejanus* too was irksome'.[2] Presumably what the uneducated spectators chiefly missed was the abundance of violent incident to which they were accustomed, and for them Jonson had gone too far in the direction of 'regular' neo-classical drama. Some of the more erudite and sophisticated members of the audience, however, may have felt there was too much action and that he had not sufficiently followed the correct rules for Tragedy. He allowed himself, for example, considerable freedom in his observance of the Unities of Time, Place and Action, adhering to the Unity of Place only insofar as the action of both plays takes place mainly within the City of Rome, and to the Unity of Time not at all—the action of *Catiline* spreads over three days and that of *Sejanus* over several weeks (historically, in fact, over several years). Although each play deals with one main action, and there are no sub-plots, he also indulged his preference for a crowded stage, and in *Catiline* there are over thirty speaking parts. More surprisingly, he admits a comic element, not far distant from the satirical comedy of *Every Man out of his Humour*. There was precedent for including satire on Court life as relief in a serious tragedy—indeed there was no less a precedent than *Hamlet*—but Dryden was able to point out this breach of Decorum with a solemnity of reproach which barely masks his pleasure at catching the master out. Equally reprehensible from the strict neo-classical point of view was the intrusion of violent incident on the stage, most notably the suicide of Silius in *Sejanus* (not even justified by historical accuracy). It is noticeable that Jonson's practice is much more rigorous in *Catiline*, perhaps because he felt that he had made concessions to popular

taste in *Sejanus* without reward and that the remedy was to aim
more directly for critical esteem. *Catiline* is still free in its
treatment of the Unities, has some comic relief in the passages between Fulvia and the other ladies, and contains scenes of horrendous
spectacle.

In the Preface to *Sejanus* Jonson admits that his tragedy is
deficient in the formal qualities expected—for example, in its lack
of a Chorus—but maintains that it would be impossible to provide
these with any hope of stage success:

> Nor is it needful, or almost possible, in these our Times, and to such
> Auditors, as commonly Things are presented, to observe the ould
> state, and splendour of *Drammatick Poemes*, with preservation of
> any popular delight.

He goes on, however, to indicate the qualities he thought of
essential importance in Tragedy:

> In the meane time, if in truth of Argument, dignity of Persons,
> gravity and height of Elocution, fulnesse and frequencie of Sentence,
> I have discharg'd the other offices of a *Tragick* writer, let not the
> absence of these *Formes* be imputed to me, wherein I shall give you
> occasion hereafter (and without my boast) to thinke I could better
> prescribe, then omit the due use, for want of a convenient knowledge.

This list is interesting as shewing the demands which Jonson felt
himself bound to satisfy. 'Truth of Argument' and 'dignity of
Persons' he guaranteed by taking his plots from Roman history;
'height of Elocution' in his own way he had; and both plays, and
especially *Sejanus*, are full of *sententiae*, those easily portable moral
apothegms which the Renaissance play-goer apparently delighted
to set down in his 'tables' (to make sure they were not overlooked,
Jonson set them off in his printed text by quotation-marks). As
long as these requirements were met, Jonson apparently felt
himself at liberty to 'preserve popular delight' by admitting comic
and violent incidents. In the event he fell between two stools, losing
the bold, if dangerous, scope which the popular playwrights
claimed, without gaining the advantages of the tightly restricted
and concentrated neo-classicism of the closet dramatists. He could
write neither an *Antony and Cleopatra* nor a *Bérénice*, and he failed
in tragedy to combine native practices and foreign theory as he had
successfully done in comedy.

The modern spectator might not be so disturbed by the lack of

violent action in these plays, though he too would probably not
escape boredom from the long speeches of Cicero. Both tragedies
in fact are essentially rhetorical. They are rather like law-suits:
Sejanus *versus* Tiberius, Cicero *versus* Catiline, and it is striking
that the denouements of both are brought about by an actual
exercise of the arts of Rhetoric—in *Catiline* by Cicero's speeches,
and in *Sejanus* by the reading of Tiberius' letter. This reflects the
high importance placed on the arts of Oratory by the Renaissance;
the orator, as the master of language, was fit to be the counsellor
of Princes, and the playwright was akin to the orator. In shewing
how Cicero saved the state Jonson was indirectly glorifying his
own art.

What is most likely to disturb a modern play-goer, however, is
the unsympathetic nature of the protagonists in *Sejanus* and
Catiline. Both of these plays are concerned with the downfall of
an evil man, and we instinctively accept Aristotle's dictum that
such a story cannot be tragic because it lacks the element of pity.
There are good characters in the plays as well—in *Sejanus* Agrippina
and Arruntius (who as a satirical and moral critic of events resembles
Asper), and in *Catiline* Cato, and of course Cicero himself—but
Jonson fails to make them attractive, and they strike us as either
petulant, or priggish, or both. Agrippina is haughty, Cato waspish,
and the trouble with Cicero is not so much that he is long-winded
as that he is intolerably self-satisfied. The honest, tetchy Arruntius
is the most satisfactory of them all, and there is real power and
feeling in some of his speeches, as when he comments on the
suggestion that 'times' in Rome are not as they were in the days of
her greatness:

> Times? the men
> The men are not the same: 'tis we are base,
> Poore, and degenerate from the'exalted streine
> Of our great fathers. Where is now the soule
> Of god-like CATO, he, that durst be good,
> When CAESAR durst be evill; and had power,
> As not to live his slave, to dye his master.
> Or where the constant BRUTUS, that 'being proofe
> Against all charme of benefits) did strike
> So brave a blow into the monsters heart
> That sought unkindly to captive his countrie?
> O, they are fled the light. Those might spirits
> Lye rak'd up, with their ashes, in their urnes,
> And not a sparke of their eternall fire

Glowes in a present bosome. All's but blaze,
Flashes, and smoke, wherewith we labour so,
There's nothing *Romane* in us; nothing good,
Gallant or great: 'Tis true, that CORDUS say's,
Brave CASSIUS *was the last of all that race.*   (*Sejanus*, I.86–104)

Failure to obtain sympathy for the characters is a limitation in
comedy; in Tragedy it is crippling. Most of us need to identify
ourselves with the tragic sufferer; we cannot identify ourselves
with Jonson's tragic heroes because they are evil, and we do not
wish to identify ourselves with his good characters because we
find them representative of ideals foreign to us.

This is not a difficulty which would not have affected the
Renaissance play-goer. His conception of Tragedy was still nearer
to the medieval idea, as Chaucer's Monk states it, than to Aristotle.
Tragedy was the downfall of a great man, and it did not make
much difference if he was good or evil. In either case the moral was
the same: put not your trust in worldly power, the gifts of Fortune,
or the favour of Princes, for all these are uncertain; only God does
not betray. Indeed the falls of mighty evil men afforded better
subjects because they had a more easily recognisable moral message:

whereas before in their great prosperities they were both feared and
reverenced in the highest degree, after their deathes, when the posteritie
stood no more in dread of them, their infamous life and tyrannies were
layd open to all the world, their wickednes reproched, their follies and
extreme insolencies derided, and their miserable ends painted out in
playes and pageants, to shew the mutabilitie of fortune, and the just
punishment of God in revenge of a vicious and evill life,[3]

—just like Sejanus. *Sejanus* is a true 'Wheel of Fortune' Tragedy,
being concerned with Sejanus' rise to power, the uncertain *stasis*
while his fortune is at its height, and his rapid and conclusive
downfall. *Catiline* is more Senecan than medieval: Catiline is the
great bad man, the scourge of God, the *lusus naturae*, similar to
Tamburlaine and Richard III, though less successful than they;
his evil is more readily contained than that of Sejanus because it is
more open, less hypocritical, and there is a just man ready to
oppose him, while in *Sejanus* ultimate power is in the hands of the
evil Tiberius. The moral in either play is ultimately the same:
men cannot master Fate nor ignore with impunity the immutable
moral law, and this was the lesson that the Renaissance audience
expected to find illustrated in Tragedy.

Jonson would have a further line of defence against the sentimental modern reader. The end of *Sejanus* is exceedingly painful;
Sejanus himself is dead, but it becomes plain that Macro is no less
evil. Instead of any kind of reconciliation or peace, we are left with
the horrible description of the punishment of Sejanus' innocent
children:

> A sonne, and daughter, to the dead SEJANUS,
> (Of whom there is not now so much remayning
> As would give fastning to the hang-mans hooke)
> Have they drawne forth for farder sacrifice;
> Whose tendernesse of knowledge, unripe yeares,
> And childish silly innocence was such,
> As scarse would lend them feeling of their danger:
> The girle so simple, as shee often askt,
> *Where they would lead her? for what cause they drag'd her?*
> Cry'd, *shee would doe no more. That shee could take*
> *Warning with beating.* And because our lawes
> Admit no virgin immature to die,
> The wittily, and strangely-cruell MACRO,
> Deliver'd her to be deflowr'd, and spoil'd,
> By the rude lust of the licentious hang-man,
> Then, to be strangled with her harmelesse brother . . .
>
> (V.839–54)

If objection were made to this, Jonson could retort that this was
what happened in fact, and that it was not his place to tamper with
History. He might indeed go even farther, and say that the moral
value of his tragedies lay exactly in the fact that they *were* true,
and not feigned fables or idle imaginings, just as part of the moral
value of his comedies lay in their fidelity to real life.

There was in fact a contemporary literary argument in progress
concerning the proper relationship between Tragedy and History.
It had long been accepted that while Comedy should be concerned
with invented stories, Tragedy must have a basis in recorded act,
though this might include what we would regard as legend or myth
rather than history. What was in dispute was the extent to which a
dramatist was bound to follow history faithfully, and how far he
could alter and invent. Ranged against Jonson were those, like
Dekker, who believed that the dramatist was not bound in any
way to historical accuracy, and should write 'as a Poet, not as an
Historian . . . these two do not lie under one hand'.[4] Jonson seems
to have taken the position that the dramatist could alter very

little: when it was clear from historical sources what a man's character was, he must be so represented, and if events were known to have followed a particular course, a dramatist could not tamper with them in order to provide a happy ending. He went indeed considerably further than this, and made a great show of his fidelity to classical sources, provoking Marson to announce scornfully in the preface to his own *Sophonisba*:

> *Know* that I have not laboured, in this poem, to tie myself to relate anything as an historian, but to inlarge everything as a Poet. To transcribe Authors, quote authorities, and translate Latin prose orations into English blank-verse, hath in this subject been the least of my labours.

Yet in this respect too, Jonson had to compromise a little. Although he was not aiming at the most restricted form of neo-classical tragedy, he was still seeking something a good deal less discursive than Shakespearian drama, and in order to meet his own artistic requirements he had to compress time, run together what were historically separate incidents, and even invent characters. (Oddly, it was those of his contemporaries who were most devoted to the principle of construction advocated by the King of Hearts who would have been able, if they had so wished, to follow the course of history exactly.)

The modern reader is still likely to remain unsatisfied. He may be prepared to accept the necessity of fidelity to history, yet still want to know why Jonson chose these two particular men as heroes of his tragedies, and picked their stories for his plots. The reason Jonson would most probably have given was that these episodes from Roman History were particularly suitable as moral examples, and moral example was something which all Renaissance critics agreed was an essential in Tragedy. At the simplest level, *Sejanus* and *Catiline* demonstrate the uncertainty of worldly fortune and the inherent instability of political success. More specifically, *Sejanus* is a demonstration of the dangers of flattery, linked, as is usual in Renaissance drama, with the evils of tyranny.[5] All Princes were expected to have favourites, for this was the natural concomitant of absolute power; it was difficult for a Prince to have a friend, for true friendship could only exist between equals. A good Prince would have good favourites, for virtue recognises and rewards virtue. This was a natural and healthy state of affairs, for these favourites would themselves use their power to reward virtue and punish vice. There was a danger, however, that a good Prince might be deceived, and put his faith in those who would abuse his trust. For this reason the Prince had to be always on his guard, and the theme of a good, if ill-judging, Prince brought to his downfall by giving his favour to an evil counsellor was a standard tragic subject. Evil Princes, naturally, attracted evil followers, who encouraged them in their wickedness, and this was the point at which a favourite became a flatterer. A good counsellor would not hesitate to speak his mind even if this meant opposing a course to which his Lord was inclined, especially if that course were wicked: thus Camillo opposes Leontes' attack on Hermione in *The Winter's Tale*. An evil counsellor, on the other hand, encouraged his Lord in his vices, and would suggest evil action, not merely concur in it:

> Flattery is midwife unto princes rage

is one of the 'sentences' in *Sejanus*. This was because in every flatterer there lurked a traitor, perhaps hoping one day to supplant his Prince and therefore willing to bring him into disrepute, or at the least aiming to render himself indispensable, and to wield the real power in the State.

This is exactly Sejanus' case. Himself an upstart, he has rendered himself indispensable to a tyrant, a Prince whose evil is unchecked by any effective force of opposition in the State. When the tragedy opens he is on the verge of complete success. Tiberius, sunk in vice and too indolent to manage the day-to-day affairs of the government, seems ready to become a *fainéant* and to allow Sejanus to become the real ruler. The only opposition to Sejanus comes from the group centred in Agrippina and it is very weak. Sejanus' first manoeuvres are to break even that slight resistance, and to remove Agrippina's sons, the lawful heirs to the throne. By the middle of the play he seems to have succeeded; and then he makes his fatal error. He asks for the hand of Livia, Tiberius' daughter, whose lover he is, and whose husband, Drusus, he has poisoned. His presumption in seeking alliance with the Imperial family arouses Tiberius' suspicions, and from that moment he is doomed. Tiberius' immediate response is to set up a counterpoise to Sejanus, in the person of Macro, a new instrument of even baser temper. Macro's declaration of his own position is brutal in its clarity:

> I will not aske, why CAESAR bids doe this:
> But joy, that he bids me. It is the blisse

Of courts, to be imploy'd; no matter, how:
A princes power makes all his actions vertue.
We, whom he workes by, are dumbe instruments,
To doe, but not enquire: His great intents
Are to be serv'd, not search'd. Yet, as that bow
Is most in hand, whose owner best doth know
T'affect his aymes, so let that states-man hope
Most use, most price, can hit his princes scope.
Nor must he looke at what, or whom to strike,
But loose at all, each marke must be alike.
Were it to plot against the fame, the life
Of one, with whom I twin'd; remove a wife
From my warme saide, as lov'd, as is the ayre;
Practise away each parent; draw mine heyre
In compasse, though but one; worke all my kin
To swift perdition; leave no untrain'd engin,
For friendship, or for innocence; nay, make
The gods all guiltie: I would undertake
This, being impos'd me, both with gaine, and ease.
The way to rise, is to obey, and please.   (III.714–35)

This is the true credo of the flatterer. Sejamus meanwhile has
passed from being a flatterer to being a traitor and, drunk with
ambition, he refuses to see the dangers of his own position or
recognise the omens of his coming downfall. Before he leaves for
the meeting of the senate on the day of his death he exalts in his
happy Fortunes:

Swell, swell, my joyes: and faint not to declare
Your selves, as ample, as your causes are.
I did not live, till now; this is my first hower:
Wherein I see my thought recach'd by my power.
But this, and gripe my wishes. Great, and high,
The world knows only two, that's *Rome*, and I.
My roofe receives me not; 'tis aire I tread:
And at each step, I feel my'advanced head
Knock out a starre in heav'n! Rear'd to this height,
All my desires seeme modest, poore and sleight,
That did before sound impudent: 'Tis place,
Not bloud, discernes the noble, and the base.   (V.1–12)

This appalling *hybris* is swiftly punished. Tiberius' letter to the
senate, at first doubtful in its phrasing but latterly unambiguously

hostile, invites the senate to turn against Sejanus and punish him as a traitor. Macro has surrounded the senate house with his guards, and Sejanus is taken off to his death.

The moral is more than the simple observation on the fickleness of Fortune which is voiced at the end of the play:

> How fortune plies her sports, when shee begins
> To practise 'hem! . . .
> Let this example moove the insolent man,
> Not to grow proud and careless of the gods . . .
> For, whom the morning saw so great and high,
> Thus low, and little, 'fore th' even doth lie.
>
> (V.888–9,898–9,902–3)

In *Sejanus*, Jonson portrays a world in which the nominal rulers, the senators, have totally lost their integrity and self-respect, and have reduced themselves to the vassals of a vicious and capricious tyrant, and in which, in consequence, the spy, the informer and the lick-spittle have become the instruments of government. The mere representation of such a society is in itself a kind of warning, which we can appreciate as much as, or perhaps even more than, Jonson's own time. It takes a man as ruthless and unscrupulous as Sejanus to succeed in such a state, but his success is likely to be ephemeral, for he will not be able to wield power temperately, and his pride and violence will bring about his fall. Jonson demonstrates this without pity, and does not allow Sejanus the degree of nobility and pathos which Shakespeare gives to the fallen Wolsey. The end of the play, in which Sejanus is supplanted by someone still more cruel and more evil—for Macro lacks the ambition which is the driving-force of Sejanus' actions, and is content to be simply the vicious tool of a vicious master—is more effective than a more conventional 'happy ending' could have been. Sejanus is gone, but the tyrant Tiberius remains. While Society itself is corrupt, it will breed such rulers, and they will always find cowards to fear and criminals to obey them.

If *Sejanus* is an essay on the evils of Tyranny and Flattery, *Catiline* is a demonstration of the dangers of political turbulence. Catiline is the pure rebel, having no cause and striving for no ideal, anxious to revenge the slight given to his pride by being rejected as a military commander, determined to possess himself of the privileges he sees enjoyed—in his eyes, without merit—by the governing class, and convinced that his past crimes cannot be expatiated and can only be justified by further evil:

> The ills that I have done, cannot be safe
> But by attempting greater. . . .   (I.79–80)

He is not, like Coriolanus (to whom he is sometimes compared), a
natural ruler whose noble qualities are vitiated by inordinate pride.
It is true that he despises Cicero as an upstart, and talks of the need
for the aristocracy to maintain its power, but he has no loyalty to
his class. In fact he despises the aristocracy as much as the mob, and
is simply resolved 'to ruin or to rule the state', resembling Milton's
Satan more than Shakespeare's hero. He is contemptuous even of
his own followers, recognising and making use of their weaknesses,
and he has no positive policy beyond revenge and the enjoyment
of absolute rule. Jonson's picture of the bold, restless, and bitter
ambition of Catiline, and the mingled blood-lust and stupidity of
his followers, is sharply drawn, and he shews particular insight into
the relationship between Catiline and his surreptitious supporters
Caesar and Crassus, a relationship between allies each of whom is
trying to make use of the other. Caesar and Crassus think they can
manipulate Catiline, profiting from his success if the rebellion
triumphs, deserting him if it fails; Cataline fully realises the nature
of their support, and is willing to accept it for what it is worth, but
one may feel sure that if he had succeeded he would have turned
on his supporters. It is a fine study of the nature of political
alliance.

However tedious he may seem to us, there is no reason to doubt
that Cicero represents Jonson's conception of the ideal magistrate,
wise, prudent, fearless and incorruptible, and there is no hint that
Jonson had any suppressed feelings of sympathy for Catiline. We
do not expect a Jacobean writer, of course, to express any admiration
for rebellion—it was hardly politic to do so. In Jonson's case the
whole tenor of his life and work suggests that he had a very
genuine veneration for established authority. The political moral of
Catiline, then, is the simple condemnation of those who would
subvert the natural order of the State. Beyond this Jonson emphasises, especially in the Choruses, another common theme of
Renaissance political thought: the tendency of states at the peak
of their prosperity to breed internal dissension. There was a simple
model for the cycle of movement in the state, analagous to the
concept of Fortune's Wheel: the progress ran from Poverty,
through War, to Peace and Prosperity; Prosperity in due course
became Luxury and Corruption, which led to oppression and Civil
War; and thus the State was brought back to Poverty again. The
Chorus after Act 1 comments on this:

> Can nothing great, and at the height
> Remaine so long? but it's owne weight
> Will ruine it? Or, isn't blinde chance,
> That still desires new states t'advance,
> And quit the old? Else, why must *Rome*,
> Be by it self, now over-come?
> Hath shee not foes inow of those,
> Whom shee hath made such, and enclose
> Her round about? Or, are they none,
> Except shee first become her owne?
> O wretchednesse of greatest states,
> To be obnoxious to these fates:
> That cannot keepe, what they doe gaine;
> And what they raise so ill sustaine!
> *Rome*, now, is Mistris of the whole
> World, sea, and land, to either pole;
> And even that fortune will destroy
> The power that made it: shee doth joy
> So much in plentie, wealth, and ease,
> As, now, th'excesse is her disease.   (I.531–50)

From this point of view Catiline himself is only a symptom of the unhealthy state of Rome and the loss of the old civic virtues in the corruption engendered by its 'dropisical' wealth. Like *Sejanus*, *Catiline* presents a clear-cut moral and political statement.

The firmness of their moral outline, together with the authenticity of their historical truth, gives to Jonson's tragedies an impressive gravity and force. It is a critical commonplace that Jonson, with all his learning, is less true to the actual life of ancient Rome than Shakespeare, because he created his characters from the outside, as Romans, while Shakespeare created his from the inside, as men. There is truth in this, although exactly how much only the Roman historian (and not even he, perhaps, with complete confidence) could assert. What is equally true is that Jonson displays a clear insight into the nature of man in so far as he is a political animal, and that it is this which was really germane to his immediate purpose. The characters in his tragedies lack subtlety, but they have a convincing consistency and clarity. Tiberius, for instance, is very little on the stage, and has only one soliloquy (that in which he voices his suspicions of Sejanus), but he emerges, as much from what is said about him as from what he says himself, as a very clear portrait of an ageing, self-indulgent, morose and unpredictable dictator. Similarly the conspirators in *Catiline* are carefully

differentiated: not much space is given to each, but they are much
more than an amorphous crowd of malcontents, as Otway's
conspirators are in *Venice Preserved* (a play which owes a great
deal to *Catiline*). In his tragedies Jonson practises greater economy
in characterisation than in his comedies; he has many characters,
but for the most part he gives only those aspects of their personal-
ities which are immediately relevant to the political situation in
which they are found. His concern, therefore, is different from
Shakespeare's. Shakespeare is as much interested in Antony and
Cleopatra as a man and a woman as he is in their roles as Triumvir
and Queen of Egypt, though he never loses sight of their political
significance; Jonson is never concerned with private life at all,
except in so far, as in Sejanus' relations with Livia, it affects the
political issues. Given this direction of interest the apparent
authenticity of Jonson's portraits is striking: he had seen the world
of politics at close quarters, and had a fine sense of its dramatic
possibilities.

The same economy and firmness are apparent in the construction
of *Sejanus* and *Catiline*: there is a resolute avoidance of side-issues
and a firm concentration on the development of the story. The
scenes between Livia and her physician in *Sejanus* and between the
ladies in *Catiline* are not 'comic relief' in the ordinary sense at all.
Eudemus the physician has an essential role to play, which is more
than to be the go-between for Sejanus and Livia and to provide
the drug which poisons Livia's husband. All his talk about cosmetics and aids to the complexion is not simply 'comical satire'
but is thematically connected with the theme of Flattery and
Treachery; he is himself a flatterer; his oils and his 'fucus' daub
over the Truth, and make corruption look beautiful. Similarly the
scene between Sempronia and Fulvia in Act II of *Catiline* is not an
irrelevant attack on the follies of women but is crucial to the plot.
By first boring Fulvia with political gossip and then insisting that
she should receive her lover Curius, Sempronia brings about the
downfall of the conspirators, for Fulvia learns the secret of the plot
from Curius, and resolving to rival Sempronia as a 'political lady',
reveals it to Cicero. Again there is a thematic significance: Jonson
underlines the essential triviality of the conspiracy, and the extent
to which it is a matter of vanity and talk. These scenes also serve
to afford some variety of tone. One of the obvious dangers of a
rigid concentration on the tragic theme is that there will be too
many scenes conducted at the highest pitch of solemnity. Jonson
has not altogether avoided this—it is part of the reason for the
comparative failure of the last acts of *Catiline*—but he does not

have the relentless consistency of mood which Dryden objected
to in French neo-classical Tragedy.

There may, however, be a deeper sense in which Jonson's
tragedies are not serious enough. Clearly the besetting sin of Sejanus
and Catiline is Pride, or Ambition. Equally clearly their downfall
is brought about by the kind of stupidity and lack of foresight which
accompanies this sin. Sejanus deludes himself in thinking that he
can manœuvre against Tiberius without the suspicious Emperor
realising his aims, and he is foolishly ready to believe in the apparent
favour in which Tiberius seems to hold him. He fails also to realise
how many of his friends support him purely for their own ends
and will betray him at the least sign of imperial displeasure: one of
the most effective scenes in the play in the last meeting of the senate,
when the senators realise that Sejanus' overthrow is imminent and
one by one remove themselves from his side—all but the gouty
Haterus, who cannot shift and whose gout keeps him 'most
miserably constant'. Catiline is less self-deluded than Sejanus; he
knows clearly what he means to do and is under no illusion about
the quality of his supporters. Yet he does not fully appreciate their
instability, and though at the beginning of the play he boasts to
Aurelia of the use he intends to make of men's weaknesses, he does
not guess that Curius' desire to impress his mistress will lead him
to betray the whole conspiracy. He fools himself in thinking that
he can stage a successful rebellion with men such as this, just as he
is guilty of wishful thinking in believing that the Allobroges will
support him in his attack on Rome. Above all he totally under-
estimates Cicero. Having begun as a portent or prodigy,
threatening universal disorder, he ends as little better than a
peevish and unsuccessful gambler, outwitted by an opponent who
has better kept his head.

Of course this kind of 'over-reaching' tragic hero can always be
accused of folly, since by definition he is bound to be ultimately
unsuccessful in his aims—even Tamburlaine cannot finally defeat
death. Marlowe, however, makes us yield emotional credence to his
heroes' overweening desires: we may know intellectually that
Faustus is doomed to inescapable failure in his struggle against the
limitations of human life, and could be called foolish to commence
it, but we feel him as a heroic if doomed figure. The ambitions of
Sejanus and Catiline move us less, and we can therefore more clearly
see their absurdity. It is in this sense that critics have spoken of
Jonson's attempt to write 'satirical tragedy'. Perhaps even more important than this, however, is a restriction of effect produced ultimately by Jonson's view of the proper nature of dramatic character. The

element of struggle or conflict is missing from the minds of Sejanus and Catiline. In accordance with the doctrine of Decorum, they are simple and consistent embodiments of evil, without redeeming qualities, and incapable of doubt or internal conflict. There is not even a part of them with which the audience sympathises, and this is one of the two major restrictions on the effectiveness of Jonson's tragedies.

The other, greater limitation on the success of Jonson's tragedies lies in the text itself, in the quality of his tragic poetry. This was the point on which T. S. Eliot fastened, when he noticed how in contrast, not only with Shakespeare, but with Marlowe, Webster, and Beaumont and Fletcher, Jonson has been paid out with reputation instead of enjoyment. Eliot's explanation was that while Jonson 'is no less a poet than these men',

> [his] poetry is of the surface. Poetry of the surface cannot be understood without study . . . Shakespeare, and smaller men also, are in the end more difficult, but they offer something at the start to encourage the student or to satisfy those who want nothing more; they are suggestive, evocative, a phrase, a voice; they offer poetry in detail as well as in design . . . But the polished veneer of Jonson only reflects the lazy reader's fatuity; unconscious does not respond to unconscious; no swarms of inarticulate feelings are aroused.[6]

In the fifty years since Eliot wrote that we have become much less favourably disposed towards poetry in which 'unconscious responds to unconscious', and innumerable exegetes have tried to make articulate our feelings about poetry, but it remains true that Jonson's plays do not offer us the kinds of satisfaction that we expect from Jacobean tragedy, and that this is primarily a question of our response to the texture of the verse. He can indeed offer 'poetry in detail', at times even achieving the sudden sharp stab of vivid imagery so characteristic of his contemporaries. In the last act of *Catiline* two such moments come within a few lines of each other: the first when Cicero commands the executioners to arrest the conspirators,

> Here, take'hem
> To your cold hands, and let'hem feel death from you,   (V.605–6)

and the second when Petreius describes Catiline leading his troops to their last battle,

> not with the face
> Of any man, but of a publique ruin. (V.642–3)

But in general the tone is weighty, grave, precise and dignified, and not urgent or exciting. It is rhetorical in a good sense; only occasionally (and principally in *Catiline*, when Jonson is trying to 'rise to the heights of Seneca') does his style become overstrained and inflated. On the other hand, only in the scenes of satirical comedy (as Eliot noted) does it become vivid, flexible and convincing as human speech. In his essay Eliot was trying, with the aid of some special pleading, to remove Jonson from the fatal comparison with Shakespeare. He was right in pointing out that Jonson's poetry was not only more accomplished and learned than that of his contemporaries, but more open and honest as well: there are no fake effects in *Sejanus* and *Catiline*. But equally there are no great heights of emotional excitement and understanding.

Paradoxically, Jonson sometimes wrote worse because he was so anxious to write well. In Tragedy his conscious artistry and control and his seriousness of moral purpose seem to have prevented him from achieving the intensity and the pathos which even the least conscientious and ill-disciplined of his contemporaries were able to touch, if only once or twice in their careers. Jonson himself bitterly recognised that writers 'who alwaise seek to doe more than inough, may sometime happen on some thing that is good and great', and write better than they deserve, but he noted that this happens 'but very seldome: and when it comes it doth not recompence the rest of their ill'.[7] Unfortunately for him our taste, since the beginning of the Romantic movement, has been exactly for the brilliant fragment, and his kind of finished craftsmanship has been out-moded. Behind his ultimate failure in Tragedy, however, lies something deeper than this. In the end, despite all his thought and care, he lacked the true Tragic vision of humanity. His *forte* was the keen observation of human life and the ability to re-create some aspects of it, not empathy or the ability to enter into the feelings of others; and in his emotional range pity played only a small part. As a result, the virtues of his Tragedies are something we can see but can hardly feel, and they move us, if at all, to something close to horrified wonder at their events, and (at the best) respectful admiration for their artistic skill.

C

II

Jonson failed to bend the tragic form to his will, and to make in it the synthesis of native and classical that he had successfully accomplished in Comedy. The Masque was a form he completely mastered, and in its short history in England his was the dominating figure. He wrote his first full-scale masque, *The Masque of Blackness*, in 1605, and in the next thirty years he produced altogether twenty-seven masques and ten other 'entertainments'. Although some of these are very short, and none, naturally, is as long as a full-length play, considerable thought went into their composition and they must have absorbed much of his creative energy; as long as King James was alive he seems to have regarded them as his major artistic commitment. He was lucky in that both his own powers and the form itself came into fruition at the same time. The Masque had a long history in England, going back at least to the late Middle Ages, but it was under the Stuarts that it reached its peak. As a form of entertainment it was extremely costly, and Queen Elizabeth was too parsimonious to indulge a taste for it herself, although she was well prepared to allow others to spend their money in entertaining her in this way. James was congenitally extravagant and had absorbed the Renaissance doctrine that a Great Man displayed his greatness by his liberal spending. He himself had written an Interlude and taken part, as 'a Christian Knight of Malta', in a masque during the festivities to celebrate the birth of Prince Henry in 1594, but he was too ungainly himself to be a successful masquer, and was frequently bored by the entertainments offered him; he suffered the Court masque mainly as a display of his own princely magnificence, and as an opportunity to admire the beauty, grace and costume of his favourites. Queen Anne, however, had a strong liking for display and dancing, a taste acquired at her home in Denmark. She commissioned the masques *of Blackness* and *of Beauty* and herself danced in these and several other masques. Other members of the Royal Family also took part, and for the aristocracy it was a great honour to be asked to perform. If Jonson sometimes felt he had lowered himself by writing for the common players, he could take satisfaction that as a deviser of masques his actors were of the highest in the land.

The origins of the Masque were complex, like the origins of all Renaissance dramatic forms. Its one invariable feature was that it involved disguise; a 'disguise' or a 'disguising' was one of the older names for a masque, as Jonson himself noted.[8] The performers were 'dressed up'; they wore costume, and sometimes masks, although the use of masks was not common in the later development of the form. Whatever its connections with folk-plays, fertility-rites, or other types of proto-drama, basically the Masque appealed to the tastes satisfied in other centuries by the charade, or the fancy-dress ball. Of the several forms which the Masque took, the most important for Jonson's work are two: the 'Greeting' and the 'Visit'. The greeting was a performance put on to welcome great personages when they arrived at a nobleman's house or entered a city. Jonson's very first 'show', the *Entertainment at Althorpe*, was of this type: it was performed in 1603 to welcome Queen Anne and Prince Henry at Sir Robert Spencer's house in Northamptonshire when they were on their way south from Scotland to join the King. His last masque, *Love's Welcome at Bolsover*, was commissioned by the Duke of Newcastle to greet King Charles and Queen Henrietta Maria when they visited him in 1634. The Visit, however, was the form in which most Court masques were cast, and which Jonson most extensively practised. It may have had its origin in the visits paid by 'stranger knights' after a tourney to the banquet presided over by the Lady of the tournament; it was quite common for knights to joust in disguise, and they may have continued to wear their costumes after the actual tilt was finished. The custom had also grown up of visiting a feast or a ball in disguise. Henry VIII visited a banquet given by Wolseley disguised as a Russian, and the visits of Berowne and his friends to the Princess and her ladies in *Love's Labour's Lost* and of Romeo and his friends to the Capulet ball are examples of the same practice. Possibly the traditional visits paid by bands of Mummers at the Christmas season also contributed to the form. Whatever the exact source, the Court masque, despite its elaboration, remained in essence a visit paid by supposed 'strangers' in compliment to the Court, and its central feature was always the dancing in which these strangers 'took out' members of the audience.

The dancing was the really important part of the proceedings, as is amusingly illustrated in the account given by Busoni, the Chaplain to the Venetian Embassy, of the performance in *Pleasure Reconciled to Virtue* in 1618. Prince Charles, whose first masque this was, and who was not physically strong, grew tired after several dances had been danced, and flagged, whereupon the King was irritated, and exclaimed: 'Why don't they dance? What did they make me come here for? Devil take you all, dance!' The Duke of Buckingham, who was an exceptionally fine dancer, came to the rescue and cut a series of graceful capers, and the King was restored to good humour.[9] Dancing was an accomplishment expected of a gentleman, and the aristocratic performers were required to do little more than dance and to carry their splendid costumes gracefully; any acting necessary was done by professionals (although Buckingham had a speaking part in *The Gipsies Metamorphosed*). Dances were arranged especially for the occasion and played and sung by professional musicians. Large orchestras were employed: Jonson's *Love freed from Ignorance and Folly* for example, although it was intended to be a less elaborate masque than usual, required no fewer than sixty-six musicians. They were usually dressed in suitable costumes and placed on the stage, rather than being grouped separately as an orchestra, so that they added to the richness of the spectacle. The singers were also often in costume—in fact they were frequently named as mythological figures, gods, and so on—and there were also choirs, usually of boys. The original purpose of the songs was to give the dancers time to regain their breath, and to change partners, but they came in time to occupy a greater space in the production. The masque *Lovers made Men*, which Jonson wrote in 1627 for the entertainment of the French Ambassador by Lord Hay, can almost be called an opera—the first in England: Jonson notes that '*the whole Maske was sung (after the Italian manner) Style Recitativo*'. There is in fact a fairly close connection between the Masque and early Opera: the staging, scenery, costumes, personages and even the plots are often similar. The opera, however, quickly developed on the Continent into a professional performance, for a paying audience, and was therefore able to continue its existence and transform itself in a way not open for the Masque.

The task of the poet, or 'inventor', as Jonson frequently calls himself, was, basically, to account for the arrival of the visitors at the Court, and to provide a coherent framework into which the dances and songs could be set. In the primitive 'disguising' this function was discharged by the 'Presenter', who merely came on and introduced the various characters, perhaps adding some brief explanation of their presence. It was Jonson's pride to make the framework of the masque an exercise in poetic fancy and moral symbolism, drawing for this double purpose on all his store of learning. Sometimes he had the scope of his 'invention' laid down for him. Thus *The Masque of Blackness* had its origin in Queen Anne's whim to appear disguised as a blackamoor, and Jonson had to devise the fable of the twelve Ethiopian ladies, daughters of the River Niger. They are represented as wandering over the world in search of land whose name ends in TANIA, and in which the Sun their enemy does not need to shine because a greater light there informs all beauty; in that land, they have been promised, they will find a cure for their black skins. This prophecy is interpreted by the Moon, who appears in her avatar as a goddess of the Ethiopians, as signifying Brit-tania, a land ruled over by a Sun—i.e. King James—

> Whose beames shine day, and night, and are of force
> To blanch an Aethiope, and revive a Cor's;

Jonson thus neatly solved the problem of accounting for the arrival of his black ladies and of including the obligatory compliment to the King. At other times no specific requirement was laid on the poet, and he was free to develop any idea which would answer the general purpose.

In composing his masques, Jonson sought first of all some central theme or symbol—what he sometimes called the 'soul' of the work —to which everything else, including the setting and costumes ('the bodily part') should be subservient.[10] An excellent example of his technique is provided by *Hymenaei*. This masque was written to celebrate the marriage (in the event, a disastrous one) between the Earl of Essex and Lady Frances Howard, daughter of the Earl of Suffolk. The aim behind the match, which was arranged by the King, was to compose the quarrels between the great noble families; another daughter of Lord Suffolk was married at the same time to Salisbury's son, so that there was to be a triple alliance between the houses of Cecil, Devereux and Howard. The theme of the masque, therefore, was 'Union', which enabled Jonson to refer as well to James's desire for the Union of Scotland and England, and to the King's mystical union to his two kingdoms. (James was fond of likening his relation with his kingdoms to that of the bridegroom to his bride.) The first scene represents a Roman wedding before the altar of Juno, the goddess of Union, whose name can be anagrammatised as 'Unio'. After a song by Hymen celebrating the glories of the King and Queen and the virtues of the two marriage partners, the Globe, which, Jonson tells us, represented the Microcosm or little World of Man, revolved, and from its interior there came forth eight male masquers, dressed to represent the four 'Humours' of Earth, Water, Air and Fire, and the four 'Affections' or Passions corresponding to them. These danced out in a 'contentious' or quarrelsome fashion, threatening the Altar and disturbing the ceremony, and thus symbolised the rebellion of the lower faculties of man against the harmony of the soul. They were quieted by the appearance of Reason, who appeared seated on top of the Globe—Reason being the highest faculty of Man. Reason, who was represented as 'a venerable personage . . . her garments blue, and semined with starres', after rebuking the Humours and Passions discoursed on the mystical significance of marriage, as the type of Union, Love and Harmony. After this the 'upper part of the Scene', which was painted to represent a cloudy heaven, opened to reveal Juno, accompanied by the second masque of eight ladies. These ladies descended on clouds, to the music of a song, and were then paired off with the male masquers by Order, the servant of Reason. There followed the dances, at the end of which the sixteen masquers formed a circle (the perfect figure) round Reason, who delivered a final speech celebrating Union. They then left the scene in pairs, to the singing of an Epithalamium. Though the philosophical basis of this is far from original—the connection between Love, Dancing, Marriage, Concord, and Harmony was a commonplace of the Renaissance—the thoroughness and skill with which the ideas are combined and expressed are remarkable.

Hymenaei is a particularly fine, though not an unique, example of Jonson's intricate construction. Not all masques could be composed with such attention to detail, though where necessary everything, including the pattern of the dances, could be pressed into service to reinforce the symbolic meaning.[11] Great attention was paid to the significance of costume, although much of Jonson's care must have been wasted on the audience: how many of the spectators would have realised, for example, when Good Fame appeared in *The Masque of Queens* dressed in white, with white wings, and wearing a collar of gold from which hung a heart, that the wings symbolised the purity and speed of Good Report, and the heart 'figured' the reputation of a Good Man? Jonson recognised this danger, and discounted it; in printing one of his early entertainments, part of the 'Welcome' given to the King by the City of London when he proceeded from the Tower to his coronation in 1604, he describes the triumphal arch at Fenchurch and the allegorical figures on it, and notes that no attempt was made to explain them to the spectators, it being enough that they would be obvious to 'the sharp and learned':

And for the multitude, no doubt but their grounded judgements did gaze, said it was fine, and were satisfied.[12]

This was bravely enough said, but there is no doubt that the interest of the masque for most spectators lay in the spectacle, and

that this assumed greater and greater importance as time went on.
Court masques were performed at night, and much emphasis was
laid on lighting effects. It was customary for the masquers to be
accompanied by torch-bearers, and lamps were placed around the
proscenium arch, and in or on whatever set was erected on the
stage; thus Jonson says of the House of Fame in *The Masque of
Queens* that:

> The *Freezes*, both below, and above, were filld with several-colourd
> Lights, like *Emeralds, Rubies, Saphires, Carbuncles*, &c. The reflexe
> of which, with other lights plac'd in the concave, upon the *Masquers*
> habites, was full of glory.[13]

These colours were produced by placing candles or small oil-lamps
behind 'glasses' or jars of coloured water. Placed on parts of the
scenery made to revolve, they must have had a sufficiently dazzling
effect, and could be used to hold the attention of the audience
while the scene was being changed. It was also possible to light
statues or buildings from within by making them of calico or oiled
paper and placing candles or lamps inside them. Clouds could be
made luminous and transparent in the same way. Much ingenuity
was exerted on sky effects: it was possible to simulate dawn or
dusk or the clouding over of a scene simply by shades over the
lamps concealed by the proscenium. A movable backcloth with
holes cut in it could produce the rising, movement and setting of
the moon and stars. Comets and shooting stars are also mentioned;
presumably they were produced as on the public stage, by a fire-
work travelling along a wire. The risk of fire was extreme, and in
fact the old Banqueting House burnt down in January 1619 because some of the oiled paper used in a masque got dry and caught
fire.

It was in the changing of scenery, however, that the masque
produced its most novel and spectacular effects. The stage manager
had at his disposal all the machinery available in the popular
theatre: characters or even buildings could rise up through trap-
doors, clouds and chariots could descend from the 'heavens',
chariots, throne, ships or islands could advance from the back of
the stage, bearing figures on them; but because the masque was
performed indoors and at night—and because he was given much
more money to spend—he could perform even more remarkable
feats. It was significant that *The Masque of Blackness*, which marked
the beginning of the collaboration between Jonson and Inigo Jones,
concentrated its action on a single set; Daniel's *The Vision of the*

Twelve Goddesses, produced in the previous year, had retained the traditional 'simultaneous' or 'dispersed' set in which the characters appeared from 'houses' in different parts of the hall. There were in fact no significant changes of scene in *The Masque of Blackness*; the important point was that by bringing all the action to one end of the hall it produced an effect more like that of a modern theatre, and established a precedent for this kind of staging (though not one that was exclusively followed). In course of time a proscenium arch became customary, framing the stage and being itself decorated; thus for *Chloridia*,

The ornament, which went about the *Scene*, was composed of Foliage, or leaves heightned with gold, and enterwoven with all sorts of flowers; and naked children, playing, and climbing among the branches; and in the midst, a great garland of flowers, in which was written, CHLORIDIA.[14]

The proscenium was closed by a 'travers' or curtain, painted to represent a scene. This could be dropped when the masque was to begin, to reveal the first scene; or the first part of the performance could be played in front of it. It could then be dropped, raised, or drawn aside to reveal the next scene, if necessary in sections, so that different parts of the main set could appear in sequence. Wings between the curtain and the backcloth could be drawn in and out in grooves, so as to shift the scene, or use could be made of triangular structures (called *periaktoi*) which could be painted with different scenes on each of their three sides, and turned round as necessary. Jones also made use of the *machina versatilis*, or revolving stage. When all these devices were combined some very elaborate stage effects were possible.

The chief effect always aimed at was surprise, and there is an almost naive note in Jonson's own descriptions of the magical transformations of scene that were made, and the magnificence and splendour of the sets. Surprise, however, is hardly an emotion that goes well with the intellectual appreciation of moral significance, and the richness of spectacle must have distracted the minds of the audience from Jonson's deeper meanings. It was almost inevitable that a quarrel between Jonson and his designer should occur. It seems that at first Inigo Jones was ready to satisfy Jonson's demands for detailed symbolism and (where appropriate) archaeollogical accuracy in his costumes and settings, but that later he gave freer reign to his artistic imagination, to such an extent that Jonson felt that his intentions were actually being obscured.[15] One cannot altogether blame Jones; he had to satisfy his patrons, who wanted fantasy and spectacle, and, if they were to appear themselves, were more interested in wearing costumes which suited them than in fidelity to a governing intellectual theme. But in any case Jones had no great sympathy for Jonson's serious concept of the masque, which he once described as 'nothing but pictures with light and Motion',[16] and he was given to introducing *coups de théâtre* for which there was no justification at all in the 'invention'. Jonson went on protesting about this to the end, but he lost the battle, as can be seen in *Love's Triumph* and *Chloridia*, the last two masques he wrote with Jones, and his last for the Court.

Inigo Jones was not alone in his view of the masque. Bacon, in his famous essay 'Of Masques and Triumphs', described them as merely 'toys', and many of Jonson's contemporaries would dismiss them as curtly as they are dismissed at the beginning of *The Maid's Tragedy*:

What think'st thou of the masque? will it be well?

As well as masques can be.

As masques can be?

Yes; they must commend their king, and speak in praise
Of the assembly, bless the bride and bridegroom
In person of some god; they're tied to rules
Of flattery . . .   (I.i.8–11)

In accordance with his general aim to dignify and ennoble whatever dramatic form he took up Jonson tried to establish the masque as a vehicle for learning and morality, expounding his deeper meaning and citing his authorities with scrupulosity and fervour. Nevertheless he could not ultimately disguise the fact that his part of the entertainment, the text, was only a minor though necessary structural feature, and that what was for the spectator the major interest was essentially visual and transitory. Indeed, he admitted this: in the introduction to *Hymenaei*, of which the text is surrounded by notes referring to classical authorities and explaining the symbolism, he first justifies himself against those who complain that 'learning and sharpness' are out of place in 'these transitory devices', but later in his account of the production he makes a moving admission that all was but 'the short bravery of the night' (as he calls it in another of his poems):

Hitherto extended the first nights *Solemnitie*, whose grace in the
execution, left not where to adde unto it, with wishing: I meane,
(nor do I court them) in those, that sustain'd the *nobler* parts. Such
was the exquisit performance, as (beside the *pompe, splendor,* or
what we may call *apparelling* of such *Presentments*) that alone (had all
else beene absent) was of power to surprize with delight, and steale
away the *spectators* from themselves. Nor was there wanting what-
soever might give to the *furniture,* or *complement;* eyther in *riches,* or
strangenesse of the *habites,* delicacie of the *daunces,* magnificence of
the *scene,* or divine rapture of *musique.* Onely the envie was, that it
lasted not still, or (now it is past) cannot by imagination, much lesse
description, be recovered to a part of the *spirit* it had in the gliding
by.   (565–79)

Jonson himself was responsible for another development in
the Masque which was bound to mitigate against its seriousness of
purpose, and this was the increase in the importance of the antimasque (or 'ante-masque' or 'antick-masque'—Jonson uses all
three forms). He used this device first in the masque which he wrote
for the wedding of Lord Haddington in 1608. Here it takes its
place properly as what Jonson calls 'a foile or false masque', being
danced by twelve boys, companions of Cupid, who represent 'the
sports, and prettie lightnesses, that accompanie Love'; they thus
complement the main masquers, who were represented as priests of
Hymen, the god of marriage. The Queen approved of this, and in
commissioning *The Masque of Queens*, 'best knowing, that a
principal part of life in these *Spectacles* lay in theyr variety', asked
Jonson to provide a *'false-Masque'* to appear before she and her
ladies danced the main dances. Jonson met this order by devising
an antimasque of twelve witches who represent the evils of Ignorance, Suspicion, Credulity and so on, and thus are the antitheses to
Fame and her Ladies who form the masque proper. The whole
masque is very cleverly put together and is one of Jonson's best,
and also one of his most scholarly: he added, apparently at the request
of Prince Henry, an exhaustive apparatus of notes and references to
support the details of his 'invention'. The antimasque caught on
and was much copied by other writers, but its popularity made it
dangerous, for it was only too liable to become irrelevant, and to
disturb the tone of the masque, which should be one of festive
solemnity. Jonson found himself compelled to give more and
more space to antimasques—sometimes even, as in *Pleasure
Reconciled to Virtue*, having to provide two for one masque—and it
became more and more difficult to relate them to his main themes.

In *The Masque of Augurs* (1622), which begins with a very long prose antimasque which has virtually nothing to do with the main part of the masque, Jonson makes one of his characters comment ironically that the more absurd an antimasque is and the farther from the purpose, the more the spectators will like it, and two years later, in *Neptune's Triumph*, the Poet (whose part may have been taken by Jonson himself) indignantly announces that he has provided no antimasque:

> neither doe I thinke them
> A worthy part of presentation,
> Being things so *heterogene*, to all devise,
> Meere *By-workes*, and at best Out-landish nothings . . .   (220–3)

He is corrected by the Cook, to whom he is speaking—cooks often seem to symbolise for Jonson the need for the popular artist to satisfy the taste of his audience—and since the conversation is in fact part of an antimasque itself, it must be an ironical admission of failure to control a demand which he had initiated but of which he did not wholly approve.

III

Jonson could not wholly check the Masque's tendency to degenerate into mere spectacle and stage-craft or into farce and grotesquerie, but he did establish it as a literary form, with its own 'rules'.[17] He appears to have seen it as a special form of comedy, in which order was restored after disorder and opposites were reconciled, usually by an unexpected revelation symbolised by a sudden and surprising change of scene. The actual presence of the King was important, since he was himself a symbol of Divine Order, and the discovery that he was present could be the surprise that reestablished harmony —a device that Jonson had first used in the original version of *Every Man out of his Humour*, where the discovery that he is in the presence of the Queen cures Macilente of his envy. In this way Jonson made the obligatory compliment to the King an integral part of the masque structure, and it is noticeable that in the few masques not written for a Court showing an essential element is felt to be missing. Jonson was as insistent in his masques as he was in his comedies on providing some conceptual basis for the action, and in some ways this was a more remarkable feat in the masque, both because of its inescapably spectacular nature, and because the action had to follow a narrowly prescribed course; particularly noteworthy in this respect is the variety of Jonson's hymeneal masques, for there was an irreducible sameness about the occasions for which they were composed and little to do except to wish Good Fortune to the happy couple. Jonson despised most of the other masque-writers—he told Drummond that 'next to himself only Fletcher and Chapman could make a masque'[18]—and he had reason to plume himself on his achievement. G. G. Smith's remark that he 'both made the masque, and controlled its short career'[19] is perhaps an exaggeration—there are several fine masques outside his work, and some better than those he wrote himself—but no one sustained so high a level in the form, and influenced it so greatly. As it happened, political circumstance dictated that it did not survive him long: Davenant's *Salmacida Spolia*, produced in 1640, is regarded as the last true masque.

Very few of us today are ever likely to see a masque properly staged, and our interest in this part of Jonson's work must be chiefly literary. His masques witness aspects of his creative magination which would not be guessed at from his comedies or even from his non-dramatic verse. The range of his 'invention' is very wide, from grave mythological allegory in a masque such as *The Golden Age Restored* to 'romantic' Arthurianism in *Prince Henry's Barriers*; similarly he can move in his verse from the grotesqueness of the witches in *The Masque of Queens*, with their uncouth, 'Gothic' charms:

> The Owle is abroad, the Bat, and the Toade,
>   And so is the Cat-à-Mountaine;
> The Ant, and the Mole sit both in a hole,
>   And Frog peepes out o'the fountayne;
> The Dogges, they do bay, and the Timbrells play,
>   The Spindle is now à turning;
> The Moone it is red, and the starres are fled,
>   But all the Sky is à burning:
> The Ditch is made, and our nayles the spade,
> With pictures full, of waxe, and of wooll;
> Theyr livers I stick, with needles quick
> There lackes but the blood, to make up the flood;   (75–86)

to the Arcadian pastrolism of this song from *The Entertainment at Highgate*:

> For, we will haue the wanton fawnes,
> That frisking skip, about the lawnes,

The *Paniskes*, and the *Silvanes* rude,
Satyres, and all that multitude,
To daunce their wilder rounds about,
And cleave the ayre, with many a shout,
As they would hunt poore *Echo* out
Of yonder valley, who doth flout
Their rusticke noyse. To visite whome
You shall behold whole bevies come
Of gaudy *Nymphes*, who(se) tender calls
Well tun'd (unto the many falls
Of sweete, and severall sliding rills,
That streame from tops of those lesse hills)
Sound like so many silver quills
When ZEPHYRE them with musique fills.
For these, FAVONIUS here shall blow
New flowers, which you shall see to grow,
Of which, each hand a part shall take,
And, for your heads, fresh garlands make.
Wherewith, whilst they your temples round,
An ayre of severall birds shall sound
An *Iö pæan*, that shall drowne
The acclamations, at your crowne.

All this, and more than I have gift of saying,
MAY *vowes, so you will oft come here a Maying.*   (136–61)

The antimasque gave him the chance to indulge a gift for the grotesque and the nonsensical which is even more unexpected; at times he comes close to Rabelais, or even Bosch, while in *The Vision of Delight* Fancy has an almost Gilbertian piece of patter:

If a Dreame should come in now, to make you afeard,
With a Windmill on his head, and bells at his beard;
Would you streight weare your spectacles, here, at your toes,
And your boots o'your brows, and your spurs o'your nose?
Your Whale he will swallow a hogs-head for a pill;
But the maker o'the mouse-trap, is he that hath skill.
And the nature of the Onion, is to draw teares,
As well as the Mustard; peace, pitchers have eares,
And Shitlecocks wings; these thing, do not mind'em.
If the Bell have any sides, the clapper will find'em:
There's twice as much musicke in beating the tabor,
As i'the Stock-fish, and somewhat lesse labour.

Yet all this while, no proportion is boasted
'Twixt an egge, and an Oxe, though both have been roasted . . .

                                                          (79–92)

Others of his antimasques are not unlike extracts from his
comedies, and often little inferior. In *An Entertainment at the
Blackfriars*, for example, which he wrote for the christening of the
Duke of Devonshire's son in 1620, there is a dispute between
Mistress Dugges, the wet-nurse, Mistress Kecks, the dry-nurse, and
Mistress Holdback, the midwife, which yields little to the quarrel
between Face, Subtle and Dol Common:

Dugges How enviously shee talkes, as if any neerer, or nobler office,
    could bee done the Childe than to feede him, or anie more necessarye,
    and carefull, then to encrease that which is his nutriment, from both
    of which I am trulye, and principallye named his nurse
Kecks Principallye? O the pride o' thy Pappes: would I were the
    ague is thy breasts, for thy sake, to bore'em as full of holes as a
    Cullender! As if there was no nutriment but thy milke, or nothinge
    could nurse a chylde, but suckinge; why if there were noe milke in
    nature, is there no other foode? howe were my ladye else provided
    against your goings to men (if the toy should take you) and the
    corruption of your milke that waye?
Dugges Howe? I goe to man? and corrupt my Milke? thou dryed eeles
    skin . . . I defy thee, I: thou onion-eater . . . Ah, 'tis pitye such a one,
    should ever come, about any good bodyes childe; thou'lt stifle it
    with thy breath one of theis mornings.
Kecks Indeed, you had like to have overlayd it, the other night, and
    prevented its Christendome, if I had not lookt unto you, when you
    came so bedewed out of the wine seller, and so watred your Couche
    that to save your credit with my ladye next morning, you were glad
    to laye it upon your innocent bedfellowe, and slander him to his
    mother, howe plentifully hee had suckt: This was none o'your drye
    jeasts nowe, this was a soaker.   (183–214)

Jonson shews the same interest in different trades and their
technical jargons in his antimasques as he does in his comedies,
but he also demonstrates a knowledge of rustic life and custom for
which there is little place in his stage plays. His most successful
exercise in this vein is *The Gipsies Metamorphosed*, which he wrote
for the entertainment of the King at the Duke of Buckingham's
mansion at Burley-on-the-Hill in 1621. Buckingham and the other
noble masquers were dressed as gipsies and told the fortunes of the

King and the other guests: this gave an opportunity for some graceful compliments, as well as some very authentic-sounding gipsy patter. The country clowns who formed the antimasque, and on whom the gipsies practised their tricks, provided another sort of rustic humour, and for good measure Jonson included a song based on the traditional explanation of how the Devil's Arse, near Burley, got its name; this might be a piece from *The Ingoldsby Legends* if it were not, as one might expect from Jonson in this mood, too coarse and outspoken. *The Gipsies Metamorphosed* was one of Jonson's greatest successes; it was repeated twice at the King's request, and of all Jonson's masques it is the most likely to make an immediate appeal to a modern reader.

As well as rustic lore, Jonson made considerable use in his masques of traditional folk customs, and also of older literature. *The Fortunate Isles*, for example, introduces Henry Scogan, Chaucer's contemporary and a legendary wit, and John Skelton, also a jest-book hero; Jonson makes some attempt at Skelton's idiosyncratic style and metre. Scogan and Skelton are brought in by the 'airy spirit' Iophiel for the entertainment of the melancholy student Mere-Foole, who is also diverted by an antimasque in which there appear, among others, Owleglass (Till Eulenspiegel), Tom Thumb, Doctor Rat (a character from *Gammer Gurton's Needle*), Skelton's Elinor Rumming, and two noted Elizabethan viragos, Mary Ambree and Long Meg of Westminister (both real women). Jonson's most charming use of folk custom, however, is in *Christmas his Masque*, written in 1616, and, like *The Gipsies Metamorphosed*, still very accessible today. *Christmas his Masque* is very close in spirit and form to one of the masque's ancestors, the Mumming. It begins with the entry of Christmas, disputing with one of the Palace guard his right to enter the Hall. He brings with him his ten children to entertain the Court: they are Misrule, Carol, Minc'd-Pie, Gambol, Post and Pair (a card game), New Year's Gift, Mumming, Wassail, Offering and 'Baby-cake'. They are joined by Venus, in the unexpected guise of a deaf 'Tire-woman' (or dressmaker) from Pudding Lane, who is searching for her son Cupid who is an apprentice to a 'bugle-maker' in Love Lane (not a maker of musical instruments, but a manufacturer of glass beads and earrings for ladies). Cupid is allowed to perform, but dries up in his speech and has to be removed by the indignant Christmas. The proceedings close with dance and song. Jonson is not wholly free from a slight tone of patronage towards the customs of the citizens of London, but for all that *Christmas his Masque* is still a delightful fantasy.

These are sides of Jonson unfamiliar to those who know only his major comedies, and there is altogether much more variety in his masques than we should expect to find in so restricted a dramatic form. Emphasis on the imagination, sometimes delicate and airy, sometimes familiar and vigorous, shewn in the antimasques should not, however, be allowed to distract attention from the 'high style' which Jonson used for the grander and more serious parts of his masques. This style, which often rivals Spenser's in its thoughtfulness, dignity and sweetness, is well illustrated by the speech in *The Masque of Beauty* in which Vulturnus, the south-east wind, describes the 'floating island' inhabited by the masquers:

> A gentler wind, VULTURNUS, brings you newes
> The *Ile* is found, and that the *Nymphs* now use
> Their rest and joy. The *Nights* black charmes are flowne,
> For being made unto their *Goddesse* knowne,
> Bright AETHIOPIA, the silver *Moone*,
> As she was HECATE, she brake them soone:
> And now by vertue of their light, and grace,
> The glorious *Isle*, wherein they rest, takes place
> Of all the earth for Beautie. There, their *Queene*
> Hath raised them a *Throne*, that still is seene
> To turn unto the motion of the World;
> Wherein they sit, and are, like Heaven, whirl'd
> About the Earth; whil'st, to them contrarie,
> (Following those nobler torches of the Skie)
> A world of little *Loves*, and chaste *Desires*,
> Doe light their beauties, with still moving fires.
> And who to *Heavens* consent can better move,
> Then those that are so like it, *Beautie* and *Love*?
> Hither, as to their new *Elysium*,
> The spirits of the antique *Greekes* are come,
> *Poets*, and *Singers*, *Linus*, *Orpheus*, all
> That have excelled in knowledge musicall;
> Where, set in arbors made of myrtle, and of gold,
> They live, againe, these beauties to behold.
> And thence in flowry mazes walking forth,
> Sing hymns in celebration of their worth.
> Whilst, to their songs, two fountains flow, one hight
> Of *lasting Youth*, the other *chast Delight* . . .   (119–46)

This fairly represents the poetical level of the best masques, and this accomplished, sonorous verse is varied by many songs of great charm and spirit, and some of Jonson's best prose. In a sense the texts of the masques as we have them are only the skeletons of a dramatic form, needing a particular—and now unreproducible—kind of staging and performance to clothe them with flesh. If we remember how absurd and jejune the librettos of even the greatest operas appear in the study, we shall better appreciate Jonson's success in turning the masque into a literary form of lasting merit.

3

THE GREAT COMEDIES

I

There is no doubt that *Volpone, Epicoene, The Alchemist* and *Bartholomew Fair* are the peak of Jonson's achievement as a comic dramatist, and critics in consequence tend to treat them as a group, seeking in them a coherent pattern of Comedy. This can be misleading, for they were spread out over nearly a decade—*Volpone* was staged by the King's Men at the Globe late in 1605 or early in 1606; *Epicoene* by the Queen's Revels (the former Children of the Chapel) in 1609–10; *The Alchemist* again by the King's Men in 1610; and *Bartholomew Fair* by the same company in 1614. They differ quite considerably from each other both in construction and, more importantly, in tone, although they share common themes: *Epicoene* and *The Alchemist*, the closest together in time, are also the closest in mood; *Volpone* is something of a transition from Jonson's earlier work to his middle period, and *Bartholomew Fair* from his middle style to his later. We have to remember also that *Catiline* (1611) comes right in the middle of the group—and perhaps we might reflect that if we could date Shakespeare's plays as closely as we can Jonson's we should not find ourselves dividing his career so neatly into 'tragic' and 'comic' periods.

Volpone has a good deal in common both with the earlier comical satires and with *Sejanus*. Although after the *débâcle* of *Poetaster* Jonson never again put himself forward on the stage in the role of the perfect satirist or the ideal poet, and indeed tended to portray himself as a jovial and slightly comic figure, in dedicating *Volpone* to Oxford and Cambridge (it had been successfully played at both universities) he took the opportunity of reaffirming the position he had earlier so stoutly maintained. He admits again that the 'too-much licence of *Poetasters*' has brought Poetry and poets into discredit, though 'if men will impartially, and not a-squint, looke towards the offices, and function of a Poet', they must admit that a true poet 'is no subject for pride and ignorance to exercise their rayling rhetorique upon'. 'Stage-poetrie' in particular has been debased by the work of writers deficient both in art and in morals, but 'that all are embarqu'd in this bold adventure for hell, is a most uncharitable thought'; it has been Jonson's study to 'stand off from them', and in *Volpone* he has 'labour'd

> for their instruction, and amendment, to reduce, not onely the ancient formes, but manners of the *scene*, the easiness, the propriety, the innocence, and last the doctrine, which is the principall end of *poesie*, to informe men, in the best reason of living.

This dedication is perhaps the clearest, and is certainly the finest written, of Jonson's statements of his position and his aims.

Volpone was thus a fresh attempt at the task of rescuing Drama from the evil days on which it had fallen, and a further attack on the problem of satisfying the scholars while still attracting the popular audience. He presented it to the universities as a show-piece, and in many ways it is the greatest of his comedies; yet many modern readers find it difficult to come to terms with. In tone it is free from the occasionally strident and hectoring note of the earlier plays, but it is almost unremittingly forceful and severe, and its effect seems somehow alien. In part this is the result of its exotic setting. *Volpone* was the last comedy which Jonson set outside England, and in practice it is the only one which has a genuinely foreign flavour. He was forced to place it in Venice because he was relying for his central plot-device on the Roman practice of *captatio* or legacy-hunting, and the giving of presents to the rich and childless in the hope of being made heir to their wealth had never become customary in England. It was not usual in Renaissance Italy either, but Jonson presumably felt that Venice was far enough away to make it credible, and as he had previously done in *Sejanus*, he set out conscientiously to reproduce the local flavour of his chosen scene. As a result the action becomes distanced from us.

Modern critics have emphasised the shock effect of the very first scene, with Volpone's impious, indeed blasphemous, invocation to his hoard:

> Goode morning to the day; and next, my gold:
> Open the shrine, that I may see my *saint*. . . .   (I.i.1–2)

The conscious use of religious language here and throughout
Volpone's first speech may well have startled the audience in the
Globe, although their reaction may not have been as simple as
present-day critics may suppose; anyone with Puritan leanings
among them may not have felt so much that it was wrong for gold
to be substituted for a saint as an object of worship, as that the
worship of gold and the worship of saints were equally deplorable
(and might quite likely go together). The moral inversion of
Volpone's world is however clear enough:

> Deare *saint* . . .
> That canst doe nought, and yet mak'st men doe all things;
> The price of soules; even hell, with thee to boot
> Is made worth heaven! Thou art vertue, fame,
> Honour, and all things else . . .   (I.i.21,23–6)

But attacks on avarice and lust for gold had a long history going
back through the homilies of the Middle Ages to antiquity, and the
Jacobean play-goer may not have immediately understood more
than that he was being presented with the figure of the Miser or
Usurer. The real shock for him may have come when Mosca and
Volpone explain the very unusual way in which Volpone makes his
money:

> . . . I gaine
> No common way: I use no trade, no venter;
> I wound no earth with plow-shares; fat no beasts
> To feede the shambles; have no mills for yron,
> Oyle, corne, or men, to grinde 'hem into poulder;
> I blow no subtill glasse: expose no ships
> To theatnings of the furrow-faced sea;
> I turne no moneys in the publicke banke;
> Nor usure private—
> *Mosca*. No sir, nor devoure
> Soft prodigalls. . . .   (I.i.32–40)

He is clearly no ordinary miser, and Jonson continues to rouse his
audience's puzzled interest for another thirty or forty lines before
he solves the mystery.

The modern spectator may in fact not notice the irreligion of
Volpone's speech nor be struck by the unexpectedness of his

methods, since for him Volpone is in any case a strange figure in a costume drama; he is most likely to feel that he is watching something odd and sinister when Volpone's household make their appearance. The fool, the dwarf and the hermaphrodite form an entourage which would be appropriate to one of the more unpleasant Roman emperors, and they may strengthen the feeling (especially if we remember the attacks on legacy-hunting in the Roman satirists) that we are really in the ancient world rather than in Renaissance Venice. Some of the atmosphere of *Sejanus* does indeed seem to have spread into *Volpone*. Basically the relations between Volpone and Mosca are the same as those between Tiberius and Sejanus, though the treachery and ambition of the flattering parasite can now only bring about disaster on a domestic scale. The political scene of *Volpone*, if it may be so called, is also not unlike that of Jonson's Roman tragedies. The majority of the characters are devotedly self-seeking, and vary only in their methods and their degree of ruthlessness. This is true not only of the main contesters for Volpone's wealth, who as their names suggest are as vicious and pitiless as birds of prey, but even of the judges of the Venetian Court, who, like the senators in *Sejanus*, are keenly sensitive to shifts of power and always ready to jockey for position. (If Mosca is only a scheming servant, then he must be condemned, but if Volpone is really dead and Mosca is the heir, then he could be a good match for a judge's daughter, and a sensible man must be ready to seize the opportunity.) As in *Sejanus*, we feel that the good characters are out-numbered and helpless in a world in which power is in the hands of the evil. In the end, because *Volpone* is a comedy, Good must triumph, but we feel that the victory is a narrow and precarious one.

Volpone comes nearer to tragedy than any of Jonson's comedies and contains more bitter and unpleasant scenes. Jonson asks us to walk a very narrow edge between laughter and disgust, and if we or the actors lose our balance some scenes may become unbearable. It is not really funny to overhear two men abusing a third who is on the point of death—

> would you would once close
> Those filthy eyes of yours, that flow with slime,
> Like two frog-pits— (I.v.56–8)

and guardedly discussing murdering him, and it depends very much on the actor playing Volpone whether we find it bearable. The scene in which Volpone attempts to rape Celia is an even

bigger problem for the producer, because it cannot be made
amusing to a modern audience without seeming tasteless, and yet
must not become too harrowing. Jonson felt the need to justify the
scene of Sordido's attempted suicide in *Every Man out of his
Humour* because it was an incident more violent than was usual in
comedy, but the scene between Celia and Volpone, on which he
did not comment, is likely to disturb us much more. Certainly
Celia's pleading has more of the note we recognise as characteristic
of Jacobean tragedy than anything in *Sejanus* or *Catiline*:

> If you have eares, that will be pierc'd; or eyes,
> That can be open'd; a heart, may be touch'd;
> Or any part, that yet sounds man, about you:
> If you have touch of holy saints, or heaven,
> Do me the grace to let me 'scape. If not,
> Be bountifull, and kill me . . .   (III.vii.240–5)

In the Dedication to *Volpone* Jonson answered those who objected
to the harshness of its ending by saying that his 'speciall ayme' was
'to put the snaffle in their mouths, that crie out, we never punish
vice in our Interludes' (the most common Puritan charge against
the theatre), but he had made something more severe than an
ordinary comic finale necessary by what he had allowed to happen
in the course of the play.

Nevertheless we are not justified in treating *Volpone* as a tragedy
or Volpone himself as a tragic figure. He is certainly an isolated
man, an 'outsider' who by his actions reveals the rottenness of
Society, but we are falling into one of the most obvious clichés
of contemporary thought if we assume that this makes him
necessarily a hero. Nor does the fact that he is surrounded by people
on the whole worse than he is make him a good man. We can see
the error in any 'noble' view of Volpone if we compare him with
Alceste in Molière's *Le Misanthrope*. Alceste is antisocial and
unbalanced, and in the last analysis ludicrously wrong in his
attitude, but his behaviour is the result of a misplaced and exaggerated idealism. We can to some extent admire Alceste and it is
not ridiculous to speak of his noble qualities. There is absolutely
no element of idealism or nobility in Volpone. His only likable
qualities are his vitality and gusto, his sheer enjoyment of his own
and Mosca's trickery. He is not motivated by greed alone as his
suitors are, however; he wants wealth, but he also wants to be
amused by the means of getting it. Indeed Volpone needs constant
stimulation of this kind, and the extent to which he depends on it,

almost like a drug, is shown after he has escaped from his trial.
As soon as he begins to recover his nerve, he immediately starts
hankering after amusement:

> Any device now, of rare, ingenious knavery,
> That could possess me with a violent laughter . . .   (V.i.14–15)

This craving for excitement is more Volpone's essential 'humour'
than any passion for gold—indeed he seems to value his gold less
for what it is in itself than as a token of his success in tricking
others; he is much more of a gambler than a miser.

An actor playing Volpone has to bring out a certain coarsening
and degradation of his character as he goes on. In the first Act he
is at his most successful and his most attractive. His deception of
Corbaccio, Corvino and Voltore seems little more than practical
joking, and given the obvious character of these 'suitors' the
audience will naturally admire Volpone's cleverness and not trouble
themselves about the morality of what he is doing. When at the
end of Act I Mosca mentions Celia, Volpone seems at first excited as
much by the opportunity of displaying his own cleverness in
another disguise as by the prospect of seeing her beauty, and in his
performance as Scoto he is at his most brilliant and amusing. The
sight of Celia is fatal to him. His desire for her clouds his judgment,
and he never again in the play shows the same mastery of the
situation as he displays at the beginning. He fully understood
Corbaccio and the others, because he was quite dispassionate in his
dealings with them and could finely estimate the degree of their
gullibility. He quite misunderstands Celia's character, because
he so desperately wants her: he thinks she will be happy to betray
her husband given a safe opportunity to do so, like the heroine of
an Italian comedy. When he realises he is wrong he loses control
of himself and threatens to rape her, and the intervention of
Bonario at this point places him in acute danger. For the third
quarter of the play he is cornered, a passive figure, while Mosca
and the others keep the action going in their efforts to release him;
when he reasserts himself at the beginning of Act V the compulsive nature of his humour forces him to seek new stimulus, and
this brings about the catastrophe.

Volpone makes a bigger fool of himself, in fact, than any of his
dupes, as he realises:

> To make a snare for mine owne necke! and run
> My head into it, wilfully! and with laughter!

When I had newly scap't, was free, and cleare!
Out of mere wantonnesse!   (V.xi.1–4)

As he has done before, he calls on Mosca for help, only to realise,
too late, that the love of his 'divine', his 'exquisite' Mosca, the
genuineness of which he had never questioned, was in fact the
flatterer's obsequious disguise for self-seeking, and that his own
gullibility has ruined him. Only then, when he is in despair, does he
reveal the truth, not from any desire to right the wrongs he has
done, but out of determination that Mosca shall not triumph over
him. The development of mood is from a jovial, assured, self-
satisfied cleverness at the beginning, through domination by the
passions first of lust and then of fear, back to a kind of desperate,
obsessive searching for amusement, and finally to a grim desper-
ation. There is no room in this for tragedy, although we may feel
if we will a kind of doomed or destined quality about Volpone (a
modern psychologist might even say that his constant flirting with
danger and discovery indicates an underlying desire to be unmasked and punished). To stress this note too much—even if an
actor could successfully indicate it—would be to over-weight the
part, and destroy much of the comic effect of the play.

In a sketchier way Mosca's character follows the same pattern
as Morose's. As a true parasite he has to be ready at all times to
satisfy his master's desire for entertainment and to suggest new
pleasures, and he clearly enjoys his job and prides himself on his
accomplishments. He directs Volpone very much like a theatrical
producer, making sure that his make-up and costume are right, and
is always ready to praise Volpone's performance. He is equally
ready to accept Volpone's applause for his own acting skill, the
irony being, of course, that while Volpone is applauding Mosca's
deception of others, he himself is the most deceived of all by
Mosca's pretence of loyalty to him. Like Volpone, Mosca becomes
infatuated with his own cleverness:

I feare, I shall begin to grow in love
With my deare self, and my most prosp'rous parts,
They doe so spring, and burgeon; I can feele
A whimsey i'my bloud: (I know not how)
Success hath made me wanton,   (III.i.1–5)

and in the end he over-reaches himself, not realising that in the
last resort Volpone, who is after all a magnifico of Venice, will not
suffer himself to be overcome by a parasite and allow his servant to

take his place. Over-confidence ruins Mosca, as it does Volpone, and
together they recall Truewit's observation in *Epicoene*: 'that falls
out often . . . that he that thinkes himself the master-wit, is the
master-fool'. We must not 'read back' the end of the play, however,
into our response to the earlier parts—this is the typical error of
thinking of drama too much as literature which we read instead of
as something which we experience sequentially in the theatre—and it
it precisely Mosca's and Volpone's excited enjoyment of their own
and each other's ingenuity that gives the tone for much of *Volpone*;
it must be brought out strongly enough by the actors to overcome
our repugnance at some of the things they do, and still more at the
things done by Corbaccio and his fellows.

   Volpone thus raises in an acute form the problem which often
faces the reader of Jonson's comedies, that of enjoying a play when
he does not really like any of the characters in it. Coleridge found
this difficulty insuperable, as he said:

This admirable, indeed, but yet more wonderful than admirable, Play
is from the fertility and vigour of Invention, Character, Language and
Sentiment, the strongest proof, how impossible it is to keep up any
pleasurable interest in a Tale, in which there is no goodness of heart in
any of the prominent characters. After the 3rd act, this Play becomes
not a dead, but a painful, weight on the Feelings.[1]

In fact it was no part of Jonson's theory of Comedy that the comic
characters should be likable, or demonstrate any goodness of heart
whatever. According to the rules of the *genre,* as he understood
them, the dramatist's task was to present persons who were ludicrous, foolish and despicable, with the object of disgusting the
spectator with their follies and stupidities. Admirable and virtuous
characters were not required in comedy: their sphere was that of
Tragedy, and perhaps also Tragi-Comedy (a 'kind' of which
Jonson never produced a finished example). In theory, at least, it
would have been an equal breach of decorum to introduce pathetic
figures, or to admit any relaxing of the hard, critical gaze at life
and human nature. In practice Jonson did not abide completely
by these principles, and in *Volpone* itself Celia is certainly pathetic,
and Bonario irreducibly, if rather woodenly, virtuous. Unfortunately Bonario's intervention to save Celia from Volpone is always
an anticlimax on the stage, and his speech extremely difficult to
deliver to a modern audience:

   Forbeare, foul ravisher, libidinous swine . . .   (III.vii.267)

This illustrates again the difficulty, which Jonson also found in his tragedies, of making ideal types of virtue credible, and vivid enough to survive changing moral fashion. Bonario suffers almost as much at the hands of his father as Celia does at those of her husband, but it would take a very good actor to make him sympathetic to us. Any other Jacobean dramatist would have done what Coleridge suggested, and made Celia and Bonario much more prominent in the action, very probably ending the play with their marriage, but though Jonson could certainly have ended the play differently if he wished, as he boasts in the Dedication, he did not want to weaken its unrelenting moral force.

Apart from Celia and Bonario, no one in *Volpone* has any genuine claim on our sympathy and admiration—Peregrine is a neutral character, and could easily be acted so as to make him seem a very nasty young man indeed—and the fact that we tend to offer our affection to Volpone may have more to do with our acquired modern approach to comedy than with Jonson's original intention. We have in England a tradition of sympathy with comic characters which is by no means common in other countries. It would be a long task to trace the history of this: it begins with Chaucer, with characters such as the Wife of Bath, and it owes an enormous amount to Shakespeare, part of whose genius lay in his capacity to present so many different types of character with understanding (it could be said that whereas Jonson could not always get sympathy for his characters when he needed it, Shakespeare appears unable to avoid getting the audience on their side even when he did not perhaps want to do so, or at least when, as with Shylock, the result is to perplex and confuse the audience's response). To this we must later add eighteenth-century Sentiment and Victorian sentimentality, and our own twentieth-century sensitivity to the feelings of the unwanted and despised. The result is that even now, although we speak of 'Black Comedy' and 'Alienation', we still expect to like comic characters even while we laugh at them, will always try to like them if we can, and (many of us) are disturbed and made uncomfortable by comedy such as Jonson's where there is no outlet for our desire to sympathise.

This is the real explanation for the sense of 'foreignness' in *Volpone*, and that general feeling of being in an alien and uncomfortable world which someone reading any of Jonson's comedies for the first time may experience. His plays seem in this aspect more 'natural' to readers not brought up in the English comic tradition and have often been (*Volpone* in particular) very successful in theatres abroad. We must be ready to subdue our gentler, humane instincts if we are to enter fully into Jonson's comic world, and prepare ourselves to enjoy humour which is hard, even cruel and brutal, and which springs from the interaction of characters very few of whom possess attractive, let alone admirable, qualities. *Volpone* is the extreme example of this unfamiliar style of comedy, and therefore the most challenging, and the fact that some critics have sentimentalised it to the extent of treating Volpone as a noble and tragic figure shews that this challenge can be difficult to accept.

II

In the point of time *Volpone* is nearer to *Poetaster* than it is to *Epicoene*, and it is also closer in spirit. Although the *persona* of the author does not obtrude as it had done in the earlier play, *Volpone* is obviously written by a close colleague of Asper (and of Crites and Horace), but the 'humours' comedy is relegated largely to the sub-plot, where the way in which Sir Politic Would-be is punished for his intolerable itch to appear the know-all 'politician' or states-man does not differ much in kind from Macilente's treatment of Puntarvolo or Buffone. The main plot of *Volpone*, however, is much nearer to the tragic satire of Juvenal, and the style, appropriately, is high and dignified; it is the unfamiliarity of this *genre* that makes it difficult for us to decide exactly how we are intended to respond to it. *Epicoene* is very different in tone, being altogether lighter, wittier and more relaxed, and it is natural to speculate whether this reflects some change in Jonson's own attitudes. It may be that having become established as a Court poet he felt less need to assert himself and harangue his audience in order to force himself on their attention; perhaps also he was anxious not to jeopardise his position with King James, who had a strong antipathy to satirical writers, having suffered at their hands before he came to England. For that matter it may simply be that Jonson was mellowing—he was nearing forty when he wrote *Epicoene*—although age does not always mellow satirists (it certainly did not mellow Swift). In the end we are left with a conundrum of a kind familiar in literary history, but still unanswerable: did Jonson simply adapt his stance to suit a subject which was less serious than *Volpone*'s, or did he choose a lighter subject to suit his own less serious mood?

Whatever the reason, the Prologue to *Epicoene* is, for Jonson, remarkably placatory towards the audience:

> Truth sayes, of old, the art of making plaies
> Was to content the people; & their praise

> Was to the *Poet* money, wine, and bayes.
> But in this age, a sect of writers are,
>   That, onely, for particular likings care,
>   And will taste nothing that is populare.
> With such we mingle neither braines, nor brests;
>   Our wishes, like to those (make publique feasts)
>   Ate not to please the cookes tastes, but the guests.   (1–9)

Despite this disclaimer Jonson retained, as always, his fundamental seriousness of purpose and his unremitting attention to form and style, but the immediate effect of *Epicoene* is of a throw-back to the Terentian comedy of *Every Man in his Humour*. Dauphine, Clerimont and True-Wit, though more polished and sophisticated, are gallants of the same type as Knowell and Wellbred, and they are fighting yet another skirmish in the never-ending battle between the younger generation and the old. Daw and La-Foole are improved versions of Stephen and Mathew, and Captain and Mrs Otter play another variation on the theme of marital warfare which in different ways Kiteley and his wife and Cob and Mrs Cob represented in the earlier comedy.

The most important 'humour' obviously is Morose's, and Jonson has been criticised for letting the play depend so much on so trivial a quality as a crotchety old man's hatred of noise. This is not the kind of objection that ever occurs to anyone in the theatre, where Morose's peculiarity is a given datum which we accept without question, as we do, for example, Marlowe's shyness in *She Stoops to Conquer*, but a closer reading of the play will shew that Jonson has 'planted' enough to make Morose a rounded character and not simply the possessor of an isolated absurdity. He describes how he was taught by his father to 'eschew' anything, and especially argument or noise, that might distract him from his reflective way of life, and learned

> that I should endeare myself to rest, and avoid turmoil: which is
> now grown to be another nature to me   (V.iii.53–4)

In effect this means that he has grown up to be solitary, self-indulgent and anti-social (a tendency to withdraw from ordinary life seems to run in the family, for Truewit accuses Dauphine of spending too much time shut up with his books in his chamber). Moreover his dislike of noise is part of a general contempt for the civilities of ordinary life ('Did you ever hear a more unnecessary question?' he asks when Epicoene enquires how he is) and although he is a gentleman he is capable of startling boorishness, as when he speaks of his future wife as 'her, whom I shall choose for my heifer'. Jonson further prevents us from sentimentalising Morose and sympathising too much with him in this 'comedy of affliction' by indicating that his quarrel with Dauphine is of long-standing, and has on Morose's side a considerable element of bitterness and envy. The whole scheme of marrying to disinherit his nephew is the produce of curdled malice, and there is a vicious note in his gleeful imaginings of how Dauphine's 'knighthood' will be reduced to starvation and beggary and in the end will have to 'make *Dol Teare-sheet* or *Kate Common* a lady, and so, it knighthood may eate'. Dauphine's dismissal of Morose at the end of the play is not exactly heart-warming—

> Now you may goe in and rest, be as private as you will, sir. I'll not trouble you, till you trouble me with your funerall, which I care not how soone it come—   (V.iv.214–17)

but even the soft-hearted audience of today is not likely to be too disturbed by it, if Morose has been correctly played.

Epicoene is recognisably a development from the Comedy of Humours as Jonson first conceived it, but the modern reader may well find it surprisingly more like what he expects from Restoration Comedy. The tone set in the very first scene by the conversation between Truewit and Clerimont is for Jonson unexpectedly free and lax, and Truewit's speeches throughout the play, with their echoes of Ovid (especially of the *Ars Amatoria*), hint at an immorality not found in the more innocent gaiety of Knowell and Well-bred. There are jokes in *Epicoene* of a kind rarely found in Jonson, such as Mrs Otter's comment when she agrees to allow her husband to take the drinking-cup he calls his 'horse' among the ladies:

> Well, I am contented for the horse: they love to be well hors'd, I know. I love it myself . . . ,   (III.i.22–3)

and her frequent references to Epicoene's 'longings'. *Epicoene* is distinguished most of all, and made more like Restoration Comedy, by the raffish, all-men-together note of much of its humour. Captain Otter in his cups would be a fitting companion for Sir John Brute: 'wives are nasty sluttish *animals* . . . I married with six thousand pound, I. I was in love with that.' But it is the Collegiate Ladies who seem to have arrived ahead of their time: they belong naturally in Wycherley's world, and the whole business of their courting of Dauphine anticipates so much of *The Country Wife* (even the references to china in *Epicoene*—Mrs Otter has kept a china-shop—are oddly appropriate).

It is easy to see how literary historians can trace a line from Jonson through his followers Brome and Shirley on to the Restoration theatre. Yet we must be careful not to overstress the similarities. The moral tone of *Epicoene* is looser and more ambiguous than that of any other of his comedies, but Jonson has certainly not completely abandoned his role as moralist. He may allow the Collegians to repeat the stock justifications for liberality in women:

> . . . why should women denie their favours to men? Are they the poorer, or the worse? . . . ladies should be mindfull of the approach of age, and let no time want his due use. The best of our daies passe first . . . ,   (IV.iii.32–3;40–2)

but we are not to suppose that he accepts or approves of them. In fact *Epicoene* is one long attack on women, in which Jonson blazes away at the targets set up by countless misogynistic writers from classical times onwards: the lustfulness of women, their extravagance, their passion for clothes, their obsession with their own appearance, their desire to dominate men, and especially to tyrannise over their husbands, their unfaithfulness and deceit, and above all, of course, their incessant chattering and noise. It is in order to demonstrate their faults and follies, not to justify them, that he allows Lady Haughty and the others have their heads. There does not seem to be anything personal or bitter in this—Jonson's relations with his own wife were perhaps not always very good[2], but *Epicoene* has nothing even remotely like the violence and vindictiveness of some of Strindberg's plays—but the theme is kept perfectly steadily before us, and it provides a consistency of intellectual and moral view-point which a Restoration comedy rarely offers.

Where *Epicoene* is least like Restoration Comedy is in its style. This was the point that Dryden fastened on when he remarked of Truewit that he is

a scholar-like kind of man, a Gentleman with an allay of Pedantry: a man who seems mortifi'd to the world by much reading . . . in short, he would be a fine Gentleman, in an University.[3]

The Restoration prided itself on having brought 'the conversation of gentlemen' to the stage, and recognised Fletcher alone as its

precursor in this. And it is true that while the conversation of
Dauphine, Truewit and Clerimont is much looser and more
'gallant', especially in the very first scene of *Epicoene*, than is at all
usual with Jonson, it lacks the polish, the epigrammatic neatness
and the rhythms of the Restoration. In general Jonson is not a
witty writer, as Congreve, Sheridan and Wilde are. His ideas of
stylistic correctness cut him off from some of the strategies on
which a wit normally relies—he disapproved, for example, of
paradox[4]—and he seems to have lacked the grace and the sense of
balance necessary for epigram, although he can always produce the
dexterous, unexpected phrase which causes an audience to explode
into laughter, such as Morose's despairing cry:

Married with a whore! and so much noise!

Epicoene demonstrates perhaps better than his other comedies his
skill in the quick and neat exchange in dialogue, for example when
Morose suddenly hits upon the happy thought that at least he will
get some peace when Epicoene is asleep:

Have I no friend that will make her drunke? or give her a little
ladanum? or *opium*?
Truewit Why, sir, shee talkes ten times worse in her sleepe.
Morose How!
Clerimont Doe you not know that, sir? never ceases all night.
Truewit And snores like a *porcpisce*.   (IV.iv.139–44)

This kind of short, self-contained passage is not so typical of
Jonson as the long interchange between two or more characters,
most often in the form of a debate or quarrel; similarly he is less
remarkable for short, pithy statement than for long tirades or
harangues. Truewit's lecture to Morose on the perils of marriage
is a fine example of this type of extended humorous passage, and
like the many others in the comedies it is carefully built up from a
mass of detail:

If shee be faire, yong, and vegetous, no sweet meats ever drew
more flies; all the yellow doublets, and great roses i' the towne will
bee there. If foule, and crooked, shee'll bee with them, and buy
those doublets and roses, sir. If rich, and that you marry her dowry,
not her; shee'll raigne in your house, as imperious as a widow. If
noble, all her kindred will be your tyrannes. If fruitfull, as proud as

May, and humorous as *April*; she must have her doctors, her
midwives, her nurses, her longings every houre: though it be for the
dearest morsell of man. If learned, there was never such a parrat;
all your patrimony will be too little for the guests, that must be
invited, to heare her speake *Latine* and *Greeke*: and you must lie
with her in those languages too, if you will please her . . . Then, if
you love your wife, or rather, dote on her, sir: oh, how shee'll torture
you! and take pleasure i' your torments! you shall lye with her but
when she lists; she will not hurt her beauty, her complexion; or
it must be for that jewell, or that pearle, when she do's; every halfe
houres pleasure must be bought anew: and with the same paine, and
charge, you woo'd her at first. Then, you must keepe what servants
she please; what company shee will; that friend must not visit you
without her licence; and him shee loves most shee will seeme to hate
eagerliest, to decline your jelousie; or, faigne to bee jelous of you
first; and for that cause goe live with her she-friend, or cosen at the
colledge, that can instruct her in all the mysteries, of writing letters,
corrupting servants, taming spies; where shee must have that rich
goune for such a great day; a new one for the next; a richer for the
third; bee serv'd in silver; have the chamber fill'd with a succession
of groomes, foot-men, ushers, and other messengers; besides
embroyderers, jewellers, tyre-women, sempsters, fether-men,
perfumers; while shee feeles not how the land drops away; nor the
acres melt; nor forsees the change, when the mercer has your woods
for her velvets; never weighes what her pride costs, sir: so shee may
kisse a page, or a smoth chinne, that has the despaire of a beard; bee a
states-woman, know all the newes, what was done at *Salisbury*, what
at the *Bath*, what at court, what in progresse; or, so shee may
censure *poets*, and authors, and stiles, and compare 'hem, DANIEL
with SPENSER, JONSON with the tother youth, and so foorth; or, be
thought cunning in controversies, or the very knots of divinitie;
and have, often in her mouth, the state of the question: and then
skip to the *Mathematiques*, and demonstration and answere, in religion to one; in state, to another, in baud'ry to a third.

(II.ii.66–80,91–123)

This type of speech can degenerate into catalogue, in which
details are heaped up for their own sake and do not contribute to
any total effect, and Jonson is sometimes guilty of this. Indeed his
greatest fault is that he often carries his love of detail to the point
of gross over-writing. He is particularly given to over-indulgence
in technical jargon—*The Alchemist* is the obvious example of this—
and one sometimes feels that he is so proud of having 'got up' the

appropriate technical language that he cannot bear to leave any of it out (this is not unusual with writers who pride themselves on reproducing the language of specialists; Kipling is another writer who indulges himself in this way). All Jonson's comedies need cutting if they are to be comfortable for the actors and acceptable to the audience, and we may hope that we are justified in this by the evidence which suggests that the plays as he printed them are longer than the versions that were acted in his own day. Critics have occasionally seen something unbalanced, even neurotic, in Jonson's tendency to provide excess of material,[5] but there seems no need to attribute it to more than a natural delight in language, together with a normal Renaissance belief in the virtue of *copia*, or abundance of matter. Perhaps we might object, in terms which he would have understood, that he tended to write with a fullness of style more suitable to an encyclopedic work such as *The Anatomy of Melancholy* (he is sometimes quite close to Burton stylistically) than to the Decorum of drama, but this was integral to his whole conception of comedy. In the long run it has not helped his reputation. His technique of accumulation, of heaping one absurdity or humorous clause on another until the audience is almost battered into laughter, works well in the theatre, but is difficult to demonstrate in a lecture-room, and because even his shorter comic passages depend so much for their effect on the context in which they occur they cannot easily be detached by the critic. We do not swap quotations from Jonson as we do from Shakespeare or Wilde, and this perhaps may have contributed to the belief that he is a slow and ponderous writer.

A visit to a production of *The Alchemist* should prove an adequate corrective to this belief. It is the most energetic and fast-moving of all Jonson's robust and vigorous comedies, a non-stop display of ingenuity and invention, centering flawlessly in the quick-change artistry of Face, Subtle, and Dol Common. The basic comic situation is the same as that of the first part of *Volpone*, with the dupes visiting the place where they are to be mulcted, but the tricksters have more roles to play than Volpone has, and a more assorted clientele, so that both the variety and the tension are greater; there is more interaction, too, between the gulls. The greatest use is made for comic effect of argument and dispute. Kastril, who has come to town to learn to quarrel, has come to the right place, for quarrelling is the dominant form of social relationship in Lovewit's house. The play begins with a violent row between Face and Subtle, which degenerates into a straightforward slanging match—

D

>   Cheater!
>   Bawd!
>   Cow-herd!
>   Conjurer!
>   Cut-purse!
>   Witch!   (I.i. 106–7)

We can trace this back if we wish to the Italian comic debates
or *contrasti*, or to the 'flytings' of medieval poetry, but its ancestry
might just as well have been the 'and you're another' exchange of
the Westminster school-yard. The argument is also a first-rate
piece of explication for the benefit of the audience, and by the time
Dol Common has joined in with her threat to leave the gang if the
others will not 'cossen kindly', the spectators have been most
effectively and quickly told all they need to know of its operations.
From this scene onwards *The Alchemist* progresses largely by a
series of quarrels. In the second scene Face, in disguise, argues with
Subtle on Dapper's behalf; in the first scene of Act II Surly and
Mammon dispute about Alchemy, and in the third scene of this
act Surly and Subtle argue the question out. Ananias then enters
the fray: he has a short brush with Subtle in Act III Scene v, a
discussion with Tribulation Wholesome in III.i. as to whether the
coining of money is lawful, and in the following scene rumbles
mutinously the whole time as Tribulation tries to smooth Subtle
down again ('I hate *Traditions*: I do not trust them. . . . They are
Popish, all. I will not peace. I will not . . .'). In IV.ii. Kastril begins
his lessons from Subtle in the art of managing a quarrel, and in
IV.iv he sets about his sister because she is reluctant to marry the
alleged Spanish Count; meanwhile, in the previous scene, Face and
Subtle have started their argument about which of them shall have
Dame Pliant. In IV.v. Mammon, who was previously warned that
Dol, in her disguise as the Lord's sister, must hear no word of
controversy, follows her in as she raves about the interpretation of
prophetic history, is scolded by Subtle, and told that her brother
is at the door 'as furious as she is mad'—a threatened quarrel that
never materialises. The great set-piece occurs in Scenes vi and vii
of this Act, when Surly reveals himself and attacks Face and
Subtle. Subtle loses his nerve, but Face sets Kastril on to 'quarrel
[Surly] out of the house', and in quick succession Drugger and
Ananias are brought into the argument. There is no better example
than this scene of Jonson's extraordinary gift for quickly turning
the action of a play. The audience has just seen Surly apparently
about to destroy the whole basis on which Face and Subtle work,

and then with magnificent speed this threat to the fabric of the comedy is not only averted but turned to new comic effect. Ananias enters with his Puritan greeting, 'Peace to the household'—a magnificent line to deliver into the middle of the violent altercation which is at this moment in full swing on the stage. Subtle tells him that the cause of the quarrel is Kastril's 'zeal' against Surly's Spanish clothes, and he is immediately launched into one of his diatribes:

> That ruffe of pride
> About thy neck, betrayes thee: and 'tis the same
> With that, which the uncleane birds, in *seventy-seven*,
> Were seene to pranke it with, on divers coasts.
> Thou look'st like *Antichrist*, in that lewd hat . . .   (IV.vii.51–5)

Jonson beautifully catches here the way in which a stupidly irascible fanatic will give rein to his own prejudices in any situation of conflict, just as earlier, in the dispute between Ananias and Subtle, he illustrates how two specialists, each speaking the jargon of his own trade, can have an argument in which neither understands a word said by the other. The out-facing of Surly in these scenes in Act IV might be regarded as Face and Subtle's finest hour because it is all improvised, whereas the discomfiture of Mammon is something they have planned long before. Effectively, as the audience actually experiences the play, both scenes contribute to the feeling that *The Alchemist* is being made up by Face and Subtle as it goes along. The whole of the last Act, after the return of Lovewit, consists of frustrated attempts by the gulls to argue him into returning their goods, and at the very end he silences Kastril, the 'angrie Child' who is berating his sister:

> Come will you quarrel? I will feize you, sirrah.
> Why doe you not buckle to your tooles?   (V.v.131–2)

Confronted with this unexpected determination on the part of his new brother-in-law Kastril compounds the final quarrel of the play.

All this gives a great sense of excitement and movement to *The Alchemist*, and like all Jonson's comedy it demands to be played quickly and without pause. It has also, as *Volpone* has, a strong atmosphere of high spirits and enjoyment. Subtle, Face and Dol, take great pleasure and pride in their trickery, and, like Volpone and Mosca, they form a little mutual-admiration society. Their language about their 'venter tripartite' is inflated and

euphoric: Subtle is 'sovereign' and Face 'general' of their 'camp';
Dol is their 'republic', their prized possession, 'our Castle, our
cinque-Port/Our Dover pier'; their camp fares

> As with the few, that had entrenched themselves
> Safe, by their discipline, against a world, *Dol*:
> And laugh'd, within those trenches, and grew fat
> With thinking on the booties, *Dol*, brought in
> Daily, by their small parties . . .   (III.iii.34–7)

Their professions of loyalty to their little commonwealth are of
course quite fraudulent, since each is always ready to betray the
others in his own interest; there is dispute between Face and Subtle
at the beginning of the play, the arrival of Dame Pliant brings out
again their distrust of each other, and once Lovewit arrives it is a
question of *sauve qui peut*. Nevertheless their way of speaking about
themselves casts an ambience of eagerness and jollity about their
activities which is not tainted, as in *Volpone*, by cruelty or violence.
Delusions of grandeur, stimulated by the promises of Face and
Subtle, affect everyone in the play: Mammon is the supreme
example, with his visions of impossible luxury and grotesque
voluptuousness, but in their humbler way Dapper and Drugger have
their own rich fantasies—Dapper with the aid of his familiar will win
their money from all the gamblers of the town, and Drugger will
have a magnet under his shop-door to draw in all the gallants by
their spurs, and will shortly be 'called to the scarlet' of his company.
Although we know that all these hopes are absurd, and will be
utterly destroyed before the play is over, we become infected by a
kind of giddy excitement in which we feel that perhaps such things
are possible, and are not wholly wrong.

   The Alchemist, indeed, lends a good deal of colour to the charge
that Jonson seems at times to approve more of his rogues than his
fools. If we bring a strict moral judgment to bear, no one in the
play is blameless. We might expect Surly, the one person who sees
through Face and Subtle, to represent honesty and virtue, but in
fact he is himself a man who lives by his wits (he is described as 'a
gamester'), and he is very quick to try and take advantage of the
opportunity of marrying Dame Pliant when it arises: what motivates
him in his attempts to expose the cheats is not love of truth, but,
as he says, his objection to being gulled. As for Lovewit, Jonson
makes him acknowledge that he may have acted in a way unbecoming
'an old man's gravity' and the 'strict canon'—that is, the rules both
of morality and artistic decorum—but he offers no excuse beyond

'what a young wife and good brains may do'. He must be played, in fact, as the sort of whimsical, humorous man—a 'jovy boy', as Kastril calls him—who would admire Face's roguery and think it served Mammon and the rest right if he refuses to give back their goods. His return ends the transformation of his house to a palace of illusion, reduces Face to his proper station in life and despoils Dol and Subtle of their ill-gotten gains, but what he brings with him is more an air of good-humoured commonsense than the pure, keen wind of moral rectitude. It is inevitable that the audience throughout the play will take its greatest pleasure in the activities of the tricksters, and it is Mammon, with his insane visions of limitless wealth and insatiable lechery, and to a lesser extent Tribulation Wholesome, the religious fanatic, who seem the real villains. It almost begins to look as if in his portrayal of 'natural follies', as he calls them in the preface to *The Alchemist*, Jonson has begun to lose sight of his sterner moral purpose.

III

Bartholomew Fair seems to confirm this shift of emphasis. The overwhelming impression it gives is inescapably one of vitality and profuse invention. In one chorus of *Every Man out of his Humour* Jonson had announced his dislike of the neo-classic restriction on the number of actors who might be on the stage at any one time:

> is it not an object of more state, to behold the *Scene* full, and reliev'd with varietie of speakers to the end, then to see a vast emptie stage, and the actors come in (one by one) as if they were dropt downe with a feather, into the eye of the spectators? (II.iii. 297–301)

and in *Bartholomew Fair* he triumphantly vindicates this preference for a crowded stage. There are over forty speaking parts: some, necessarily, are slight, but even apart from Zeal-of-the-Land Busy and Ursula the Pig-Woman, which are obviously the 'fattest', there are a surprising number which provide the actor with enough on which to base a detailed characterisation—Knock'em, for example, the 'horse-courser', or Captain Whit, the Irish pimp. Unfortunately *Bartholomew Fair* is less often staged than the other major Jonsonian comedies (very largely precisely because it does demand so numerous a cast) and this is a pity, because it is much better seen than read—indeed reading it for the first time can be a baffling experience. It is an extraordinary *tour-de-force*, both as an example of dramatic construction, and as a kind of blue-print from

which we can re-create in our own theatre a whole section of
Jacobean London life. But if we challenge it for its moral significance
it does not immediately seem to have much to offer. Essentially it
is based on the age-old comic formula of deflating pomposity and
making everyone who is in any way 'stuck up' or pretentious look
absurd. All those in the play who claim any sort of authority over
their fellow human-beings are humbled. Littlewit, who is accused
of being insolent and 'overdoing' with his wit, is discomforted by
discovering the wife of whom he is so proud in the dubious company of a bully and a bawd; the choleric Waspe loses his power over
his stupid master when he is put in the stocks for drunken quarrelling; Dame Purecraft, the 'sanctified sister', has to renounce her
claims to spiritual superiority and is reduced to seeking the love
of a madman; more importantly to Jonson, her religious mentor
Busy is defeated in his attack of the puppets, and reduced to silence.
The greatest fall is that of Overdo, the officious magistrate, who, in
the fashion of the Duke in *Measure for Measure*, sets himself up as
'God's spy' and visits the Fair secretly to reveal the 'enormities'
that he is convinced are practised there. Having been consistently
wrong in all his judgments, humiliated in each of his disguises,
and cheated, by his own stupidity, of his control over the ward
from whose marriage he expects to profit, he is finally cast down
when his own wife reveals her drunken disgrace just as he is about
to mete out punishment to the assembled 'Batholomew birds', and
he is left with nothing to do but to accept Quarlous' advice:

> remember you are but *Adam*, Flesh, and blood! you have your
> frailty, forget your other name of *Overdoo*, and invite us all to
> supper.   (V.vi.96–8)

We should be misreading Jonson if we thought that there was
anything revolutionary in *Bartholomew Fair*; he is not, as a modern
writer might be, attacking all authority, but simply mocking those,
whether they are magistrates, watchmen or pastors, who have
power over others without having the wisdom to use that power
correctly. Overdo, who sees himself as 'the true top of formality,
and scourge of enormity', has a glimpse of the truth when he says
that men have before his time seen 'many a foole in the habit of a
Justice', but this does not mean that every magistrate is a fool.
Nevertheless there is a strong hint in *Bartholomew Fair* of the most
basic of all comic occasions, the *Saturnalia*, in which all order is
inverted and licence reigns.

From the reference to '*Tales, Tempests*, and such-like drolleries' in the Induction to *Bartholomew Fair* it seems that Jonson had been irritated by the new vogue current from about 1610 onwards for pastoral tragi-comedy, and particularly by Shakespeare's versions of the genre. In part he may have been annoyed by the introduction into the popular theatre of masque-like elements, both because it represented an inacceptable mixture of 'kinds' and because he resented poaching on his own especial territory; but obviously he objected also to the fantasy and unrealism of this type of drama, being himself, as he said, 'loth to make Nature afraid in his *Playes*'. Not that he ever fell into the opposite extreme and denied the importance of Imagination: Drummond records **him** as saying of du Bartas, who had a towering European reputation **as** a didactic author, that he was 'no Poet, but a Verser, because **he** wrote not fiction'.[6] Essentially he accepted Horace's dictum in the *Ars Poetica: Ficta voluptatis causa sint proxima veris*—in Jonson's own translation 'Let what thou fain'st for pleasure's sake, be neere The Truth', or as he adapts it in the Second Prologue to *Epicoene*,

> ... *Poet* never credit gain'd
> By writing truths, but things (like truths) well faind. (9–10)

In *Bartholomew Fair* Jonson brought his fiction closer to the truth—that is, closer to the actual everyday London in which he lived—even than in *The Alchemist*, and in so doing he produced a gallery of characters who illustrate the complete range of what could be comprehended under the general concept 'humour'. Waspe is a pure choleric, Cokes a phlegmatic; Trouble-all, the madman, with his obsessive enquiry after Justice Overdo's warrant, is the victim of a compulsive *idée fixe*; Zeal-of-the-Land Busy, according to Quarlous, 'affects the violence of Singularity in all he does' and reproves others out of 'vaine-glory', the implication being that his profession of puritanism is not simply hypocritical, but an affectation adapted in order to distinguish himself from the common herd. Littlewit has the rather pathetic humour of delighting in his own feeble playing upon words, this being his way of trying to distinguish himself; Knock'em, Cutting and Whit, with their game of 'vapours', are up-dated versions of Bobadil and Cavaliero Shift, the perennial types of braggarts, bullies, petty thieves and bawds, with a new type of blustering jargon. The rear is brought up by the watch and the various showmen, who are merely quickly sketched contemporary types. The skill with which all these characters are established and brought into action is stupendous, but there are so many of them and so much going on in the play

that Jonson has little room to develop any didactic purpose, beyond
a generalised injunction to us to Know Ourselves and not to
presume above our capacities, and a more particular defence of the
theatre against its traditional enemies, the Puritans (championed by
Busy) and the City fathers (represented by Overdo, who regards
actors as a 'licentious quality' and thinks puppetry 'little better
than Poetry'). Today's audience is not likely to complain about the
absence of moralising, but it does seem that in moving steadily
towards greater realism and contemporaneity Jonson had also
retreated from the heroic position he took up in his first group
of plays.

IV

It is possible, in fact, to feel a certain general disappointment at
the scope of Jonson's satire. Asper's bold assertions may be discounted as part of the dramatic portrayal of the Juvenalian satirist,
but Jonson was ready enough to let himself be identified with his
own portrait of Horace, who though more urbane and less frenzied
than Asper, is still a stern and incorruptible judge of men and
manners, and he never hesitated to declare himself one

> at feud
> With sin and vice, though with a throne endued.[7]

In actual fact he never enjoyed the independence of which he
boasted. If he had really meant to act out in reality the role of the
fearless exposer of the vices of his day, he could have found a very
good subject in the extravagance and homosexuality of the court
of King James, but to have ventured on this he would have had to
be, in Donne's phrase, 'hungry for an imagined martyrdom'; it
was literally more than his life was worth to have touched on such
a subject. We cannot blame him for not risking too much; he did
not have even the degree of freedom which Pope and Swift had a
century later. We may still feel that he would have been truer to
his pretensions if he had ventured on something as relevant to the
political concerns of the day as Middleton's *A Game at Chess*
(which he despised), or had been as bold to stand up for what he
believed was right as William Prynne.

Once he had accepted that Comedy should sport with human
follies and not with crimes, however, Jonson was debarred from
anything resembling the savagery and penetration of *Gulliver's
Travels*, and in selecting 'humours' as his prime target he was

condemning himself inevitably to a degree of ephemeral triviality. Of course the kind of behaviour which he satirised, even at its most transient and silly, is still the product of genuine and recurrent aspects of human nature. There are plenty of people today who are as ridiculous as Brisk or Sir John Daw and as ready to embrace any literary or sartorial fashion in their efforts to keep up with the times, or are as enamoured as Puntarvolo or Sir Politic Would-be of the ludicrous behaviour which, they believe, marks them off from the common herd. The 'apes' that Asper set out to scourge still flourish. Yet although we could claim for Jonson that in this respect his range was extensive—there can have been few eccentricities or follies around him which he did not notice and incorporate into his own world—if there were no more to him than this we could not say that his satire went very deep. We would have to place his comedies on the same level as Thackeray's *Book of Snobs*, and this is not the level of great satire.

In each of Jonson's plays, however, we can distinguish some underlying moral theme which forms the basis for the satirical attack and adds depth to the more superficial satire of behaviour. In *Cynthia's Revels* it is Vanity, or self-love, in *Epicoene* women's desire for mastery over man (no trivial affair to Jonson, but a gross inversion of the natural order of the universe), in *The Staple of News* the inordinate craving for novelty, and so on. Usually this theme is quite explicit, and sometimes it is expressed not merely negatively but positively, by direct moralising: in *Poetaster*, for example, the theme may be said to be true artistic value, and this is shown not merely by the satire of Demetrius and Crispinus and the final banishment of Ovid, but by an actual demonstration of the highest form of poetry—the Epic as practised by Virgil. This kind of overt didacticism tends to decrease later in Jonson's career, although it makes a reappearance in *The New Inn*, with Lovel's disquisitions on the nature of Love. There is never much difficulty in perceiving the particular moral lesson which Jonson wishes to teach; what is often not apparent to the modern reader, is the extent to which Jonson relates apparently trivial episodes to his main theme. The incident in *Volpone* when Sir Politic Would-be, believing that he is about to be arrested by the agents of the Venetian State, conceals himself in a tortoise-shell has often been criticised as an irrelevant piece of rather feeble farce, but it has been convincingly shown to have a real place in the texture of the play. The tortoise was an emblem not only of Policy, the statesmanship which Would-be most wishes to demonstrate that he possesses, but also of Silence, a characteristic which he equally lacks, so that he is simply physically clothing himself in the trappings of qualities which he has always falsely claimed to have.[8] There are many other examples of this kind of invention in Jonson's other plays.

It could still be alleged that the object of Jonson's attack varies too much from play to play, and that there is no unifying principle in their different themes. If this is so Jonson fails to answer the demand we must make of the satirist if we are to accord him our highest praise—that he has a central position which he is prepared to defend, and is not simply a carper at others with no positive principles of his own. This is the charge which T. S. Eliot made when he said that Jonson's satire has no source 'in any precise emotional attitude or precise intellectual criticism of the actual world'[9] and this, in Jonson's own eyes, would be the worst thing that could have been said of him. Many defenders have tried to rebut the allegation, and to find some vice, other than mere affectation, which Jonson can be said to attack consistently in all his plays.

Greed is one candidate to fill this place. In its simplest form as avarice it is a dominant in *Volpone*, *The Alchemist*, and *The Devil is an Ass*, and it plays a significant role in other comedies—for example, *The Staple of News*. If we extend its meaning further, so as to cover all forms of covetousness or desire for possession, it could be found in nearly every play. Jonson himself equates desire for gold with desire for woman in both *Volpone* and *The Alchemist*: in fact both Volpone and Sir Epicure Mammon—two dedicated if self-indulgent voluptuaries—endanger themselves by allowing lust for a woman to distract them from the main object of their desire. Many of Jonson's lesser characters are dominated by a longing to possess something—a reputation for learning (like Sir John Daw and Lady Would-be) or gentility (like Matthew or Sogliardo or Sir Amorous Lafoole), or beauty, or wit, or even fine clothes. A passionate, blind desire to possess anything, even something as trivial as an embroidered cloak, can make a man ridiculous and a fit subject for Comedy. It can also make him a tragic hero, or a villain; for Greed, as the homilists of the Middle Ages insisted, is closely related to Pride. Together they constitute the sin known to Jonson's contemporaries as 'Surquedry'—that is, arrogance, unnatural and impious presumption, and a compulsive urge to triumph over men and circumstances. This is the sin of which Marlowe's heroes are guilty, and critics have rightly pointed out the Marlovian ring in some of Volpone's and Mammon's speeches.[10] As we should expect, Jonson treats of it most fully in his Tragedies, for it is liable to become too serious a subject for Comedy, but it is not only Volpone and Mammon who have something in common with Catiline and Sejanus: the same drives towards domination can be seen in characters as different as Macilente and Meercraft. Another aspect of this insolence is the habit Jonson's characters have of setting themselves above the ordinary run of mankind, either alone (like Overdo) or as a group (like Face, Dol and Subtle). Morose is another who attempts to shut himself off from the ordinary life of mankind and make a little world for himself obedient only to his own selfish caprice. The idea these comic figures hold of themselves as a sect, a chosen few superior to the multitude, is reflected in their parodies of religious observance: they seem to want to set up their own religions, as Volpone does with his worship of gold or Morose with his cult of silence. A general concern with the unbridled assertion of personality may also explain why love and sexual desire play so comparitively small a part in Jonson's world, for in it desire for woman is merely another manifestation of the desire to dominate, similar to, but no more important than, the desire to possess wealth or power. In very crude terms, the world is interpreted through an Adlerian rather than a Freudian psychology.

Blinkered obsession and over-weening pride are traditional subjects for the comic writer, yet are serious enough to rebut any charge of flippancy or triviality. While they could be traced in many of Jonson's comedies, however, the definition would have to be stretched very thin, and some plays—*Every Man in his Humour*, for instance, or *The Magnetic Lady*—have very little direct relation to this theme at all. There is another vice, related to these, yet still more basic, against which Jonson consistently directed his attack in all his comedies—and for that matter in his tragedies and many of his masques as well. This is the vice of relying on what his age called 'Opinion'. In Renaissance psychological theory the Imagination was very much a subordinate faculty, its prime function being to present to the mind images of things so that they could be considered and judged by the Reason.[11] It was also, however, potentially a very dangerous power, for two reasons, one being its ability to summon up false pictures of things which were not only present in reality but never had or could have been present, and the other its close link with the passions. A mental image very quickly stirred up emotion, as when the lover summoned up the image of his absent mistress, and conversely a strong emotion would stimulate the imagination to produce the appropriate mental picture—

Or in the night imagining some fear,
How easy is a bush supposed a bear![12]

It was very necessary, therefore, for the Imagination to be kept
firmly under the control of the Reason, for only on a true, rational
apprehension of reality and a considered use of Judgment could
right action be based. If the Reason was inactive or temporarily
enfeebled in some way, a false image of reality might be taken as
the truth, and a man might be led into rash, uninformed or inappropriate decisions. Such shallow and ill-considered judgment
constituted Opinion: the French psychologist Charron defined it
thus (in a passage actually quoted by Jonson in *Discoveries*):

Opinion is a light, vaine, crude and imperfect thing, settled in the
Imagination; but never arriving at the understanding, there to obtaine
the tincture of *Reason*.[13]

Jonson only brought the opposed faculties of Opinion and true
Judgment into open conflict once, in the masque *Hymenaei*, in
which Opinion appears claiming to be Truth, and is finally defeated
by the champions of Truth itself, but the struggle is implicit in
all his comedies. It is closely related to the opposition between
Appearance and Reality—a theme treated in so many of Shakespeare's plays—because Opinion was essentially a superficial
valuation based on outward show, whereas Judgment penetrated
to the real inner nature of things. Jonson's fools—and this includes
several who pride themselves on their own wisdom—are always
taken in by appearances: there could be no clearer case than that
of Morose. Vanity is a passion very likely to lead to the errors of
Opinion because it puffs its victim up with a belief in his own
cleverness and so makes him very gullible:

self-love never yet could looke on truth,
But with bleared beames; slieke flatterie and shee
Are twin-borne sisters,

says Echo in *Cynthia's Revels* (I.ii.36–8), and the whole of that
play demonstrates this fact. Self-love makes Morose easily deceived,
but he is rendered even more vulnerable by his mean desire to
disinherit Dauphine; he *wants* Epicoene to be the wife he desires
and is really asking to be deceived. Any strong passion is liable
to inflame the Imagination and distort the Judgment, and produce
the will to believe even in the teeth of the evidence. Mosca recog-

nises this in Volpone's suitors, who will reject anything they do
not want to be true:

> Eache of 'hem
> Is so possesst, and stuft with his owne hopes,
> That any thing, unto the contrary,
> Never so true, or never so apparent,
> Never so palpable, they will resist it.   (V.ii.23–7)

In the same way Mammon is so dominated by greed and lust that
he readily takes Subtle for a pious and humble devotee of the
alchemical art and Dol Common for an intellectual noblewoman,
while Surly, who is not inflamed by desire, has no difficulty in
seeing them for what they are. The other comedies are full of like
errors of judgment, the most common being the result of judging
a man by his own account of himself, as Stephen and Matthew
judge Bobabil—'the sign of the soldier' Justice Clements calls him,
and he is indeed as painted and sone-dimensional as an inn-sign—
or by his dress and behaviour: the nadir in this respect is reached
by Cokes, who believes the puppets are real people. The basis of
Jonson's frequent attacks on vanity in dress lies here:

> A number of these popenjayes there are,
> Whom, if a man conferre, and but examine
> Their inward merit, with such men as want;
> Lord, lord what things they are![14]

With a true man, as Jonson said of himself,

> his clothes shall never bee the best thing about him . . . hee will
> have somwhat beside, either of humane letters, or severe honesty,
> shall speake him a man though he went naked.[15]

Satire of women's love of fashion and their dependence on cosmetics
to disguise their real appearance has the same gravamen, but
women are no worse than the men who love them for this artificial
beauty. Here the palm is taken by the tailor in *The New Inn* who,
whenever he has made a new dress for a client, dresses his wife up
in it and takes her into the country to make love to her in her
borrowed finery. He must have been a real person, for Jonson
mentions him also in *Discoveries*, and he was guilty of the most
absurd sin imaginable—'committing adultery with a suit of
clothes'. The moral behind all this is clearly expressed in the preface
to *Cynthia's Revels*:

It is not pould'ring, perfuming and every day smelling of the
taylor, that converteth to a beautiful object, but a mind shining
through every sute, which needes no false light, either of riches or
honours, to helpe it.

All forms of ostentation are both a product of a yielding to Opinion
and an attempt to influence Opinion in others, and the real seriousness of any cultivation of singularity or affectation was that it
distracted the mind from the apprehension of true value:

Why, that's the end of wealth! thrust riches outward,
And remain beggers within: contemplate nothing
But the vile sordid things of time, place, money,
And let the noble, and the precious goe,
Vertue and honesty . . .[16]

The flaw common to all of Jonson's comic characters is their
failure to appreciate the true nature of the people and the circumstances with which they come into contact. Their misapprehensions
may be trivial or radical, and may have consequences ranging from
the farcical to the near tragic, although this range is limited by the
Decorum of comedy. Any yielding to Opinion is at once an
intellectual and a moral failing, since it springs from a defect of
reason, and can lead only to irrational, and therefore immoral,
action. One critic has said

Jonson's didactic theory is more philosophical than moral, more
literary than monitory;[17]

in fact all four adjectives in this sentence can well be applied to his
'doctrine'.
   The wise man, like Asper, is not a 'parasite to time, place, or
opinion' (Asper, as Macilente, had the gift of seeing through the
pretensions of the other characters); on the contrary he

   never goes the peoples way
But as the Planets still move contrary,
To the worlds motion; so doth he, to opinion . . .[18]

Here 'Opinion' is the common judgment of the world, that is
popular report or reputation, and it is characteristic of the irrational
person to be swayed by this even against the evidence of his own
senses. Truewit thus characterises the Collegiate ladies:

> Why, all their actions are governed by crude opinion, without
> reason or cause; they know not why they doe anything: but as they
> are inform'd, beleeve, judge, praise, condemne, love, hate, and in
> æmulation one of another, doe all these things alike.[19]

There is something very modern about this description of the
kind of fatuous prejudice characteristic of any self-satisfied social
group—indeed we can recognise around us today example after
example of what Jonson intended. He lived just long enough to see
the beginnings of the commercial management of Opinion by the
newspapers: today he would be saddened, though perhaps not
surprised, to see how we have elevated the diffusion of precipitate
and shallow judgment into an industry.

In Jonson's plays true Judgment, whenever it is found, at once
reveals the falseness of Opinion, as the mock virtues in *Cynthia's
Revels* are unmasked as soon as they come into the presence of
Cynthia, Crites and Arete. Whenever the moment of truth comes
—normally it is at the end of the play—all misapprehensions are
removed and reason and order are re-established. As a dramatist,
Jonson naturally wanted these moments to be exciting as possible;
the most striking is the revelation of Epicoene's true sex, which
surprises everyone on the stage except Dauphine. As a moralist he
could justify this by the need to make a sharp impression on the
minds of the audience; it was necessary to demonstrate that Truth
is invincible, and that once it is revealed men can do no other than
accept it. From two different starting points Jonson was led to
the 'surprise ending'.

The great enemy of Truth was Ignorance, and this was something more than stupidity or lack of education. 'I know of no
disease of the Soule', Jonson noted in *Discoveries*, 'but Ignorance':

not of the Arts, and Sciences, but of it selfe: Yet relating to these, it is a
pernicious *evill*, the darkner of man's life: the disturber of his *Reason*,
and common Confounder of *Truth*: with which a man goes groping in the
darke, no otherwise, then if hee were blind.[20]

In *The Masque of Queens* the twelve witches of the coven represent
in order Ignorance, Suspicion, Credulity, Falsehood, Murmur (or
rumour), Malice, Impudence (or lack of shame), Slander, Execration, Bitterness, Fury and Mischief (which would have a stronger
sense of evil to Jonson than it carries today). These derive one
from another, and Ignorance is their parent. Jonson also connected Ignorance with Envy, with especial reference to the attack

by the ignorant upon the glory of Art; altogether Ignorance
represented for him a complex of evils inimical to the whole mode
of life to which he had dedicated himself. Opinion was based upon
Ignorance, and could only exist as long as Ignorance survived. A
person as apparently brilliant and sophisticated as Volpone might
be truly called ignorant, because his vanity prevented him from
seeing the truth which Reason makes plain, that Virtue is the only
Good. Men like him suffer from the true 'disease of the soul', the
most dangerous form of Opinion, which is a mistaken apprehension
of the nature of Man and the end for which he was created.

Jonson expected the spectators themselves—or the judicious
among them—to avoid the errors of Opinion. However amusing
and attractive he made the comic parts of his work they were not
to be satisfied only to appreciate this superficial pleasure—unlike

> the vulgar sort
> Of Nut-crackers, that onely come for sight—[21]

but should make the effort to penetrate to the inner moral meaning
of his plays. Only then would they truly be in the ranks of the
'understanders'—

> attentive auditors,
> Such as will joyne their profit with their pleasure,
> And come to feed their understanding parts.[22]

For these 'ripe judgments' Jonson was prepared to 'melt his brain
into invention'. He constantly lamented that they were so few, and
the enemies of Art so many, but the fact that he kept before him
the need to satisfy the severest judgments of the critic and the
moralist gives his comedy its stability and ballast. His satirical
attacks had a real, identifiable objective, and it was balanced by a
self-consistent moral and aesthetic theory: not original, truly, but
to all appearances sincerely, even passionately, held. Jonson never
faltered in his aim to achieve 'the principal end of poesie': to inform
men in the best reason for living.[23]

4

THE LAST PLAYS

I

With the notable exception of Swinburne, critics have been hard on Jonson's later comedies ever since Dryden called them his 'dotages'. The context of Dryden's remark is often overlooked: it is made in parenthesis in the *Essay on Dramatic Poesie* when he is engaged in claiming a very high place indeed for Jonson:

As for Jonson . . . if we look upon him while he was himself (for his last plays were but his dotages) I think him the most learned and judicious writer any theatre ever had.[1]

In dismissing the least satisfactory part of Jonson's work so summarily he may, like a practised orator, have been deliberately conceding the weak points in his case before they could be urged against him. Nevertheless, there is no pretending that Jonson ever wrote as well again as he had done in *Bartholomew Fair*, and *The Devil is an Ass*, although it appeared only two years later, seems to mark a clear decline in his powers. If we knew less than we do about Jonson's life we might be tempted to regard 1616 as a watershed: realising that his best days as a playwright were over, we might surmise, Jonson abandoned the popular stage, perhaps in intention for ever, only returning to it ten years later when compelled to do so by his poverty. Jonson may indeed have intended to give up the public theatre for good in 1616, though there is no direct evidence of this, but it is very unlikely that he felt driven to this by a sense of any loss of vigour; 1616 may more likely have seemed to him the beginning of his period of greatest success.

The publication of his *Works* in a massive Folio of over a thousand pages had been the crowning stroke of his struggle to dignify the position of the playwright. It contained no play later than *Catiline* (although the masque section includes *Mercury Vindicated*, which was performed in January 1616) and all the nine plays included had gone through a process of careful revision, most obvious in the case of *Every Man in his Humour*, where the changes go far beyond those made necessary by the transference of the scene from Italy to England, and amount to a substantial re-writing with the aim of bringing it closer to the plays which followed it. Jonson saw the *Works* through the press himself with quite exceptional care, and it set a standard of printing very much higher than any book of plays had reached before (there is in fact a visible improvement in the printing of plays after it). The publication was greeted with considerable ridicule, for '*Works*' was a title reserved for the collected efforts of theologians and philosophers, not for the trivial effusions of popular dramatists. Even thirty years later Suckling could make affectionate fun of Jonson by representing him in *A Session of the Poets* claiming the right to be crowned by Apollo before all the other poets 'For his were called *Works*, where others wrote but Plays'.[2] But Jonson carried his point, and it is almost certainly to his example, even if not to his personal initiative, that we owe the Shakespeare First Folio.[3] Despite the mockery and the malicious comment, Jonson may justifiably have felt satisfied with this achievement.

He could take satisfaction, too, in the following decade in his position at Court. Up to the death of James I he was in regular demand as a provider of masques—he called himself

A kind of *Christmas Ingine*: one that is used, at least once a year, for a trifling instrument, of wit, or so—[4]

and although he was never officially given the title of Poet Laureate, which it seems he hankered after, he held the position in all but name. He was recognised, too, by the academic community. Oxford, in 1619, made him an honorary M.A., perhaps through the influence of his friend Richard Corbett, Dean of Christ Church (best known as the author of 'Farewell, rewards and fairies'). When it became known in 1621 that Donne was to become Dean of St Paul's, the newsletter writer John Chamberlain wrote

. . . and then we are like to have our new Deane Dr Dun at Paules, so as a pleasant companion said that yf Ben Jonson might be made deane of

Westminster, that place, Paules, and Christchurch should be furnished
with three very pleasant poetical deanes.[5]

That this could be said even as a joke indicates the extent to which
Jonson, the bricklayer and strolling player, had succeeded in
identifying himself as a figure in the country's intellectual life. In
the same year it was rumoured that he was on the point of being
knighted by King James, but had managed to avoid the honour,
which he did not want; he was, however, given the reversion of the
office of Master of the Revels.[6] Sufficiently free of financial worry
not to have to tempt the uncertain favour of the theatre public, he
was able to devote himself to his scholarly interests. 'An Execration upon Vulcan', the poem he wrote on the fire which took place
in his lodgings in 1623, provides information about his various
projects—a commentary on Horace's *Ars Poetica*; an account in
verse of his journey to Scotland in 1618; a history of the reign of
Henry V; a translation (asked for by the King himself) of *Argenis*,
a Latin prose romance by the Scots writer John Barclay; and—
rather unexpectedly—his 'humble gleanings in Divinity'. To the
same period belong the meetings in the Apollo Room at the Devil
Tavern, near Temple Bar, where the group of young poets who
became known as 'the sons of Ben' foregathered: the exact membership of the club is not easy to determine, but certainly besides
Fletcher (a friend of long-standing) it included Herrick and
Lovelace. All in all this may have seemed a golden period to
Jonson.

The death of James I in 1625 brought it abruptly to an end.
Although Charles I was kind to his father's old servant he clearly
never had the same affection for him as James had had, and it is
easy to see why. Jonson, with his earthiness, his boisterousness
and his pedantry, is very much a Jacobean figure, and he never
seems to fit in as a 'Caroline' author; although many of the poets
we accept under this head owed much to him, he himself lacked
the lightness of touch, the gallantry, and the easiness of morals
which characterises them. He was still employed from time to time
as a masque-writer, but he finally lost this link with the Court in
1631, after the production of the twin masques *Love's Triumph
through Callipolis* and *Chloridia*. This was not because they were
unsuccessful, but because he foolishly again provoked a quarrel
with Inigo Jones; Jones, now Surveyor General, was in high
favour with the King, and Jonson was no longer a match for him.
In 1628 he acquired another source of income when he was appointed
City Chronologer at an annual stipend of 100 marks: unfortunately

he appears to have regarded this post as a sinecure, which was not the view of the City Fathers. They expected their Chronologer to write glowing accounts of notable events in the City, and when none were forthcoming they stopped his pay until he should present them with 'some fruit of his labours'. Jonson commented indignantly in a letter:

Yesterday the barbarous Court of Aldermen have withdrawn their Chander-ly Pension, for Verjuice and Mustard.[7]

Some of his friends intervened and got his salary restored, and his pension from the King was increased. It was one thing to be granted a pension, however, and another to get it paid, and Jonson wrote a series of begging poems to various officials pointing out that he had had neither his money nor his allowance of Canary wine. Throughout the last period of his life he was in debt, and also in illness: he suffered a stroke in 1628 or early 1629, from which he never properly recovered, and was largely confined to his house. It was in these circumstances that he tried to write stage comedy again, beginning with *The Staple of News* in 1626, and perhaps it is less surprising that these plays do not have the vigour of his earlier work than that he succeeded in producing them at all.

One difficulty he faced was that of reminding the theatre-going public of his existence, after a ten-year absence from the stage. A quarter of a century had passed since he had made his name with *Every Man in his Humour*, and the extent to which he was felt to be a figure of the past is indicated by a curt note written in 1632 by a letter-writer: 'Ben Jonson (who, I thought, had been dead) hath written a play against next terme called the Magnetick Lady'.[8] It is noticeable in all the last plays that he frequently refers to himself and his past successes and, as he had not done since his early plays, takes pains by means of Choric figures to explain his aims and methods: clearly he was trying to establish himself again as the dominating figure he had once been. Thus the 'gossips' Mirth, Tattle, Expectation and Censure, who form the chorus of *The Staple of News*, refer explicitly in their first 'Intermean' to *The Devil is an Ass* ('he is an arrant learn'd man that made it, and can write, they say, and I am foully deceiu'd, but hee can read too'), and this has a point greater than a simple reminder of his last production, for *The Staple of News* and *The Devil is an Ass* have a considerable amount in common

Obviously both are modernisations of older forms of English drama. *The Devil is an Ass* begins with Pug, a junior devil, appealing to Satan for permission to travel to earth to tempt mankind. With him he wants to take the devil's traditional companion on the stage, a 'Vice'; Iniquity, the vice assigned to him, speaks in the old 'fourteener' measure of early drama:

> What is he, calls upon me, and would seeme to lack a *Vice?*
> Ere his words be halfe spoken, I am with him in a trice;
> Here, there, and every where, as the Cat is with the mice:
> True *vetus Iniquitas*.   (I.i.44–7)

It would not need the reference later on in Iniquity's first speech to the moral interlude *Lusty Juventus* to tell the Jacobean audience that Jonson was aiming at an up-dating in parodic form of the familiar type of semi-religious, semi-comical morality play representing the various temptations to which mankind is subjected. This kind of use of outmoded convention is very common in the theatre, for actors and playwrights seem to take a particular pleasure in affectionately mocking styles current in their parents' day or their own childhood, and especially in parodying what was once fashionable in the popular theatre: John Osborne's *The Entertainer* is a modern example. This can degenerate into a kind of professional jokiness, but with Jonson it was elevated to something approaching a principle. He held an organic view of the development of Comedy, which he expressed in the commentary to *Every Man out of his Humour*: the Old Comedy of Aristophanes had given rise to the Greek New Comedy, from which Roman comedy was derived; these forms in turn provided the material and the examples from which Renaissance comedy, including his own, could develop. Although he never explicitly said so, he seems to have felt that a similar kind of development could and should take place from older native comedy. Certainly he made use from the beginning of ideas and material from English stock,[9] and the only new feature of *The Devil is an Ass* and *The Staple of News* is that this use is more central to the structure, and that he is at pains to make sure that the audience realises what he is about.

This tendency to look back to the past of English comedy as well as to classical antiquity, and to equate the two as foundations upon which modern comedy might be built, may be reflected in Jonson's otherwise puzzling use of the term *Vetus Comedia*. When Cordatus says that *Every Man out of his Humour* is 'somewhat like *Vetus Comedia*' he seems clearly enough to be referring to the comedy of Aristophanes, but Jonson used the term quite differently when he was talking to Drummond about *The Devil is an Ass*:

a play of his upon which he was accused the Divell is ane ass, according to Comedia Vetus, in England the divell was brought in either with one Vice or other, the Play done the divel caried away the Vice, he brings in the divel so overcome with the wickedness of this age that [he] thought himself as ass.[10]

Here 'Comedia Vetus' is obviously medieval English drama. There was yet another contemporary sense of the term. Attacking 'Martin Marprelate' in his *Pasquill's Return* in 1589, Nashe says

Me thought *Vetus Comedia* began to prick him at London in the right vaine, when she brought forth *Divinite* with a scratched face. . . ,[11]

and here and elsewhere he is apparently referring to the satirical plays which are known to have been performed as part of a Marprelate controversy, but have not survived. Jonson presumably knew of these plays, and it is tempting to speculate whether he may have seen likenesses, as Nashe apparently did, between this type of satirically didactic comment on contemporary intellectual questions and Aristophanic comedy, and whether these have coloured his reference to *Vetus Comedia* in the Induction to *Every Man out of his Humour*.

There is one other way in which he may have linked up the history of ancient comedy with the development of comedy in England. Behind the Greek Old Comedy were supposed to lie the 'satyr plays', and satyrs, to Christian thinkers, were undoubtedly minor devils; Burton includes them among his list of 'terrestial devils', along with trolls, fauns, fairies, and 'the bigger kind' of fairies

called with us Hobgoblins or Robin Godfellows that would in those superstitious times grind corn for a mess of milk, but wood, and do any manner of drudgery work . . .[12]

The 'Satyre' who is the main figure in Jonson's *Entertainment at Althorpe* actually combines the characteristics of the classical satyr and Robin Goodfellow; he is a haunter of the woods and a follower of Pan, but he is called 'pug' (= Puck), and is represented as a mischievous, teasing, pranksome creature who maliciously interferes with the welcome being given by the Queen of the Fairies to Queen Anne and Prince Henry. Pug in *The Devil is an Ass* has no especially satyr-like qualities, but Satan regards him as only equal to hobgoblin tricks such as laming cows, souring cream, and (like

Puck in *A Midsummer Night's Dream*) 'keeping' the churn 'that the
butter come not'. It is again tempting to wonder whether Jonson
was not looking back even behind the native equivalents of Aristophanic Old Comedy and seeing the English 'devil plays' as approxi-
mating to the Greek 'satyr plays'; if so he had an English as well as
a classical lineage for his own form of Satirical Comedy.

This can only be speculation, but the use of older native dramatic
material and convention is part of an aspect of Jonson's mind for
which there is much more solid evidence. This is his attachment
to things natively English. Jonson is often joined with Dickens as
an example of the typical metropolitan writer, interested in little
beyond the boundaries of the city. This is hardly true even of
Dickens, and it is completely untrue of Jonson, although this may
not be apparent to those who know only his comedies and tragedies.
There is much in his poems in praise of country life, and though no
doubt some of this is a conscious echoing of the Latin poets, not
all is convention. The use of rural and popular love and custom in
the masques has already been noted. This is a side of Jonson that
becomes more evident as he grows older: indeed the last comedy he
ever put on the stage, *The Tale of a Tub*, is his only play completely
set in rural England—in what were then the villages of Tottenham,
Kilburn and Marylebone. It must be added that there is controversy
as to when *The Tale of a Tub* was written, many scholars (including
the editors of the great Oxford edition) maintaining that although
it was undoubtedly staged in 1633 (and again in 1634) it was in fact
an early play, brought out of the drawer and refurbished as part of
a last desperate attempt to discredit Inigo Jones.[13] This issue is too
intricate to discuss here, and is complicated by the fact that the
text we have is almost certainly not the original acting version,
the attack on Jones having been partly cut out and partly modified
on the instructions of the Lord Chamberlain, to whom Jones had
complained. Whether it is early or late, however, there is a real
country atmosphere to *The Tale of a Tub*, and although the rustic
characters are humourously portrayed they are not maliciously
satirized; there is none of the cockney's contempt for the turnip-
eaters. The heroine, Audrey, daughter of Tuby Turfe, High
Constable of Kentish Town, is an engaging figure, and particularly
touching in her despairing cry in the middle of the play, when the
counter-plotting of her various suitors has resulted in a total
stalemate:

Was ever silly Maid thus Posted off?
That should have had three husbands in one day;

> Yet (by bad fortune) is possest of none? . . .
> Husbands, they say grow thick; but thin are sowne.
> I care not who it be, so I have one.   (III.vi.27–9,43–4)

The tone of *The Tale of a Tub* is also deliberately archaic. It is set in the early years of Queen Elizabeth's reign, and its style of comedy is often akin to that of plays such as *George-a-Green, the Pinner of Wakefield*, with much mistaking of words and an old-fashioned clown, who even on occasion breaks, like Iniquity, into fourteeners.

There is the same chronological uncertainty about *The Sad Shepherd*, which was found unfinished among Jonson's papers after his death. It may perhaps be the same as the pastoral *The May Lord* which he told Drummond in 1618 that he had in hand,[14] but its Prologue refers to the poet as one 'that hath feasted you this 40 yeares', and this could hardly have been written before 1635. *The Sad Shepherd* is a pastoral tragi-comedy of the type first successfully staged in England by Fletcher with *The Faithful Shepherdess*, but Jonson departs from the established convention by setting it not in Arcadia or some other idyllic never-never land, but firmly in the English countryside. Aeglamour, the shepherd-hero, is a stock figure of romance, but Earine, the love whom he believes drowned, was lost not in some faerie stream but in the River Trent, and the groves in which he laments her are in the vale of Belvoir. In fact Earine has not been drowned at all, but captured by the wicked witch Maudlin and her clottish son Lotel, aided by her familiar 'Puck-hairy'—the hobgoblin Puck or Pug again; opposed to this wicked crew are Robin Hood, Maid Marion, and Robin's Merry Men. This is, indeed, English pastoral with English characters and an English setting, and there is not only a genuine love for the countryside in it, but a moving recognition that much of Old England was passing away: Robin and his friends lament the decline of rustic mirth and jollity under the attacks of 'the sourer sort of Shepherds' (that is, of course, the Puritans; Jonson makes the same point as Corbett in 'Farewell, rewards and fairies'). *The Sad Shepherd* breaks with convention, too, in being in part realistic and humorous. In the Prologue Jonson complains:

> But here's an Heresie of late let fall;
> That Mirth by no meanes fits a *Pastorall*;
> Such say so, who can make none, he presumes:
> Else, ther's no *Scene*, more properly assumes
> The Sock. For whence can sport in kind arise,
> But from the Rurall Route and Families?

> Safe on this ground then, wee not reare to day,
> To tempt your laughter by our rustic *Play*.[15]

Implicit in this is once again the traditional derivation of Comedy from rustic 'satyr plays' of the Greek villagers, and *The Sad Shepherdess* can be seen as yet another attempt at bringing together in a new combination classical and neo-classical forms, older native drama (the 'Robin Hood plays'), and native traditional lore. In the Prologue Jonson for the last time asserts his right to experiment, and attacks those hidebound by their respect for critical prescription:

> As if all *Poesie* had one character:
> In which what were not written, were not right.   (56–7)

In both form and content, whenever it was written, *The Sad Shepherd* is one of the most original and unexpected of Jonson's creations.

The traditional English element in *The Devil is an Ass* is confined to its use of the morality framework; in substance it is very 'modern' —more so, in fact, than *Volpone* and *The Alchemist*. The devices used by the confidence tricksters in those plays to fleece the greedy were old: Volpone's methods go back to classical antiquity, and after all the other most famous account of false alchemists in England is Chaucer's in the *Canon's Yeoman's Tale*, written almost 200 years before Jonson was born. Meercraft in *The Devil is an Ass* was an absolutely contemporary figure, making use of a notorious economic abuse of the day.[16] His device of offering his dupe Fitzdottrel a choice of fantastic get-rich-quick schemes for which he could hope to be granted a State monopoly is also completely intelligible in our own time, since it is the exact equivalent of persuading investors to put their money into dud companies or non-existent gold-mines. The combination of the traditional, the contemporary, and the timeless is brilliant, and it is difficult to see why *The Devil is an Ass* is not a better play than it is. The basic idea of a devil coming to earth to tempt mankind, and finding men are a good deal worse than he is was not a new one (it had been used in the anonymous *Grim the Collier of Croydon* and in Dekker's *If it be not a good play, the Devil is in't*), but it was still capable of development. Pug, praying in prison for Satan to come and bear him off to Hell, provides a nice ironic counterpart to the most famous 'Devil play' of all, *Doctor Faustus* (still on the stage in 1616) and Jonson deliberately echoes Faustus'

O lente, lente currite noctis equi!
The starres move still, time runnes, the clock will strike,
The devil will come, and Faustus must be damned . . .

in Pug's

Well! Would it once were midnight, that I knew
My utmost. I think Time be drunk and Sleepes;
He is so still, and moves not!   (V.vi.9–11)

There is also a further ironical twist to the situation in the Fifth
Act when Fitzdottrel, whose 'humour' at the beginning of the play
has been a yearning to see the devil, but who has stubbornly refused
to realise that he actually has a devil as his servant, is forced to
pretend to be 'possessed' by a devil in order to get himself out of
his difficulties. It is impossible not to feel, however, that Jonson
had failed to make full use of the possibilities of his theme.

Some critics have seen the basic flaw as lying in the character of
Fitzdottrel. It is true that in order to maintain his place as the
connecting link between all the different strands in the intrigue
he has to combine several kinds of folly, demonstrating not only
his itch to see the devil and the avarice, vanity and ambition which
make him a ready prey for Meercraft, but also the uxoriousness of
Littlewit, the fashion-consciousness of Fungoso, and Sogliardo's
naïve snobbishness in the presence of fine ladies. In practice this
does not matter, for an audience is usually ready enough to accept
the most unlikely collection of attributes if the actor puts them
forward with enough confidence. It is a fair criticism, however, to
say that *The Devil is an Ass* has too many different sorts of comedy
in it, and that Jonson fails to connect them firmly enough together.
The objection has also been made that Pug, who after all is the
eponymous hero of the play, seems to drop into the background
in the second half and becomes almost completely passive. This
again is not likely to be noticed in performance, for while Pug
takes little initiative in the action in the latter part of the play,
he is actually on stage much of the time; it is easy when
reading a play to fall into the trap of thinking that if a character is
not saying anything he is unimportant on the stage, whereas on
occasion an actor may dominate the stage even though he has no
single line to say—it is Pug's horrified and bewildered reactions
to what is happening that are comical. It is in any case quite consistent with the conception of the play that Meercraft should usurp
Pug's place as the chief intriguer, for this sustains the thesis that

modern villains are worse than devils: in fact Jonson could have afforded to make Meercraft an even more vigorous and dominating figure than he is.

Logically the biggest flaw in the play lies not here but in the treatment of Wittipol's courtship of Mrs Fitzdottrel. Wittipol's intentions are obvious, and Pug seizes on the opportunity to further them. In his attempts to encourage Mrs Fitzdottrel to cuckold her husband, however, he is rebuffed by her virtue and her suspicion of him, and he complains bitterly of her chastity (II.v). It is possible that Mrs Fitzdottrel, angered by what she believes is a trick by her husband to use Pug to sound her out, may be beginning to show Wittipol some favour in the following scene (II.vi), but Pug spoils this by bringing Fitzdottrel to discover them; this illustrates his gaucheness, as Satan complains—'[thou] hinder'est (for ought thou knowst) a deed of darkness'. Whether or not we are supposed to suspect that Mrs Fitzdottrel is tempted in the scene, in the end her virtue is triumphantly asserted, in a speech to Wittipol reminiscent of Celia's appeal to Volpone:

> I am a woman,
> That cannot speake more wretchednesse of my selfe,
> Then you can read; match'd to a masse of folly;
> That every day makes haste to his owne ruine;
> That wealthy portion, that I brought him, spent;
> And (through my friends neglect) no joynture made me.
> My fortunes standing in this precipice,
> 'Tis *Counsell* that I want, and honest aides:
> And in this name, I need you, for a friend! (IV.vi.18–26)

Spurred on by his friend Manly ('O friend! foresake not/The brave occasion, venture offers you,/To keep you innocent . . .') Wittipol renounces his dishonourable intentions and embraces the role of aid and comforter: 'Vertue shall never ask my succour twice!'. All this is very edifying, but it hardly sustains the satirical import of the play, which should be that the world is so corrupt that even the efforts of devils cannot make it worse. To be consistent Jonson should have made Mrs Fitzdottrel eager to yield to Wittipol without any need of encouragement from Pug. The tone in this scene becomes very similar to that of eighteenth-century Sentimental Comedy, in which the characters are always liable to be overcome by virtue at critical moments, whereas what was needed was the tone of the Restoration. This illustrates once again that Jonson is often closer to the Augustan writers than to those in the latter part of his own century, and it demonstrates, too, the restriction that his moral views put upon the range of his satire. However much the logic of his plot might demand it, he would have felt it 'indecorous' to represent a good woman yielding to an adulterous passion in a comedy: this would be a tragic subject, and would require the punishment of the sinner. Since the audience, especially today, is likely to be more interested in Mrs Wittipol and her sufferings than in the antics of her husband, the total effect of *The Devil is an Ass*, despite the brilliance of its ideas and the vigour of many of its scenes, is of a play that has pulled its punches.

There is, however, no shortage of vitality and invention in *The Devil is an Ass*, although there is a weakening, compared with *Bartholomew Fair* only two years before, in control of the material and manipulation of the action. Perhaps Jonson was feeling the loss of Beaumont, who may have helped him with the plotting of his greatest plays.[17] In *The Staple of News* and the plays which follow it, there is some decline of energy and a more marked loss in richness of texture. These are comparative judgments. In Jonson's earlier plays—up to and including *The Devil is an Ass*—nothing is more striking than his fertility and the lavishness of his imagination. There is always a tremendous amount in one of Jonson's plays—more than there is in the work of any comparable dramatist. This is not so much a question of action in the strict meaning of movement about the stage, for in fact many scenes in Jonson are virtually static (this is one reason why his plays broadcast well). It is in terms of the number of good parts, the amount of material provided for the actor, and the richness both of intellectual content and verbal embroidery, that his plays are so exceptionally generous. His last plays are certainly not empty, but they are less closely-packed than before, with a more relaxed tempo and a certain thinness or lack of idiosyncratic detail in the characterisation. This is common in the later works of many dramatists—Shakespeare and Shaw, for example—but it matters more in Jonson, precisely because his early plays rely so much on attack and fullness.

Another quality which seems to emerge in the late plays of dramatists with a long writing career is a tendency towards idealisation or the allegorical treatment of intellectual or emotional concepts (this is marked in Ibsen), and this too is visible in Jonson. *The Staple of News* makes direct use of Allegory. Structurally it belongs to the type of the 'Prodigal Plays' which recounts the adventures of a rich young man and the temptations by which he is beset, and its theme could be well stated in the title of a late example of this type of moral interlude, *The Contest between Liberality and*

Prodigality—a play which Jonson may well have known. Penniboy Junior, the hero, represents Prodigality, and the play opens in the traditional manner with him lavishing his newly-inherited money on the collection of grasping tradesmen—tailor, haberdasher, barber and so on—who traditionally gather round a young heir. The opposite extreme is represented by his covetous uncle, Penniboy Senior, who is of Volpone's religion—'a slave and idolater to *Pecunia*'. The end is very predictable: when Penniboy Junior's father is revealed not to be dead at all and his false friends and suitors desert him in his poverty, he realises the vanity of his ways and resolves to lead a better life, and is given a chance to demonstrate his repentance and redeem himself when he is able to counter a plot against his father's estate. The obvious moral is pointed by the heroine, Pecunia:

> And so *Pecunia* her selfe doth wish,
> That shee may still be ayde unto their uses,
> Not slave unto their pleasures, or a Tyrant
> Over their faire desires; but teach them all
> The golden meane: the *Prodigall* how to live,
> The *sordid*, and the *covetous*, how to dye: ...   (V.vi.60–5)

Gossip Mirth spells out Jonson's intentions for any of the audience who have failed to realise his strategy. She asks her companions 'How like you the *Vice* in the play?', and when they complain that there are no 'proper' old-fashioned Vices, with their traditional wooden daggers, she explains:

> That was the old way, Gossip, when *Iniquity* came in like *Hokos Pokos*, in a Juglers jerkin, with false skirts, like the *Knave of Clubs*! but now they are attir'd like men and women o' the time, the *Vices*, male and female!   ('Second Intermean', 14–7)

A modern audience could hardly be expected to gather the import of Mirth's references, but it would be difficult to miss the allegorical status of the heroine with her resounding name ('Aurelia Clara Pecunia, Infanta of the Mines') and her household—Mortgage the nurse, Statute and Bond her waiting-women, and Rose Wax, her chambermaid. Jonson had not put anything so overtly allegorical on the stage since *Cynthia's Revels*, though he had made consistent use of allegory in his masques. It may be, as critics have suggested, that in coming back to the theatre after the ten-year gap he automatically transferred to it the techniques in which he had become practised at Court, and the second element in the play, the Staple of News itself, does incorporate and develop material from his masque *News from the New World*. Jonson's drama had always moved in the direction of Allegory, however, since this was the easiest, and consequently in the Renaissance the commonest, way of satisfying the demand that Literature should Instruct and Delight: Allegory could offer an attractive exterior for the pleasure of the superficial spectator together with a didactic core for the edification of the percipient. A writer of Jonson's period could hardly be expected not to write allegorically, and perhaps it is surprising that his stage comedies do not make greater use of the mode.

It is important to note that it was to Allegory and not to Symbolism, as we understand it today, that Jonson naturally tended. So much attention has been paid by the recent generation of Shakespearean critics to image and symbolism in Shakespeare's plays that inevitably some of this approach has spread across into the criticism of Jonson. Some useful insights have been gained in this way, but sometimes at the cost of blurring a fundamental distinction between Shakespeare and Jonson as writers. We are probably safe in supposing that Shakespeare rarely worked out in advance the dominant images or metaphors in his plays, and that they emerged instinctively as he wrote; it is another thing to suggest, even by implication, that Jonson worked in this way. We can hardly maintain that Jonson had no subconscious mind, but it is obvious that he was an extraordinarily careful and self-conscious writer, and that little was allowed to stand in the text of his plays for which he could not give a rational justification. Nor does the pursuit of 'dominant images' in Jonson take us very far. In *Epicoene*, for example, evidence has been found for a theme of 'infertility', expressed in the symbol of a frozen river[18]. An equally valid 'symbol' in the play might be that of a bear at the stake; this is obviously appropriate for Morose, and there are several allusions to bear-baiting in the play. The point is not so much that alternative 'symbols' may be found, as that this kind of approach to Jonson is ultimately disappointing. The symbolism of the 'unclean birds' or predators in *Volpone* is undoubtedly there, and we need not doubt it was intended by Jonson, but neither this nor the 'infertility' images in *Epicoene* have any real development, nor do they lead us very far to any deeper meaning in the play. Volpone's suitors are obviously ruthless and greedy, Morose's marriage will obviously be infertile: the images may crystallise a truth, but they do not hint at something otherwise inexpressible. Significantly the richest rewards of this kind of investigation come in *Cynthia's Revels*, where Jonson has clearly and most carefully worked out his allegorical meaning and where the symbols are given precise intellectual significance. Behind this is something of vital importance in the assessment of Jonson as a writer, and especially as a poet, and it is a pity that some enthusiasts for Jonson, in their efforts to claim for him the poetic and dramatic qualities which are currently fashionable, should put him into competition with Shakespeare at a point where he is bound to be at a disadvantage.

The 'modern' part of *The Staple of News* is that concerned with the Staple itself—and it is modern for us, too. Historians of the press trace the origins of the newspaper to the almanacs, newsletters and 'corantos' which began to be issued in the 1620s to satisfy an increasing public appetite for news of prodigious events at home and bloody wars and sieges abroad. The news they provided was often false and their proprietors fraudulent; Jonson refers specifically to two, a certain Captain Gainsford, who was dead when *The Staple of News* was first performed, and a stationer turned newsvendor, Nathaniel Butter, who was very much alive. The commonest fault of these journalists (a term not yet current) —apart from their general unreliability—was their tendency to re-issue stale news again and again in a slightly altered form ('*buttering* [it] over again', Jonson calls this); the ostensible aim of the Staple is to obviate this by cataloguing all news under different heads and issuing it to customers with a guarantee of its genuine freshness, just as real merchant-staples were accustomed to warranting goods.

The structural connection between the Staple and the rest of the play is slight: it hangs on little more than the fact that the Staple is set up in the house in which Penniboy junior is staying, that his barber Thomas becomes one of its clerks, and that its Master, Cymbal, is his rival for the hand of Pecunia. There is little possibility of development in the concept—it is more like a revue sketch than part of a play—and Jonson gets rid of the whole thing at the beginning of the last act simply by saying that when Pecunia decided not to remain with Cymbal the Staple was 'exploded' or dissolved. Thematically, however, the links are strong. Greed for novelties, marvels and 'inside information' is easily related to greed for money, and the prodigal's glorying in the outward trappings of wealth and the public's credulous reception of the wonders offered to them, are both species of Opinion. Closer to Jonson's own personal interests was the intolerable fact that

Pecunia could, even if only for a time, remain at the Staple—i.e. that ignorant and ill-educated scribblers like Butter could become successful professional writers. His resentment was akin to Pope's and Swift's attitude towards the hacks of Grub Street; writers of this kind not only prostituted an art which should be dedicated to the propagation of Truth and Morality, but dragged down with them the reputation of the intellectuals and scholars who alone were fit to be trusted with the power of the written word. This reaction, a compound of high-mindedness and genuine concern for the public good, together with snobbishness and a jealous envy of the success of people less ostensibly well qualified than themselves, has been the usual response of the highly educated whenever there has been an increase in literacy among the common people, and it is still present in the fashionable contemporary attitude to the 'mass media'. In Jonson's mind it was exacerbated by the very direct and urgent connection he made between good writing and moral virtue: he never doubted—publicly at least—the absolute necessity for the good writer of being a good man. It followed that Butter and his friends could not write well, because they were not writing morally, and conversely that because they wrote badly, they must be morally suspect.

Behind this lies a less obvious tissue of interconnected ideas. Cymbal and the Clerks of the Staple make their living by spreading lies, gossip and rumours, and when the Staple is 'exploded' they revert to their former role as 'jeerers'. 'Jeering' is a kind of spiteful and stupid party-game like 'vapours' in *Bartholomew Fair*; ever since *Cynthia's Revels* Jonson has shewn an interest (similar to Swift's in *Polite Conversation*) in this kind of coterie pastime. The jeerers pride themselves on their malicious wit—they are prototypes of the smart comparison-makers of Restoration Comedy—and they specialise in slanderous observations. In their different capacities, then, they run the range of what might be termed 'ill report', and one theme of *The Staple of News* is the power and the evil of gossip and malevolent talk. At one point Jonson refers specifically to Chaucer's House of Fame, and he seems to connect, as Chaucer does, the uncertainty of public opinion with the fickleness of Fortune: a man's reputation and even his wealth can be at the mercy of chance rumour and idle chatter—just as Jonson's play itself is subject to the favour of the 'Gossips'. Ultimately the enemy is again Ignorance, the mother (as in *The Masque of Queens*) of rumour, slander, misunderstanding and all similar evils.

The theme of the abuse of speech is elaborated further in the concept of the Canters' College, or school for jargon, which forms a counterpart to the Staple. This is an idea put forward by Penniboy junior's father, who accompanies his son through the play in the disguise of a canting beggar. As Penniboy Canter, he represents both Liberality, or the Golden Mean between the Prodigality of his son and the excessive Frugality of his brother, and Truth, in which capacity he acts as commentator on the action throughout, and at the end of the play cures his brother, who has run mad, and drives away the jeerers who are mocking him. In the eyes of Truth the jargon of lawyers, politicians, heralds or any other professional group is no different from beggars' or thieves' cant: all, like the joking of the jeerers, are ways of imposing on the innocent and credulous, and asserting an unjustified superiority to the common herd. More than this, they represent a sickness or corruption of language, and where language is corrupt reason and virtue cannot flourish. Jonson notes in *Discoveries*:

Wheresoever manners, and fashions are corrupted, Language is. It imitates the publicke riot. The excess of Feasts, and apparell, are the notes of a sick State; and the wantonesse of language, of a sick mind.[19]

Extravagance and self-conscious eccentricity were therefore as fit subjects for satire when they were found in speech as they were when they were pursued in manners or dress, and Jonson was fulfilling his functions of corrector of his age as much in attacking the one as the other; Asper had proclaimed his intention of correcting 'these ignorant *well-spoken* days'.

When Jonson said Comedy required 'Language, such as men do use' he was not simply stating a need for verisimilitude in language, although he may have felt it was the duty of the comic writer to be a repository of the spoken language of his day, as Terence was regarded as the treasure-house of spoken Latin. In part he was echoing the commonly held opinion that a man's talk was the clearest revelation of his personality: 'Language most shewes a man; speak, that I may see thee.'[20] The same view underlies his proclamation in the Prologue to *Cynthia's Revels* that he aimed to provide

Words, above action; matter, above words.

In saying this he was not only dismissing the extravagant rough-and-tumble and violence of much Elizabethan drama but, more importantly, indicating how he proposed to create his characters: not so much by what they did as by what they said. This was the

E

pure water of Renaissance doctrine, and again the concept of
Decorum was involved:

> In Commedies, the greatest Skyll is this, rightly to touche
> All thynges to the quicke: and eke to frame eche person so,
> That by his common talke, you may his nature rightly know:
> A Royster ought not preache, that were too straunge to heare,
> But as from vertue he doth swerve, so ought his woordes appeare:
> The olde man is sober, the younge man rashe, the Lover triumphing
> in joyes,
> The Matron grave, the Harlot wilde and full of wanton toyes.
> Whiche all in one course that in no wise doo agree:
> So correspondent to their kinde their speeches ought to bee.[21]

That Jonson was at great pains to give his characters a vocabulary
and style appropriate to their nature and profession hardly needs
illustration, but it is worth noticing how fully they are realised in
their words: Bobabdil is never more himself than when he is
elaborating his scheme for confounding the Queen's enemies by
defeating each one of them in turn in single combat, and the whole
atmosphere of *Epicoene* changes when the 'silent woman' finds her
voice and her new personality emerges with it. It was vital to the
dramatist that he should be able to master the varieties of common
speech in this way and reveal character in language, but to Jonson
it would have been a dereliction from his plain moral duty if he
had attempted no more than recording and reproducing; it was
necessary to ridicule and attack all abuses of language. Jonson does
this implicitly in many plays, but he is most outspoken in *The
Staple of News*. Despite its morality structure, it is the misuse
of language in all its aspects rather than the misuse of wealth
that is the play's major subject.

The Staple of News is by no means simply a hasty putting-
together of ill-assorted parts to meet a financial crisis, and there is
much lively comic invention in it as well as a serious intellectual
theme. It evinces, however, a quality which had always been
present in Jonson, but which became more obtrusive in his later
years. Jonson had a quick and robust sense of humour, but a very
idiosyncratic one, and like other people of his type he found it
difficult to understand that what seemed so obviously ridiculous to
him could fail to amuse others. There is always something off-hand
or take-it-or-leave-it about Jonson's comedies even at their best,
and in his later years he often does little more than present characters
whom he thinks funny, without making it plain exactly what the

audience is expected to laugh at, or concretely demonstrating the absurdity that he himself sees. This is true of the comic characters in *The Staple of News*, although to some extent this is disguised by the nature of the framework in which they are presented. It is even more true of the low-life comedians in *The New Inn*, who are merely paraded before the audience like a small army of grotesques. No doubt this was partly why this play was a failure when it was performed in 1629. Jonson thought the fault lay with the actors, and when he printed *The New Inn* he described it on the title page as 'A COMEDY. As it was never acted, but most negligently play'd, by some, the Kings Servants. And more squeamishly beheld, and censured by others, the Kings Subjects'. In the Dedication he attacks the 'fastidious impertinents' who were there at the first performance 'to see, and be seen', but who understood nothing; against 'the pompe of their pride and solemn ignorance' he invokes the 'rustic candor' of the Reader. However it was acted, *The New Inn* deserved to fail; it is the only really bad play that Jonson ever wrote, and the only one which would yield nothing in revival.

This was in part because Jonson was writing against the grain. Queen Henrietta Maria had brought with her from France an admiration for the cultivation of refined and idealised sentiment which was fashionable there under the influence of romances such as d'Urfé's *Astrée*. As a result there was in the 1630's a vogue in Court circles for neo-Platonic theories of love, high-flown gallantry, excessive sensibility, and nice speculations on questions of honour —all of which is reflected in what we call 'Cavalier poetry'. *The New Inn* was written to catch this taste. The core of the play consists of two long scenes (III.ii and IV.iv) in which the hero, Lord Lovel, demonstrates and defends the nature of True Love and True Valour. If Jonson was looking back to any earlier kind of drama here it was to the proto-drama of the *estrifs* or debates in the medieval Courts of Love, but he chose to put his set-pieces in a plot of the Plautine type which he had not used since *The Case is Altered*. An attempt to summarise this plot is an interesting exercise in précis. The hero, Lovel, has long loved the heroine, Lady Frampul, but believes her to be in love with a young nobleman who is his ward; he has therefore not pressed his suit and is indeed trying to avoid her. In his melancholy despair he comes to the New Inn, where the jovial Host tried to cheer him up, and mocks his 'philosophical' speculations, such as

> poring through a multiplying glasse,
> Upon a captiv'd crab-louse, or a cheese-mite

> To be dissected, as the sports of nature,
> With a neat Spanish needle! Speculations
> That doe become the age, I doe confess!   (I.i.29–33)

(There is a foretaste here of Swift's attitude to the experiments in
the Academy of Lagado, and indeed Lovel has something of the
air of a later seventeenth-century *Virtuoso*.) To the Inn comes
Lady Frampul, together with her maid Prudence and the Lords
Latimer and Beaufort, the latter being Lovel's ward. Lovel tried to
avoid them, but instead is caught up in the festivities, as part of
which he has to deliver his disquisitions on Love and Valour;
Lady Frampul is so moved by his eloquence on these subjects that
she is overcome by love for him. As part of the entertainment Lady
Frampul and Prudence take the Host's son and dress him as a
girl. Lord Beaufort falls in love with 'her' and marries her secretly—
which removes Lovel's scruples about courting Lady Frampul. It is
then revealed in quick succession that 'she' is a boy, and then that
she is a girl, after all, and not only that, but Lady Frampul's sister;
for the drunken, one-eyed Irish nurse who originally brought the
child to the Inn turns out to be Lady Frampul's mother, who many
years before had left her husband because, she thought, his affection
for her had cooled after she had presented him with two daughters
only, and no son. The dialogue at this point is a little too much:

Lady Frampul Sister, O Gladnesse! Then you are our mother?
Nurse   I am, deare daughter.
Lady   On my knees, I blesse
              The light I see you by.
Nurse   And to the author
              Of that blest light, I ope my other eye,
              Which hath almost, now, seven years beene shut,
              Darke, as my vow was, never to see light,
              Till such a light restor'd it, as my children,
              Or your deare father, who (I heare) is not   (V.v.73–8)

After this it is hardly a surprise when the Host removes his beard
and cap and shines forth as the long-lost Lord Frampul, who had
left home and estate to roam with the gipsies, in his distraction and
grief at the loss of his wife.

Jonson realised that this was confusing, for in the edition of 1631
he prefaced the text with a summary of 'The Argument' and an
annotated *Dramatis Personae*. It is so unlike what we expect from
him that many critics have been tempted to suppose that the whole

play is intended as a parody, a satirical attack on the current Court fashion.[22] There is no evidence to support this interpretation, and it is unlikely that Jonson would have risked this attack when he so desperately needed a success. The Epilogue to the play is genuinely pathetic in its plea for favour:

> Playes in themselves have neither hopes, nor feares,
> > Their fate is only in their hearers eares:
> If you expect more than you had to night,
> > The maker is sick, and sad. But doe him right,
> He meant to please you: for he sent things fit,
> > In all the numbers, both of sense, and wit,
> If they ha'not miscarried! If they have,
> > All that his faint, and faltring tongue doth crave,
> Is, that you not impute it to his braine.
> > That's yet unhurt, although set round with paine,
> It cannot long hold out.　　　　　　　　　(1–11)

We may be surprised to find Jonson seriously holding forth on the subject of Love, if not to hear Jonson the old soldier expatiating on Valour, but this kind of treatment of abstract virtues is common enough in the masques. There are, indeed, passages of strained rhetoric. Lady Frampul is moved to heroic simile by her admiration of Lovel's bravery in subduing a drunken quarrel among the roisterers in the tavern:

> 　　　　　　　I nere saw
> A lightning shoot so, as my servant did,
> His rapier was a *Merteor*, and he wav'd it
> Over 'hem, like a Comet, as they fled him!　(IV.iii.11–14)

and Lovel himself reaches no less high a pitch in his emotional despair:

> 　　　　　　　O my braine!
> How art thou turned! and my blood congeald!
> My sinews slackned! and my marrow melted!
> That I remember not where I have bin,
> Or what I am? Only my tongue's on fire;
> And burning downward, hurles forth coals, and cinders,
> To tell, this temple of loue, will soone be ashes!　(IV.iv.257–63)

This is approaching the fervent extravagances of Heroic Tragedy—Dryden was born in the year that *The New Inn* was published—but we cannot be certain that Jonson did not mean it to be taken seriously. What we can see is that he is—unusually—permitting the high style in Comedy, perhaps simply because he was aiming at an aristocratic audience. He had done the same in *Cynthia's Revels*, also intended for the taste of the Court, and the verse of the 'debates' in *The New Inn* is, like some of the verse in *Cynthia's Revels* (and still more like the verse of many masques), of a dignified, orotund kind:

> But put the case, in travayle I may meet
> Some gorgeous Structure, a brave Frontispiece,
> Shall I stay captive i'the outer court,
> Surpris'd with that, and not advance to know
> Who dwels there, and inhabiteth the house?
> There is my friendship to be made, within;
> With what can love me againe: not, with the walles,
> Dores, windo'es, architrabes, the frieze, and coronice.
> My end is lost in loving of a face,
> An eye, lip, nose, hand, foot or other part,
> Whose all is but a statue, if the mind
> Move not, which only can make the returne.
> The end of love is, to haue two made one
> In will and in affection. . . .   (III.ii.140–53)

As we should expect, Lovel here argues—rather like Spenser in *The Four Hymns*—for the love of the mind, the love of inner virtue, as against Fancy or Opinion, the shallow and fickle love of the eye. Similarly in discussing Valour he praises the Golden Mean between sluggish and shameful cowardice on the one hand and rash vain-glory on the other (Beaufort represents the opposite side in both arguments, maintaining the importance to a man of defending his 'reputation' in matters of honour at all costs, and actually demonstrating, in his own sudden infatuation for the Host's disguised son, a sensuous and superficial love). Lovel's defence of Love and Honour is essentially rational and measured, and he is unequivocal in his condemnation of the fictions of the romances, which he dismisses as

>   publique Nothings,
> Abortives of the fabulous, darke cloyster,
> Sent out to poison courts, and infest manners . . .   (I.vi.126–8)

It may well be that the gentlemen-courtiers who saw *The New Inn* found it not so much a parody of their views as an intolerably stuffy and old-fashioned account of their favourite topics of speculation; they wanted something more extreme and with altogether more *panache*.

For a modern audience the main drawback to *The New Inn* would be its static quality. Although the plot when set down looks complicated enough, in fact all the revelations come close together, and for most of the play nothing very much happens except rather formal debate. The 'comic relief' is equally event-less: the below-stairs 'militia' under their colonel Sir Glorious Tiptoe, a stilted, vainglorious warrior with an exaggerated admiration of everything Spanish, form a kind of antimasque to their betters, but, as a contemporary critic noted, their comedy extends little further than their names ('Fly', 'Jordan', 'Jug, the tapster', 'Peck, the ostler,' 'Trundle, a coachman') and once they have been presented to the audience little more is done with them. Given the original conception of the play this lack of movement and excitement was perhaps inevitable, but Jonson seems to have chosen to emphasize it deliberately, and at the same time to stress the theatricality of the situations by frequent references to plays and playacting.[23] The result is to give *The New Inn* almost the feel of a piece of amateur play-making—certainly the entertainment that Lady Frampul and Prudence devise is the equivalent of what in a later century would have been a game of charades at a country-house party—and it seems oddly unprofessional for a playwright like Jonson near the end of his career.

Stung by the failure of *The New Inn*, Jonson wrote one of his finest and most energetic poems, his 'Ode to Himself', in which he expressed for the last time his contempt for the taste of the popular audience and those who wrote to satisfy it, and asserted his sense that his own superiority of mind doomed him to failure in a profession he despised:

> Come leaue the lothed stage,
>   And the more lothsome age:
> Where pride, and impudence (in faction knit)
>   Usurpe the chaire of wit!
> Indicting, and arraigning every day
>   Something they call a Play.
>   Let their fastidious, vaine
>   Commission of the braine
> Run on, and rage, sweat, censure, and condemn:
> They were not made for thee, lesse, thou for them.   (1–10)

He goes on to castigate the audience for their desire to see 'some
mouldy tale, Like Pericles' which, re-worked and padded out with
the stale common-places of the theatre, 'May keepe up the *Play-
Club*', and declares his desire to abandon drama for poetry:

> Leave things so prostitute,
>   And take the *Alcaick* Lute;
> Or thine owne *Horace*, or *Anacreons* Lyre;
>   Warme thee, by *Pindares* fire:
> And though thy nerves be shrunke, and blood be cold,
>   Ere yeares have made thee old;
>   Strike that disdaine-full heate
>   Throughout, to their defeate:
> As curious fooles, and envious of thy straine,
> May, blushing, sweare no palsey's in thy braine.   (41–50)

No doubt he sincerely wished he could leave the theatre for good,
but circumstances demanded that he should make one more attempt
to win favour.

In writing *The Magnetic Lady* in 1632 he followed his usual
practice when he was uncertain of his reception and wanted to
make sure his intentions were not misrepresented, and provided a
chorus. It consists of two Gentlemen, Mr Probee and Mr Damplay,
whose function is largely to make disparaging and unintelligent
remarks about the play and to be put right by 'a Boy of the house'.
This boy-actor emphasises that *The Magnetic Lady* is in a consistent
line of development from Jonson's earliest work, looking back
not merely to *The New Inn* (as *The New Inn* had looked back to
The Staple of News and that in turn to *The Devil is an Ass*), but
nearly thirty-five years, to the first Humour Plays. He also states
once again Jonson's reliance on the 'understanding' spectator as
against those who 'judge only by show':

> careless of all vulgar censure, as not depending on common appro-
> bation, hee is confident it shall super-please judicious Spectators,
> and to them he leaves it to worke with the rest, by example, or
> otherwise.   (Induction, 122–5)

One sign of Jonson's determination to win back the favour of
the learned is his explicit defence, put in the mouth of the boy, of
the structure of *The Magnetic Lady*, as being in accordance with
the best neo-classical principles. References to the structural
principles on which he worked occur throughout his career, but

they became more common in his last plays, probably because critical precept was in general becoming more stringent, and Jonson himself was learning more about it; he appears, for example, to have become familiar only in the later 1620's with the work of the great Dutch critic Daniel Heinsius.[24]

The particular plan he follows in *The Magnetic Lady* is usually called 'the four-fold structure', because it implies a division of the plot into four distinct movements.[25] This theory had its origin in a well-known commentary on Terence by the fourth-century Latin grammarian Donatus, who analysed Terence's comedies into four parts, which he called *Prologue, Protasis, Epitasis* and *Catastrophe*. Of these the *Prologue* was extraneous to the play proper and might contain matter not germane to it (for example, an apology for the Author), so that one was left with a three-fold division of the acting matter proper, which corresponded well enough with Aristotle's demand that a drama should have a beginning, a middle and an end. In the sixteenth century, however, the Italian scholar Julius Caesar Scaliger subdivided the *Epitasis* or middle of the play into two parts, so that when Jonson started to write it was correct to hold that a comedy should consist of an introductory part, the *Protasis*, in which the characters were introduced and the problem or situation adumbrated; an *Epitasis* in which the action commenced; a third movement, called by Scaliger the *Catastasis*, 'the full strength and crisis of the fable', during which the plot was at its most complicated; and finally the *Catastrophe*, in which every difficulty was resolved and tranquillity restored.

Many of Jonson's earlier plays follow this pattern. In *Volpone*, for example, Act I forms the *Protasis*, in which Volpone, his household and his various suitors are introduced and his method of gaining wealth is explained. The *Epitasis* consists of Acts II, III, and IV, in which Volpone attempts to gain Celia, is nearly destroyed by the intervention of Bonario and is rescued by Mosca and Voltore. The *Catastasis* begins with the first scene of Act V and is concerned with the device of Volpone's pretended death and the advantage Mosca takes of this; the *Catastrophe* comes right at the end when Volpone reveals himself. *Epicoene* has the same kind of structure. Act I is again the *Epitasis*, and by its end all the major characters have appeared or have been described, and the central relationship between Dauphine and Morose has been established; Acts II and III are the second movement, in which Truewit tried to dissuade Morose from marriage but has the opposite effect of confirming him in his intention, the marriage is solemnised, and Epicoene finds her voice; the *Catastasis* takes up Acts IV and V, with Morose's attempts to escape from the marriage, culminating in the scene with the bogus Canon and Civil lawyers; the *Catastrophe* is the revelation of Epicoene's true sex, which resolves Morose's problem, secures Dauphine what he wants, and incidentally discomforts Daw, La Foole and the Collegiate ladies.

Jonson appears not to have been completely satisfied with this scheme at its simplest and to have modified it to suit his own ideas. Scaliger apparently thought of the *Catastasis* only as the most involved stage of the plot, but Jonson seems to have taken it, as Dryden was later to do, as a counter-movement or new intrigue, which disappoints the spectator of an apparent solution for the earlier problem and introduces a new complication. Dryden uses the metaphor of

a violent stream resisted by a narrow passage,—it runs round to an eddy, and carries back the waters with more swiftness than it brought them on.[26]

Both *Volpone* and *Epicoene* illustrate this. In his later work Jonson also modified the conception of the *Catastrophe*, which originally was only the final unravelling of the complications of the play— most straightforwardly, as in *Volpone* and *Epicoene*, by a simple revelation that the central character was not what he was supposed to be. His final ideas are illustrated by the commentary on the action of *The Magnetic Lady*. In the 'Intermean' after Act I the Boy refers to what has so far passed as the *Protasis*: little, so far, has been accomplished beyond putting the audience in possession of the necessary facts, so that they know that Placentia, Lady Loadstone's niece, comes of age that day, they have seen or heard of her suitors, and they have been told that she has suddenly fallen ill. In Act II there is a violent quarrel between two of her suitors which so frightens her that she collapses, and at the end of Act III, which is introduced as the *Epitasis*, it is announced that she has given birth to a child. Act IV constitutes the *Catastasis* (although the term is not used); in it Compass, the hero, overhears a quarrel between Lady Loadstone's companion Polish and the nurse Keep which reveals that Placentia is really Polish's daughter and Lady Loadstone's true niece is the waiting-woman Pleasance. Compass immediately sets in train a plot to marry Pleasance, for whom he has previously expressed affection; the Act ends with a scheme concocted by Polish and Keep to conceal the birth of Placentia's baby and thus preserve her reputation. In Act V, which is spoken of as the *Catastrophe*, Placentia's suitors, who have not unnaturally been somewhat discouraged by the news that she has had a child, come flocking back, but Compass forces the revelation of the truth. In what is called the 'conclusion' Placentia is finally discredited and married off to her lover (who is revealed to be one of Lady Loadstone's servants), and Compass gets the true heiress and her fortune.

It would seem from this that Jonson later not only saw the *Epitasis* and *Catastasis* as two distinct movements within the play but regarded the *Catastrophe* as possibly forming yet another movement: the fifth Act of *The Magnetic Lady* contains, besides the unsuccessful attempt to rehabilitate Placentia and its defeat by Compass, a completely new though very slight sub-plot in which Pleasance's uncle, the usurer Sir Moth Interest, is gulled with false news of hidden treasure. In *The Magnetic Lady* Jonson is concerned to show that he has mastered the latest critical theory, so that it is perhaps not safe to assume that he had previously taken this view of the proper distribution of the parts of a comedy. Both *The Devil is an Ass* and *The Staple of News*, however, introduce what are virtually new plots in their last acts, and even in *The Alchemist* the return of Lovewit precipitates a new situation at the beginning of the last Act and forces Face into a series of manœuvres, first to try to keep him out of the house, then to persuade him that nothing has gone wrong, and finally (and successfully) to win his forgiveness by offering him the chance to marry the widow Pliant. A Jonsonian comedy may therefore be expected to begin with a more-or-less static *Protasis*, often occupying the whole of the first Act and sometimes extending further, which introduces the characters and establishes the situation. Movement or development of the intrigue commences in Act II, and carries on to a point somewhere between one-half and two-thirds of the way through the play, at which point a new intrigue starts and fresh characters may be introduced. In most of the earlier plays this movement, the *Catastasis*, continues until the very end, when a revelation or series of revelations occur which resolve the conflict and bring the play to an end; in later plays a third intrigue (and sometimes more than one) begins in the last Act, whether the previous action has been concluded or not, and this forms the extended *Catastrophe*, which is finally resolved in a 'conclusion'.

This may represent an attempt to solve a problem which bothered Renaissance critics—how to reconcile a four-act structure with the five Acts dictated by Horace and Cicero: it is possible to imagine a Comedy (though Jonson never wrote it) in which Act I constituted the *Protasis*, Act II the *Epitasis*, Act III the *Catastasis*,

Act IV the *Catastrophe* and Act V the 'Conclusion'. Perhaps more probably it reflects a determination to give his audience value for money and to hold their interest to the end. In *The New Inn* the Host is made to speak of his wish

> like a noble Poet, to have had
> My last act best,   (V.i.26–7)

and Jonson clearly liked to keep the audience guessing and astonish them if he could; in the Chorus before Act V of *Every Man out of his Humour* Cordatus replies to Mitis' objection that most of the characters have not yet been taken 'out of their humour' by saying:

> Why, therein his art appeares most full of lustre, and approcheth nearest the life: especially, when in the flame, and height of their humours, they are laid flat, it fils the eye better, and with more contentment.   (IV.viii.166–9)

This explicitly justifies Jonson's structural practice by reference to the canon of Verisimilitude and to a postulate concerning audience-satisfaction, and also, less obviously, rationalizes one effect of the principal of Decorum on the handling of character. The static consistency of 'decorous' characters meant that development was virtually impossible, and change could only come about by some form of conversion, change of heart, or sudden apprehenion of the truth, if it were to come at all (and it does not always come in Jonson—there is no indication, for example, that Morose will be any less self-centred in the future, or Mammon less ridiculously voluptuously-minded; Jonson does not have Dickens' evangelical faith in the powers of conversion). Surprise is therefore even more of a necessity in Jonsonian than it is in other forms of comedy; whether it conduces as much to the pleasure of the audience as Jonson apparently believed it did is open to question. It would certainly not seem to be especially 'near the life'—sudden revelations of concealed truth and strippings-off of disguise are not every-day occurrences—and too much emphasis on shock-effect is likely to produce diminishing returns. In fact, of all Jonson's plays only *Epicoene* depends entirely on a surprise-ending, and even *Epicoene* is perfectly viable as a comedy to someone who already knows the truth (or has the wit to guess the significance of the title). There is a general tendency, however, for the characters to be assembled together in the final scene of a Jonsonian comedy, and for some sort of argument or trial to take place, in the course of which a truth which has been hidden from at least some of the characters is revealed. In part this is a consequence of Jonson's virtual abandonment of the love-story as a plot-element, which cut him off from the stock kind of 'Jack-shall-have-Jill' conclusion; few of Jonson's comedies—and none of his greatest—have this sort of 'happy ending'. It was imperative for him, therefore, to find plots which were not only capable of sustaining the audience's interest up to the last moment, but could culminate in a 'big scene', and in this he most often succeeded. Behind this again one senses a desire on his part to dominate his audience, to keep them at his mercy until the play ended and to send them away astonished at his dexterity, and this suspicion is given credibility by the frequency with which he calls attention to his own skill in the manipulation of plot and characters.

It is not quite possible to postulate a characteristic Jonsonian situation, as one can speak of an 'Ibsenesque' dramatic situation and pattern of development, in which the tensions and the bitter history behind the apparent unity of a group or a family are gradually brought to the surface. The Renaissance would have recognised the Ibsenesque type of movement as a form of Tragedy, which, it was laid down, should begin in tranquillity and end in disaster (*Hamlet* is—among other things—an Ibsenesque play). The correct movement for Comedy was from disorder to harmony or peace, and in fact some of Jonson's plays—*The Alchemist*, *Epicoene* and *Bartholomew Fair*, for example—either begin or are conducted for most of their length in literal disorder and noise, and are suddenly restored to silence and tranquillity at their close. In other plays Jonson experimented with different ways of providing the required pattern, and indeed it would have been unlike him not to experiment, and try to give his own imprint to whatever he could learn from the theory or example of others. This is the significance of his motto '*Tamquam Explorator*'—a phrase from one of Seneca's letters in which Seneca speaks of himself as entering the camp of his intellectual enemies, not as a traitor or a deserter, but 'like a spy', in the attempt to gain useful information; Jonson inscribed this tag in his books. Jonson's attitude to authority was plain:

I m not of that opinion to conclude a *Poets* liberty within the narrowe limits of lawes, which either the *Grammarians*, or *Philosophers* prescribe.[27]

He believed that any theory should be tested against experience, and refused to 'bee tyed to those strict and regular forms' which the

'niceness' (or over-scrupulousness) 'of the few' would make
mandatory; Beaumont was praising him as he would have wished
when he said 'thou has squar'd thy rules, by what is good'.[28]

This is borne out in Jonson's handling of the celebrated 'Unities'.
He comes closest in *The Alchemist* to strict obedience to the Unities
of Time and Place: 'the time-elapsed' in the play is six hours, which
is well within the broad interpretation of the 'Rule' that the action
of a play should take place 'within one revolution of the sun', if
not quite in accordance with the purist view that the time elapsed
in the play should be exactly equivalent to the time actually taken
in performance. Similarly the events all take place in Lovewit's
house or just outside it, which is not quite Unity of Place as the
French critics understood it, but very close to it. *The Alchemist*
is an exception, however (and Jonson is at some pains to point out
his skill in it); elsewhere he is satisfied if the action takes place
within twenty-four hours, and if all the events occur in the same
city or the same stretch of country. He is boldest of all in his treatment of the Unity of Action, which is the most directly relevant
to the question of structure.

Although he would appear unjustifiably free to the seventeenth-
century French critics in his treatment of Time and Place, Jonson
is still very restricted in comparison with most of his English
contemporaries, and the effect is one of concentration, both
geographically and chronologically. Within these limits, however,
the richness and complexity of his plots seem very far removed
from the spareness and simplicity we expect from neo-classical
drama. We are conditioned here by what we know of Racine,
Corneille and Molière; the critics of the earlier Renaissance—who
in this respect were following Aristotle more faithfully than their
successors—did not insist that the action of a play should be
'simple' in the sense that it must rigorously exclude everything not
absolutely essential to the development of the main plot. Provided
that the Action as a whole was 'one and entire' it might include
many parts or strands. Jonson has a long passage on this point in
Discoveries (2678 ff) in which, following Heinsius, he maintains
the superiority of the complex action over the simple, provided
that all the parts are properly integrated with each other and all
'tend to the same end'. It was in this sense that *The Faerie Queen*
could claim to have Unity of Action, and some theorists of the
drama justified the double plot in this way. Jonson does not go as
far as this, but he does accept the view, also based on the authority
of Aristotle, that a dramatist may introduce 'episodes' into his main
action, that is, scenes which are not essential to the advancement of

the plot but are by-products of it. He says of such 'digressions in the Fable' that they are 'the same as household stuff, and other furniture in a house'—not an essential part of the structure but playing a vital part in the function of the whole.

In general it seems to have been Jonson's view that it was the duty of the playwright to elaborate his material as much as he could, provided that he introduced nothing irrelevant or not properly grafted into the main structure of the play, and this was the way he himself worked. For this reason the simple 'linear' approach suggested by the concept of the 'four-fold structure' is inadequate as a method for analysing his plays. Although the story of Morose and his marriage forms the backbone of *Epicoene*, for example, much time is taken up with the activities of the fops, the Collegiate Ladies, and Captain and Mrs Otter; all of these have a part to play in the main action, but some of the scenes in which they appear can properly be classed as 'episodes'. Jonson often surrounds his protagonists in this way with groups of minor characters who have little intrigues of their own as well as some part in the main plot, but only rarely are they quite detachable from the play, as Tipto and his 'militia' are in *The New Inn*. Some plays have several plots of nearly equal importance which together form a complex Action. *Every Man in his Humour*, for example, has the four-stage movement, but it also has four different intrigues: Knowell's attempt to spy on his son and Brainworm's gulling of him; Kiteley's jealousy of his wife (and her later suspicions of him); Bobadil's friendship with Stephen and Matthew and his quarrel with Downright; and the love affair between Edward Knowell and Bridget Kitely.

Jonson also experimented in *Every Man in his Humour* with a device for structuring his material which he later used frequently, that of bringing all his characters together at different stages of the play at what might be called nodal points. In *Every Man in his Humour* these are the Tavern, Kitely's House, Cob's House, and finally Justice Clement's. In *Every Man out of his Humour* the rallying places are Puntarvolo's house, the Court, and the Mitre. In *Bartholomew Fair* the Fair itself is one big meeting-place, and the events of the play result from the inter-action between the showmen and the four groups who invade their territory: the 'Littlewit party', consisting of John and his wife, his mother-in-law, and Zeal-of-the-Land Busy; the 'Cokes' party, which comprised Cokes, his servant Waspe, his fiancée Grace Welborne, and Mistress Overdo, her guardian's wife; the gallants Winwife and Quarlous; and finally Mr Justice Overdo, *solus*. Localised within the Fair, however, are several points where these groups encounter each other: the Pig-Woman's booth, Leatherhead's stall, the stocks, and the puppet-show, at which they are all finally assembled. There may be in this a survival of the traditional 'simultaneous décor' in which the stage was set with different 'houses' and the actors proceeded from one to another as the play progressed; certainly *Bartholomew Fair* cries out for this kind of setting. Other plays have less movement from place to place, and instead some centre is required to which all the characters may logically come— Volpone's lodging or (most successfully of all) Lovewit's house in *The Alchemist*. (*The Alchemist* is the most interesting of all Jonson's plays from the point of view of the history of stage-craft, since it requires a practical built-up set representing the inside of Lovewit's house and the street just outside, both of which must be simultaneously visible to the audience; this is the first clear example in England of this kind of stage arrangement.) It is because of his desire to group his characters naturally together at intervals in his plot that Jonson is so fond of setting his action in places of public resort—the Court, Taverns, Courts of Law, the 'centre aisle of Paul's,' and so on—and of feasts, parties, drinking-bouts and other convivial occasions.

In some plays the four-fold movement is not present at all, or is so overlaid that it is hardly noticeable, and a quite different mode of construction is followed, which has been compared to a web or net.[29] The image of a net is a good one, for essentially what is involved is the interweaving of various strands of action which can be as it were knotted together at the nodal points. *Every Man out of his Humour* was Jonson's first exercise in this mode, and *Bartholomew Fair* was his greatest success. The design of *Bartholomew Fair* is so intricate that it almost defies analysis, but something can be learnt by picking a single character and following his movements. Waspe, the choleric servant, appears first in the fourth scene, when he comes to Littlewit's house to fetch the licence for his master Cokes's marriage to Grace Welborne. In the following scene he is persuaded against his will to accompany Cokes to the Fair, and we next see him there with Cokes, Grace and Mistress Overdo listening to Overdo haranguing the crowd in his disguise as 'Mad Arther of Bradley'; Cokes' pocket is picked, and Waspe beats Overdo, whom he suspects of being in league with the thief. He does not reappear until Act III, when he goes with Cokes and his party to Leatherhead's booth, and there quarrels with Quarlous. Cokes's pocket is picked again, and this time Overdo is arrested for the theft. Quarlous, however, has seen the cutpurse Edgeworth stealing the purse, and employs him to filch the marriage licence, which Waspe has taken back from Cokes into his own keeping, because Cokes's pocket has already been picked twice. Having washed his hands of Cokes, whose folly he feels he cannot control, Waspe appears next at the Pig-Woman's booth drinking with Edgeworth and the other rogues, and playing the game of 'Vapours'; this ends in a quarrel, during which Edgeworth steals the licence. Waspe is arrested and put in the stocks, along with Zeal-of-the-Land Busy. They both escape, and Waspe rejoins his party at the puppet-show, only to find at the end that he has lost the licence (which Quarlous has used to marry Dame Purecraft) and with it his authority over Cokes. His little Odyssey has been a series of peripities in which all those whom he has insulted and reproved have triumphed over him, and in the course of his adventures he has been involved at one time or another with all the other characters in the play. Similar accounts could be given of the adventures of many of the other characters, and there is a striking resemblance to the technique Joyce used in *Ulysses* (Joyce was an admirer of Jonson). The organisational skill required for this type of plotting is considerable, and in his later plays Jonson simplified and restricted his action much more, though if *The Tale of a Tub* is in fact a late play, then he was still capable at the end of his life of an exercise of the same kind as *Bartholomew Fair*.

In the Induction to *The Magnetic Lady*, the 'Boy' speaking of a good play, uses the metaphor of a skein of silk

> which, if you take by the right end, you may wind off, at pleasure ... how you will: But if you light on the wrong end, you will pull all into a knot, or elfe-lock ...
>
> (136–40)

The 'clue' in this play is that it is Pleasance, the waiting-maid, who is the true niece to Lady Loadstone, just as the clue to *Epicoene* is that the silent woman is a boy. Jonson must have been particularly anxious after the disaster of *The New Inn* to avoid being 'taken up wrong' by the audience, either by being suspected of personal reference where he intended none, or by having his intention and drift misunderstood: in the Induction the boy speaks of everything in the play being done '*in foro*'—in the open—'as a true Comedy should be'. This is true of most of Jonson's plays: he rarely conceals anything from the audience and he was always ready, through a chorus or through the characters in the play, to explain his

mechanisms and his aims. Perhaps he was too ready; some readers
are irritated by Jonson's habit of pointing out that he has everything
under control and that there is really nothing for the spectator to
do but admire. We are not always prepared to accept the doctrine
which Master Probee lays down in *The Magnetic Lady* to his
'brother' Master Damplay:

> our parts that are the Spectators, or should heare a *Comedy*, are to
> await the processe, and events of things, as the *Poet* presents them,
> not as wee would corruptly fashion them. Wee come here to behold
> *Playes*, and censure them, as they are made, and fitted for us; not
> to beslaver our owne thoughts, with censorious spitle tempering the
> *Poets* clay, as wee were to mould every *Scene* anew: That were a
> meere Plastick, or Potters ambitions, most unbecoming the name
> of a *Gentleman*.   (Chorus after Act IV, 10–9)

Jonson might have been better loved as a writer if he had been a
little more careless, a little readier to allow the audience to contribute
something from their own imagination. The vast difference between
the amount of critical commentary on Shakespeare and on Jonson
is not just a simple measure of their respective greatness. In all of
Shakespeare's plays we, whether as spectators, readers, critics or
actors, are given something like a set of building-blocks out of
which we can build our own characters, our own play, and part
of the fascination is that not only can many different patterns be
made, but that often no pattern is completely satisfactory. There
is no scope in Jonson for this kind of imaginative re-creation: his
blocks can only be assembled in one way—his; and if an attempt
is made by a producer or actor to invent a new interpretation the
result is distortion and strain. Denied in this way of our chance to
contribute from our own store of creative energy we may well feel
cheated, and resentful of the very masterfulness and clarity which
Jonson expected us to admire.

The Magnetic Lady seems a little swamped by the critical
apparatus which surrounds it, and Swinburne's enthusiasm does
not ring wholly true:

> The higher genius of Ben Jonson as a comic poet was yet once more
> to show itself in one brilliant flash of parting splendour before the
> approaching sunset.[30]

Nonetheless it is a very competent and viable play. A formal critic
might fault it because Lady Loadstone, who ought to be 'the

magnetic lady', is not truly the centre of attraction, though she is in the end very properly married off to Captain Ironside; nor for that matter are all the 'humours' in the play 'reconciled', though there are some scenes of reconciliation. The humorous figures are well enough defined, if not very vigorous, and they bring out again the connection between 'humour' and the 'character'—two 'epigrams' or 'characters' are quoted in the play, and attributed to 'a great Clarke As any is of his bulke (*Ben: Jonson*)'. *The Magnetic Lady* will not stand comparison with Jonson's great plays, but will hold its own with contemporary plays such as those of Brome or Shirley, or with those of a later playwright such as Colley Cibber. In some ways, indeed, it seems more like a later play. Attempts have been made, for reasons best known to producers, to stage *The Alchemist* and *Epicoene* in eighteenth-century costume–with little success, because they are so inescapably Jacobean in tone and 'feel'. *The Magnetic Lady* could easily be staged as if it had been written a hundred years later, and would not lose much in the process; in mood it could quite well be an eighteenth-century play, or, if transposed into another mode, its plot would serve well enough for an eighteenth-century novel. It is extraordinary to find Jonson, only five years before his death, still experimenting not only with form and structure, but able to suggest a capacity for yet further development and change.

The readiness to experiment, to try new forms of drama, was characteristic of Jonson. Carew, one of his 'sons', said of his comedies:

> Though one hand shape them, & though one brain strike
> Soules into all, they are not all alike;[31]

and to a certain extent generalisations about 'Jonsonian comedy' can be misleading. Certainly Jonson had some fixed principles. Comedy to him was a serious matter—almost, indeed, no laughing matter: in *Discoveries* he noted:

> Nor, is the moving of laughter alwaies the end of *Comedy*, that is rather a fowling for the people's delight, or their fooling. For, as *Aristotle* saies rightly, the moving of laughter is a fault in Comedie, a kind of turpitude, that depraves some part of a mans nature without a disease.[32]

He was thinking here of 'scurrilous' laughter, the laughter of the malicious buffoon, who mocks men's infirmities. Even Aristophanes was to blame for ridiculing Socrates personally in *The Clouds*: this, Jonson says, was

truly leaping from the Stage to the Tumbrele againe, reducing all witt to the original Dungcart.[33]

The 'moving of laughter' was permissible if it was not directed maliciously at individuals, but tended towards the reformation of manners; delight could be freely given the audience, provided instruction was also present. There is earnestness of moral purpose in all Jonson's comedies, but it is not always, or even usually, obtrusive. Only occasionally does Jonson come forward and lecture the audience: usually his moral committment is plain, but not forced upon us. Critical commentary may often suggest that the moral significance of his plays is more prominent than in fact it is: we may rise even from a performance of *Volpone* without realising we have witnessed quite the excoriating flagellation of the baseness of human nature to which critics will assure us we have been exposed. Similarly, while it is true that examination of any of Jonson's plays will reveal the remarkable degree of thought and care which has gone into the writing, in the theatre we are not conscious all the time of what C. H. Herford called 'the perverse prodigality of his elaborating intellect'. When we are actually watching a performance we are more likely to be aware of the richness and vigour of his invention, and of the relentless speed of his attack.

It is indeed vital to Jonson that the plays should be seen in performance, and not judged solely from the printed page. There is a persistent belief that he does not act well, but the falsity of this is demonstrated every time one of his best-known comedies is acted. Since he is not a witty writer, much of his effect depends on the actual physical presence of his characters and the situations in which they find themselves. His most characteristic comic effect is one of accumulation, the steady building up of absurdity and ridiculousness. A fine example is the scene in *Epicoene* in which the bogus lawyers are brought in to advise Morose. The immediate source of laughter is the miserable Latin which the two produce; behind this is a double recognition on our part of the pretentious absurdity of the professional jargon of lawyers and of the fact that Cutbeard and Otter are in fact not lawyers at all, but a barber and a retired bear-warden. Similarly we realise that all this performance is being put on for Morose's benefit, and that while he is suffering the torture of the noise of the argument, and is alternately encouraged and depressed by the escape-routes which are first offered and then denied to him, all is completely unnecessary, since he has never been married at all. Stern critics have objected even to this scene as being unrealistic—how have Otter and Cutbeard learned even this much dog-Latin?— and not consistent in tone with the rest of the play. It would require a very hard heart, however, not to warm to it:

Otter I, or if there be *morbus perpetuus, & insanabilis, as Paralysis, Elephantiasis,* or so—
Dauphine O, but *frigiditas* is the fairer way, gentlemen.
Ott. You say troth, sir, and as it is in the *canon,* master Doctor.
Cutbeard I conceive you sir.
Clerimont Before he speakes.
Ott. That *a boy, or child, under yeares, is not fit for marriage, because he cannot reddere debitum.* So your *omnipotentes*—
Truewit Your *impotentes,* you whorson Lobster.
Ott. Your *impotentes,* I should say, are *minime apti ad contrahenda matrimonium.*
Tru. Matrimonium? Wee shall haue most un-matrimoniall *latin,* with you: *matrimonia,* and be hang'd.
Dau. You put 'hem out, man.
Cut. But then there will arise a doubt, master Parson, in our case, *post matrimonium*: that *frigiditate prœditus,* (doe you conceive me, sir?)
Ott. Very well, sir.
Cut. Who cannot *uti vxore pro uxore,* may *habere eam pro sorore.*

(V.iii.177–98)

It is a curious defect in some critical studies of Jonson that they sometimes fail to suggest that his comedy is in any way funny. He is certainly not to everyone's taste: his hard, tough, unsympathetic tone may give rise to dislike, even distress. He illustrates perfectly Bergson's theory of Comedy; it is true, for example, that many of his characters are funny because they behave in a stereotyped, invariable way, like machines, and also that, because of their enslavement by Opinion, they often act in a way inappropriate to the real situation in which they find themselves, and are thus absurd. Not many English comic writers fit so neatly into this pattern, and in some ways Jonson is an un-English writer. This has not prevented him from having a profound influence on English literature: we can trace the 'comedy of humours' through later seventeenth-century and early eighteenth-century drama through into the novels of Fielding and Smollett, and so on to the nineteenth century: it is almost an invariant that the traditional English novel should have its quota of low-life comic 'humours'. But Jonson lacked a sentimentality or whimsy, and we are accustomed to meeting both of these in our comic writers. Within his limits, however, and consistently with his settled principles, he explored different ways of achieving the comic effects he desired, and his variety, as well as his consistency, requires to be recognised.

JONSON'S POETRY, PROSE AND CRITICISM

I

Considering that he wrote the best-known lyric in the English language, Jonson has had comparatively little attention as a poet. The reason for this is not hard to see. As with his plays, he had a very clear idea of what he wanted to do in poetry and what his principles were, and he remained largely independent of fashions and schools. In consequence his poetry does not quite fit into the usual categories of English literary history, and while its obvious qualities have always gained it respect, it has never been fully in accord with the taste of any period. Jonson yielded to no one in in the high value he placed on poetry, but he saw it as essentially an Art, rather than as the expression of personality or a way of conveying a unique perception of Truth. Skill was the quality most inescapably demanded of the poet. Certainly he had to be born a poet, and equally certainly he needed Inspiration, in some sense of that difficult word, but no man can rely on these alone and think

hee can leape forth suddainely a *Poet*, by dreaming hee hath been in *Parnassus*, or, having washed his lipps (as they say) in *Helicon*. There goes more to his making, then so. For to Nature, Exercise, Imitation, and Studie, *Art* must be added, to make all these perfect. And, though these challenge to themselves much, in the making up of our Maker, it is Art only can lead him to perfection, and leave him there, as planted by her hand.[1]

The position maintained is straightforwardly neo-classical. In order to write well, the first necessity was, as Horace had said, to master the subject; then, to know how other writers had treated it so as to be able to make use of their work. Originality and Inspiration, as the Romantics understood them, do not, or need not, enter into this. There is one poem of Jonson's—'That women are but men's shadows' (*Forrest*, vii)—which we know was written to order, having been given to him as a 'penance' by the Countess of Pembroke. It is not a very distinguished poem, but it has interest because it shews Jonson carrying out his precepts in practice; having been set his task, he looked for a suitable model to imitate, found it in a lyric by the early sixteenth-century Latinist Barhélemi Aneau, and adapted this to his purpose. This is in miniature the technique he used when he had to fulfils a commision for a masque, such as *The Masque of Blackness*, and indeed it seems to have been his natural method whenever he set himself to compose anything, large or small.

Mastery of the matter to be conveyed and familiarity with the best models for imitation were as important even in a brief lyric such as 'That women are but men's shadows' as in Tragedy and Comedy. Next after them came the logical disposition of the matter and proper attention to detail. In the preface to *The Alchemist* Jonson draws a distinction between energetic but careless writing, and proper composition:

> ... there is a great difference between those, that (to gaine opinion of *Copie* [that is, copiousness or fertility of imagination]) utter all they can, however unfitly: and those that use election and a meane. For it is only the disease of the unskilfull, to think rude things greater than polish'd: or scatter'd more numerous than compos'd.

The true craftsman-poet must be ready to polish and revise, to 'bring all to the forge and file again', and if necessary to expunge, and this is what lies behind his comment when the players mentioned it as an honour to Shakespeare, 'that in his writing . . . he never blotted out line'. In rejoining: 'Would he had blotted a thousand' Jonson certainly did not mean that he wished there was less of Shakespeare's writing, but that he felt that Shakespeare managed his genius badly and would have been an even better writer if he had revised more.[2] In his own way Jonson would have accepted the dictum that poetry must possess all the virtues of good prose, and indeed he told Drummond that

> he wrott all his ⟨verses⟩ first in prose, for so his master Cambden had learned him.[3]

This sounds like an exaggeration—it is difficult to believe, for example, that all his lyrics can have begun in this way—but it may well be largely true, and there are certainly places where Jonson can in fact be seen to be versifying his own or others' prose.

The next demand that poetry had to meet was for perspicuity and naturalness of diction. Simplicity and directness, however, were not to decline into emptiness and insipidity. Jonson distinguished between what he called 'men's poets' and 'women's poets', the latter being typified for him by Daniel:

> Others there are, that have no composition at all; but a kind of tuneing, and riming fall, in what they write. It runs and slides, and onely makes sound. Womens-*Poets* they are call'd: as you have womens-*Taylors*.
>
> *They write a verse, as smooth, as soft, as creame;*
> *In which there is no torrent, nor scarce streame.*
>
> You may sound these wits, and find the depth of them, with your middle finger. They are *Creame-bowle*, or but puddle deepe.[4]

For this kind of writing Jonson had no patience, but he objected as much to the other extreme of deliberately 'strong' or harsh poetry:

> *Others*, that in composition are nothing, but what is rough and broken: *Quae per salebras altaque saxa cadunt.* And if it would come gently, they trouble it of purpose. They would not have it run without rubs, as if that stile were more strong and manly, that stroke the eare with a kind of unevennesse.[5]

This was a 'humour' like affecting a 'singularity' in the cut of one's beard; Jonson complained of it in Donne, a poet whom he otherwise greatly admired (he told Drummond 'that Done for not keeping of accent deserves hanging' and that 'Done himself for not being understood would perish'[6]).

In versification, then, Jonson desired what was 'numerous' or harmonious, but not boringly regular. He tried his hand at a number of different metres, even experimenting with the Pindaric Ode, a form little practised by the Elizabethans, and indeed not very well understood by them; Jonson's scholarship gave him an advantage here, though he was not temperamentally suited for such a rhapsodic form, and could only sometimes bring it off. In general he had no taste for wild and irregular beauties: he said of style that it should be smooth, gentle, and sweet; like a Table, upon which you may runne your finger without rubs, and your nayle cannot find a joynt; not horrid, rough, wrinckled, gaping, or chapt.[7]

Perhaps most revealing of all is a remark that Drummond records:

That Southwell was hanged yett so he had written that piece of his ye burning babe he would have been content to destroy many of his.[8]

Southwell was a Catholic martyr, and for a long period of his life Jonson was a member of the Roman Church, but it was probably not so much the religious content of *The Burning Babe* that he admired as its combination of gravity of subject, fervour of feeling and firm stylistic control. In his own work the same combination of qualities can be found, as in his 'Epigram' on the death of his first son:

> Farewell, thou child of my right hand, and joy;
>   My sinne was too much hope of thee, lov'd boy.
> Seven yeares tho'wert lent to me, and I thee pay,
>   Exacted by thy fate, on the just day. . . .

The union of smoothness and strength is especially valuable in this poem because it so successfully contains what might easily have become mawkish and sentimental; this is truly 'masculine' poetry.

Jonson defined his ideal diction clearly in *Discoveries* (in what is actually a paraphrase from Quintilian):

Pure and neate language I love, yet plaine and customary.[9]

He took his stand, that is, with Cheke, Ascham, Sidney and those other humanists who believed in 'dignifying the vernacular' by 'purifying' it, freeing it from obscurity, rusticity, clumsiness and affectation, whether this last took the form of self-conscious archaism or of pedantic importation from ancient or modern languages. English was to be transformed into an expressive and worthy literary language by revealing its true genius, not by divorcing it from the actual speech of men, 'upon the which', Jonson says in his unfinished *Grammar*, 'all precepts are grounded, and to the which they ought to be referred'. 'Custom' or usage was the ultimate sanction, but this did not mean accepting the standards of the vulgar:

Yet when I name Custome, I understand not the vulgar Custome: For that were a precept no lesse dangerous to Language, then life, if wee should speake or live after the manners of the vulgar: But that I call Custome of speech, which is the consent of the Learned; as Custome of life, which is the consent of the good.[10]

As always the link between purity in diction and purity in life was a vital one to Jonson, and in neither sphere must the good man be corrupted by evil practices. On the other hand it was wrong to be too precious in diction, or to attempt to astonish by inflated grandness of style:

The true Artificer will not run away from nature, as hee were afraid of her; or depart from life, and the likeness of Truth; but speake to the capacity of his hearers. And though his language differ from the vulgar somewhat; it shall not fly from all humanity, with the *Tamerlaines* and *Tamer-Chams* of the late Age, which had nothing in them but the *scenicall* strutting, and furious vociferation, to warrant them to the ignorant gapers. Hee knowes it is his onely Art, so to carry it, as none but Artificers perceive it.[11]

Jonson's own vocabulary has been extensively studied, and the statistical evidence supports those who have emphasised the Englishness of his language against the older view expressed by Dryden—'he did a little too much romanise our tongue'.[12] The modern reader may well be struck by apparent Latinisms in Jonson, but it must be remembered that many words of Latin origin were common in the Renaissance but have since passed out of currency. Jonson himself is credited with the introduction of only about 100 words from Latin, many of which are now quite domesticated —'candidate', for example, 'connection', 'frugal', 'gesticulate', 'petulant', 'preside', 'reciprocate', and 'terse'. This incidence of borrowing is low for an Elizabethan writer, and, oddly, it is lowest in Jonson's Roman tragedies. As might be expected he borrowed less still from Greek, though here again some of his important loans are now naturalised—'analytic' is one, and so are 'exotic', 'heroine' and 'plastic' (as an adjective). More obvious than his importations are his usages of words derived from Latin or Greek in their original rather than their English meaning, such as his use of 'front' to mean 'forehead' or 'frequent' to mean 'crowded' or 'well-attended' ('a frequent Senate'). Many of these senses were common in his day, and, of course, to the educated among his audience, to whom Latin was as familiar as English, they would not have seemed strange.

In his actual vocabulary, then, Jonson may be classified as only

moderately Latinate, and certainly well removed from the affected
Latinism which he satirised in the characters of Juniper in *The Case
is Altered* and Crispinus in *Poetaster*.[13] His language is more often
given an exotic appearance by his readiness to interrupt normal
English word-order. The 'hanging' or misplaced clause is an
example of this:

> If you had bloud, or vertue in you, gentlemen, you would not
> suffer such eare-wigs about a husband, or scorpions, to creep
> between man and wife. . . .   (*Epicoene*, V.iv.6–8)

> If there be never a *Servant-monster* i'the *Fayre*, who can helpe it?
> he sayes; nor a nest of *Antiques?* . . . (*Bartholomew Fair*, Ind.127–8)

A similar strangeness may come from a more minor displacement
of the expected run of a sentence, as when he notes in *Discoveries*
that 'Men are decay'd, and *studies*', or refers in the dedication
to *Volpone* to the 'invading interpreters' (or unauthorised commentators on others' work) 'who cunningly, and often, utter their
owne virulent malice, under other mens simplest meanings', where
we would expect 'often cunningly'. His ellipses also sometimes
produce odd effects, as in these lines from the first Prologue to
Epicoene (which also contain one of Jonson's characteristic
negatives):

> Our wishes, like to those (make publique feasts)
> Are not to please the cookes tastes, but the guests.
> Yet, if those cunning palates hether come,
> They shall find guests, entreaty, and good roome;
> And though all relish not, sure, there will be some,
> That, when they leave their seates, shall make 'hem say,
> Who wrote that piece, could so have wrote a play:
> But that, he knew, this was the better way.   (8–15)

Together with Jonson's frequently heavy punctuation, these
idiosyncrasies often produce both in prose and verse a broken-up,
jerky impression which may at first reading be difficult to follow
(though the difficulty often disappears if the passages are heard
or read aloud). Sometimes in the plays this can be justified
as reproducing the movement of a character's thought or the
forms of colloquial speech, but it is not always possible to maintain
this. No doubt Jonson was affected by the movement of taste at
the end of the sixteenth century away from the polished 'Ciceronian'
style towards a rougher, more abrupt and colloquial-seeming

manner. The older balanced and ornate mode appears in him only in parody, as in Puntarvolo's address to his wife's gentlewoman:

> To the perfection of complement (which is the Diall of the thought, and guided by the Sunne of your beauties) are requir'd these three specials: the *gnomon*, the *puntilio*'s, and the *superficies*: the *superficies*, is that we call, place; the *puntilio*'s, circumstance; and the *gnomon*, ceremony: in either of which, for a stranger to erre, 'tis easy and facile, and such am I. (*Every Man out*, II.ii.19–23)

Jonson wrote in both the stock forms of 'baroque prose', the 'curt,' most familiar to us from Bacon's *Essays*, and the 'loose' or 'dispersed', of which the extreme example is perhaps Burton's *Anatomy of Melancholy*; both are well illustrated in *Epicoene*, mainly by Truewit, who is something of a virtuoso of 'modern' eloquence. But Truewit to some extent parodies himself, and Jonson was aware, as Bacon was, that in the end those who set out to avoid the ornateness of the Ciceronian style might fall as easily as their predecessors into that error 'when men study words and not matter'. In all probability Jonson's experimenting with word-order was not so much a conscious attempt to be fashionable as a wish to give English the more flexible word-order of Latin, and in this sense perhaps he was a 'romaniser'. His ultimate principles were never in doubt: 'I would rather have a plaine down-right wisdome, than a foolish and affected eloquence'.[14]

Jonson's borrowings from foreign languages are few, and can usually be accounted for by the need to provide local colour. *Volpone*, for example, has a number of loans from Italian, and *The Devil is an Ass* many from Spanish, since in that play there is some incidental satire of the contemporary vogue for Spanish fashions and manners (of which Jonson, born and brought up in Elizabethan England, disapproved). Some of the words he introduced have become established: 'caress' (as a noun) and 'disgust' (as a verb), both from Italian; 'casuist' and 'responsible' from French; 'drill' and 'furlough' from Dutch—remembered perhaps from his days as a soldier. He has none of the excessive dependence on French and Italian which characterised some of his contemporaries, and indeed satirises it in his fops. He is similarly sparing in his use of dialect and archaism; his comment on Spenser is famous: 'in affecting the Ancients [he] writ no language.'[15] Altogether in the 'enrichment' of English he was conservative—extremely conservative in comparison with Spenser or Shakespeare—and he was equally conservative in drawing on native resources. All writers of his period show an extraordinary facility in substituting one part of speech for another and in giving new meanings to established words. Jonson is the first recorded authority for over 1,000 such usages, but this is little in comparison with Shakespeare. Nor was he very inventive in coining compound nouns and adjectives, in which Elizabethan English was particularly rich. 'Book-worm' is one of his creations, and so are 'half-witted', 'pig-headed', and 'close-mouthed'. Some of his inventions have failed to survive, and this is perhaps a pity: 'egg-chinned', 'shrewd-bearded' and 'squirrel-limbed' might be useful additions to our vocabulary. Significantly he was most creative in constructing new terms of disparagement or abuse; the speeches of Tucca and Buffone are rich in this respect, and so are those of Face. But in general Jonson's strength lay not so much in the richness or fecundity of his language, as in its perspicuity, preciseness and straightforward vigour.

The qualities of Jonson's prose are not easily isolated in his comedies, for the simple reason that he was there mostly writing 'in character'. Although he accepted Aristotle's dictum that the 'low style' was appropriate for Comedy, this did not obviate the need for variety of tone, and in practice he uses different styles for description, exposition, narrative, and so on. More obvious, however, is that much of the speech that he puts into the mouths of his characters is pastiche, or downright parody. This has somewhat confused critics, so that one can claim 'it is probable that in Jonson more than in any contemporary dramatist we have the pattern of Elizabethan and Jacobean English', while another can declare that 'his dramatic speech is a unique language never heard off the stage'.[16] Certainly Jonson did not, any more than any other dramatist, reproduce exactly the everyday speech of real people: the tape-recorder has made us all painfully aware how dull, repititious and undramatic this can be. On the other hand it is not fair to say, as one scholar has done, that

he could mimic successfully only a language stamped with oddness or derangement. . . and his inability to portray the speech of healthy normalcy make one limit to his immense gift as a mimetic artist.[17]

When he had no particular interest in bringing out the oddity in a character's speech—in the (admittedly few) words given to Bridget Kitely, for example, or indeed in the speeches of her brother when he is being 'the merchant' rather than 'the jealous man'—he probably comes as near to the ordinary speech of his time as any dramatist could. Language was his chosen way, however, of establishing character, and since so many of his people are eccentrics, their language must be expected to be to that extent idiosyncratic and 'unnatural'. What counts is whether it interests and convinces us as a *possible* way of speaking, and, when Jonson is at his best, this it does. No doubt nobody ever spoke like Bobadil, but we are willing to believe that somebody might have done; just as, to take a different sort of example, we are willing to accept Truewit even at his most elaborately rhetorical for the sake of the pleasure he gives us.

It may have been a sign of weakness in Jonson, as some have suggested, that so much of his comic writing is parodic, in that it may indicate an infertility in original creative impulse and the need to have a 'kicking-off point' for his imagination. On the other hand Jonson was setting out to write satirical comedy, and parody is the weapon readiest to the hand of the literary satirist. What is certainly true is that he was the master of a fine prose style of his own when it was appropriate to use it. It is at its most dignified and cogent in the dedication to *Volpone*, and at its richest in the descriptive passages of some of the masques. *Discoveries* should also be mentioned here, for although nearly all the ideas in the collection are borrowed, the expression of most of them is Jonson's own. At times Jonson aspires too closely to the 'Senecal' terseness thought appropriate for the essay—*Discoveries* is after all a notebook—but for the most part *Discoveries* is clearly, plainly, but energetically and roundly expressed, and at times it reaches a noteworthy grandeur and solemnity.

The stylistic qualities which Jonson desired were those which we would tend to think of as the qualities of good, plain prose, but he looked to see them in poetry as well. The prescriptions he laid down were those for the 'plain' rather than the 'high' or ornate style, and this choice radically limited his range as a poet.[18] It prescribed the type of poem he wrote, for by the laws of Decorum the plain style was only appropriate to certain 'kinds', in general those that were at once 'familiar' and moral. Jonson's *Epigrams*, which he called 'the ripest of my studies', fall under this heading. They are not the bitter, sharp, 'snarling' epigrams fashionable at the time he wrote his first Humour plays, although some of them are satirical (Jonson never in fact uses 'satire' to describe any of his poems), nor are they always, or even usually, witty and pointed. The lack of wit was commented on by contemporary critics, and Jonson acknowledged the complaint. His second epigram, however, should have made it plain that he was not offering specimens of the *genre* so popular at the end of the previous century:

To My Booke

It will be look'd for, booke, when some but see
    Thy title, *Epigrammes*, and nam'd of mee,
Thou should'st be bold, licentious, full of gall,
    Wormewood, and sulphure, sharpe, and tooth'd withall;
Become a petulant thing, hurle inke, and wit,
    As mad-men stones: not caring whom they hit.
Deceive their malice, who could wish it so.
    And by thy wiser temper, let men know
Thou are not covetous of least selfe-fame,
    Made from the hazard of anothers shame:
Much lesse with lewd, prophane, and beastly phrase,
    To catch the worlds loose laughter, or vaine gaze.
He that departs with his owne honesty
    For vulgar praise, doth it too dearely buy.

To the 'meere English Censurer' who complains that his poems are not true epigrams of the old-fashioned sort, Jonson retorts (*Epigram* xviii) that they are not a new kind but in 'the old way and the true', and he seems to be thinking of the epigrams of Martial, who said that the epigram should constitute a kind of letter. Many of Jonson's epigrams are addressed to his friends, and except in length there is little difference between them and his longer 'Epistles'; even the shorter, more satirical epigrams are often addressed to imaginary recipients. 'Epigram' could also cover epitaph, and in fact the famous *Epitaph on Salamon Pavy* was printed among them; even this is in a way a letter, since it is addressed to the audience: 'Weepe with me all you that read/This little storie . . .' . In tone and mood, however, Jonson is nearer Horace than Martial, and he may have been aiming at providing an English equivalent of Horace's *sermones*—'conversational poems' or, literally, 'talks'.

In Jonson's hand the epigram was a versatile 'instrument', and he added to it the ode, the elegy, the lyric, as well as some other poems not so easily classifiable. He was cut off, however, not only from Heroic poetry—so that the closest he comes to the Epic style is in his tragedies—but, by his own decision, from love poetry as well. In *Poetaster* he had relegated erotic poetry to a subordinate place in the canon, and we should not therefore expect to find him devoting his talents to it; in fact he seems to have tried to make himself the kind of poet he represents Horace as being in that play. Perhaps there were personal reasons as well, but if so we cannot now discover them: the little humorous poem 'Why I write

not of love', which was printed as the first poem in *The Forrest*
tells us nothing. In fact he did write some 'elegies' of love, but they
form a very striking contrast to those of Donne, for example. They
have little of Donne's wit, of which Jonson did not wholly approve,
although he could at times approximate to it; more significantly
they are hardly passionate, though sometimes fervent, and reveal
little sensuous feeling. On the whole they use the language and
manner of erotic verse with some skill, but with a kind of constraint. The group of poems 'To Charis' in *The Underwood* may
perhaps express some real incident in Jonson's own life,[19] but they
are marked by a note of self-conscious irony, and the last two are
frankly humorous. Moral considerations probably came into play
here; it was not the part of the truly good man to celebrate passion
or sensuality, and one safeguard was to introduce the pose of one
who 'ever cometh last in the dance of love' and does not take it
all too seriously. The Elegy no. xlii of *The Underwood* sets Jonson's
usual tone:

> Let me be what I am, as *Virgil* cold;
>   As *Horace* fat; or as *Anacreon* old;
> No Poets verses yet did ever move,
>   Whose Readers did not thinke he was in love.
> Who shall forbid me then in Rithme to bee
>   As light, and active as the youngest hee
> That from the Muses fountaines doth indorse
>   His lynes, and hourely sits the Poets horse?
> Put on my Ivy Garland, let me see
>   Who frownes, who jealous is, who taxeth me.
> Fathers, and Husbands, I doe claime a right
>   In all that is call'd lovely: take my sight
> Sooner then my affection from the faire.
>   No face, no hand, proportion, line, or Ayre
> Of beautie; but the Muse hath interest in:
>   There is not worne that lace, purle, knot or pin,
> But is the Poets matter: And he must,
>   When he is furious, love, although not lust . . .

Thereafter it turns into a satire on women. Jonson would not have
the same reasons for restraint, however, in his religious poetry,
where he sounds sincere enough, but equally frigid, and it becomes
obvious that the real limitation was stylistic.

The criteria which Jonson imposed on his own style were
directed towards clarity and harmony, but they virtually precluded

F

a complex and plastic use of words. This results in what T. S. Eliot called the 'superficiality' of his poetry, noting that his words lack

a network of tentacular roots reaching down to the deepest terrors and desires.[20]

Eliot was writing especially of the poetry in the tragedies, but it is generally true that Jonson's poems provide little for the exegete using the methods of 'close reading'; he lacks the interlocking of connotation and evocation and the buried image-chains for which critics are now trained to look. The first stanza of 'Drink to me only with thine eyes', for example, has a reasonably complex structure of meaning—indeed Professor Empson brought it, perhaps a little forcedly, within the compass of *Seven Types of Ambiguity*.[21] Eyes can be liquid; they can literally 'brim over' with tears; their gaze can be intoxicating. Kisses, too, are not inappropriate in a cup; we are accustomed to the idea of tasting someone's lips, drinking in beauty, and so on, and 'kisses like wine' has become a cliché. After this, however, the poem dwindles into little more than graceful compliment, although possibly a determined commentator might see in the conceit of the unwithered branch a suggestion not only of the immortality of love but of the mistress as a fertility-goddess.

From this point of view Jonson is rather an unrewarding poet, just as he is unrewarding as a poetic playwright, and one disappointed critic has committed himself to the surely damning judgment:

Jonson's imagery . . . resembles that of a philologist who could also write poetry.[22]

Jonson may well, like Joyce and Milton, have had a primarily verbal rather than pictorial imagination, although in any case his insistence on the logical disposition of the matter of a poem (to say nothing of the practice of first writing his poems out in prose) would militate against an unconscious logic of metaphor. The major point, however, is that Jonson's views of the proper use of words drove him towards what we should call a denotatory use of language, in which the 'dictionary meaning' is the most important aspect of the word. In this, as in some other aspects of his thought, Jonson anticipated the doctrines of the later seventeenth century; perhaps it would be truer to say that the movement to 'ennoble' the English language by purifying it, to which he belonged, was that which eventually triumphed over its rivals and emerged as the

dominant force in the latter part of the century. In general terms
the strength and weakness of Jonson's poetry are very much the
strengths and weaknesses of the poetry of Dryden and Pope,
although it could not be confused with theirs, and could only in a
limited sense be called 'Augustan'. (To Dryden and Pope, Jonson's
verse was insufficiently pure and refined, not correctly versified,
and altogether lacking in 'politeness'; Jonson for his part would
have disapproved, among other things, of Dryden's persistent use
of the High Style for inappropriate subjects, and of Pope's devotion
to epigram and paradox.)

One significant characteristic of Jonson's verse is that it often
draws its strength from objects rather than giving strength to
them. A good example is this stanza, from the fourth of the series
of poems 'To Charis'—*Her Triumph*:

> Have you seene but a bright Lillie grow,
> 　　Before rude hands have touch'd it?
> Have you mark'd but the fall o' the Snow
> 　　Before the soyle hath smutch'd it?
> Have you felt the wooll o' the Bever?
> 　　　　　　　Or Swans Downe ever?
> Or have smelt o' the bud o' the Brier?
> 　　　　　　　Or the Nard i' the fire?
> Or have tasted the bag o' the Bee?
> O so white! O so soft! O so sweet is she!　　　　　(21–30)

There is no question of the effectiveness of this, but it depends on
reminding us of the actual physical qualities of the objects mentioned,
and then transferring the sense-traces thus evoked to the idea of the
mistress; Jonson does not, through his language, *convey* the sensual
impressions to us, or modify them in any way. The same is true of
much of his pastoral poetry, in a lyric such as this (from *Pan's
Anniversarie*):

> Strew, strew, the glad and smiling ground
> With every flower, yet not confound
> The Prime-rose drop, the Springs own spouse,
> Bright Dayes-eyes, and the lipes of Cowes,
> 　　The Garden-star, the Queene of May,
> 　　The Rose, to crowne the Holy-day.
>
> Drop, drop, you Violets, change your hues,
> Now red, now pale, as Lovers use;

And in your death go out as well
As when you liv'd, unto the smell;
  That from your odour all may say,
  This is the Shepherds Holy-day.   (11–24)

Apart from the rather subdued conceit of the violets' breathing
their last in odour nothing *happens* to the flowers in the poem; they
are not even described, or given any qualities, and the effect of the
piece depends on the reader's recalling them to his memory and
producing in himself the stock attitude towards them.

 This is not to say that Jonson's use of language is never creative.
Characteristically, however, he is most forcible when he is dealing
with things which in themselves generate emotion, and corre-
spondingly at his most effective when expressing the emotions
which are most readily aroused by the actual physical presence of
objects. Desire and Aversion are the feelings he can most readily
convey, and he habitually does so through reference to physical
objects. Volpone thus attempts to convey his feelings for Celia
through a catalogue of the riches he will shower on her:

See, here, a rope of pearle; and each, more orient
Then that the brave *Egyptian* queene carrous'd:
Dissolve, and drinke'hem. See, a carbuncle,
May put out both the eyes of our *St. Marke;*
A diamant, would have bought *Lollia Paulina,*
When she came in, like star-light, hid with jewels,
That were the spoiles of provinces; take these,
And weare, and lose'hem . . .   (III.vii.191–8)

This seems natural in Volpone: we may be more surprised to find
the Host in *The New Inn* celebrating a more 'spiritual' matter—
the death of the happy lover—in similar terms:

    A death
For Emperours to enjoy! and the Kings
Of the rich East, to pawne their regions for;
To show their treasure, open all thier mines,
Spend all their spices to embalme their corpse,
And wrap the inches up in sheets of gold,
That fell by such a noble destiny!   (II.vi.236–42)

Not only do sexual desire and Avarice seem closely connected in
Jonson's mind; he seems to need the tangible symbols of wealth to
convey passionate longing and the desire for possession.

Jonson is still more original in his expression of scorn, hatred or contempt, and is most likely in this mood to create images which stick fast in our minds. Critics usually illustrate his vitality in this respect from some of the famous pieces of description in his comedies—such as Face's description of Subtle's complexion:

> Stuck full of black, and melancholique wormes,
> Like poulder-corns, shot, at the *artillery-yeard* . . .   (*Alch.* I.i.30–1)

As well as their sonorous and dignified passages in the high style, however, the two tragedies have some sharp imagery of this kind. In *Sejanus* Jonson twice brilliantly evokes the shiftiness and cunning of the time-serving Roman politicians, once when Sabinus commented to Silius on their lack of pliancy and ambition:

> Wee have no shifts of faces, no cleft tongues,
> No soft, and glutinous bodies, that can sticke,
> Like snailes, on painted walls;   (I.7–9)

and again when Arruntius describes a group of Senators anxiously whispering together:

> I, now their heads doe travaile, now they worke;
> Their faces runne like shittles, they are weaving
> Some curious cobweb to catch flies.   (III.22–4)

In his non-dramatic verse, too, there is no doubt that a new note of vigour and urgency appears when Jonson is on the attack, as for example in the 'Expostulation with Inigo Jones', or the 'Execration upon Vulcan'.

There is a critical fallacy to be avoided here. The modern reader is conditioned to find the violent and the sordid more exciting and therefore more 'real' than the harmonious and beautiful, and to think that what excites him most in a poet must be the produce of what is 'deepest' in that poet's personality. It is tempting to base interpretation of Jonson's own character on the fact that he seems most vital when he expresses desire or repugnance in terms of physical objects; it may be safer to accept the fact that his concept of poetry and his view of language were bound to limit the emotional range of what he wrote. He may have felt himself free to express emotion only when he was confident that this could be justified morally: the dramatic expression of inordinate desire by characters who are clearly held up for disapproval, and the satirical description of real or imaginary opponents of virtue were privileged occasions. We cannot ignore the presence of much fine verse of a generally philosophical or ethical kind among his poems and in his masques; that this moves us less may be partly because the ideas he expresses no longer mean much to us, and because the expression of them is restricted by his demand for perspicuity and logic.

Jonson's best poems, naturally enough, are in those 'kinds' to which his critical theories were best adapted—the epistle and the lyric. An epistle such as that to Edward Sackville, Earl of Dorset, manages to combine the familiar and the grave in a balance that can properly be called 'masculine', as Jonson understood the term:

> If, *Sackvile*, all that have the power to doe
> Great and good turns, as wel could time them too,
> And knew their how, and where: we should have, then,
> Lesse list of proud, hard, or ingratefull Men.
> For benefits are ow'd with the same mind
> As they are done, and such returnes they find:
> You then, whose will not only, but desire
> To succour my necessities, tooke fire,
> Not at my prayers, but your sense; which laid
> The way to meet, what others would upbraid;
> And in the Act did so my blush prevent,
> As I did feele it done, as soone as meant:
> You cannot doubt, but I, who freely know
> This Good from you, as freely will it owe;
> And though my fortune humble me, to take
> The smallest courtesies with thankes, I make
> Yet choyce from whom I take them; and would shame
> To have such doe me good, I durst not name:
> They are the Noblest benefits, and sinke
> Deepest in Man, of which when he doth thinke,
> The memorie delights him more, from whom
> Then what he hath receiv'd.   (1–22)

The more famous 'To Penshurst' has the same use of objects for the evocative power that resides in them as Jonson's poetry of Desire and Loathing, but here adapted to the creation of a picture of harmonious and civilised rusticity:

> Each banks doth yeeld thee coneyes; and the topps
>   Fertile of wood, *Ashore*, and *Sydney's* copp's,

To crowne thy open table, doth provide
   The purpled pheasant, with the speckled side:
The painted partrich lyes in euery field,
   And, for thy messe, is willing to be kill'd.
And if the high-swolne *Medway* fails thy dish,
   Thou has thy ponds, that pay thee tribute fish,
Fat, aged carps, that runne into thy net.
   And pikes, now weary their owne kinde to eat,
As loth, the second draught, or cast to stay,
   Officiously, at first, themselves betray.
Bright eeles, that emulate them, and leape on land,
   Before the fisher, or into his hand.
Then hath thy orchard fruit, thy garden flowers,
   Fresh as the ayre, and new as are the houres.
The earely cherry, with the later plum,
   Fig, grape, and quince, each in his time doth come:
The blushing apricot, and woolly peach
   Hang on thy walls, that every child may reach.   (25–44)

The list of fruits in the last few lines is more than a catalogue, for
it is modified by the very last phrase, 'that every child may reach';
the fruit is harmless, it is freely bestowed, it is plucked in innocence. The tone established is intensified in the lines immediately
following:

And though thy walls be of the countrey stone,
   They'are rear'd with no mans ruine, no mans grone,
There's none, that dwell about them, wish them downe;
   But all come in, the farmer, and the clowne . . .   (45–8)

This invocation of simple, innocent but ordered and cultivated
rural living is far removed from the bustling city life of the comedies,
but it echoes the atmosphere of *The Sad Shepherd* and of some of
the masques. 'To Penshurst' and the epigram 'Inviting a friend to
supper' (no. ci) are Jonson at his most urbane and 'Roman', and
at his closest to the Augustans:

To night, grave sir, both my poore house, and I
   Doe equally desire your companie:
Not that we think us worthy such a ghest,
   But that your worth will dignifie our feast . . .

No one would deny that these poems represent a largely conventional pose, or that we may be closer to the 'real' Jonson in the

nervous indignant energy of the 'Expostulation with Inigo Jones'. They do represent, however, Jonson as he would have liked to see himself, and (more importantly) successfully writing the kind of poetry he set himself to write.

Jonson's reputation as a lyric poet has suffered much from Swinburne's judgment that he was 'a singer who could not sing'. This may seem an odd description of the poet who wrote the 'Hymn to Diana' from *Cynthia's Revels* ('Queene, and *Huntresse*, chaste and faire'), and the less-known Echo's song from the same play:

> Slow, slow, fresh fount, keepe time with my salt teares;
> Yet slower, yet, o faintly gentle springs:
> List to the heavy part the musique beares,
>   Woe weepes out her division, when shee sings.
>   Droupe hearbs, and flowres;
>   Fall griefe in showres;
>   Our beauties are not ours:
>   O, I could still
> (Like melting snow upon some craggie hill,)
>   drop, drop, drop, drop,
> Since natures pride is, now, a wither'd daffodil.   (I.ii.65–75)

There are many other lyrics in the masques which could be quoted to refute Swinburne. His judgment requires the elucidation provided by another passage:

> The case of Ben Jonson is the great standing example of a truth which should never be forgotten or overlooked: that no amount of learning, of labour, or of culture will supply the place of natural taste and native judgment . . .[23]

There is no pretending that Jonson's lyrics read like 'the spontaneous overflow of powerful feelings'; they are undoubtedly 'artificial'—a term which Jonson would have taken as one of approval, as indicating the proper exercise of the craft of the artificer-poet—and they certainly evince learning and care. But they are not therefore bad, unless one is prepared to dismiss all poetry of this kind as inferior; they are certainly good examples of their 'kind'. The song from *Epicoene* is a fair representative:

> Still to be neat, still to be drest,
> As, you were going to a feast;

Still to be pou'dred, still perfum'd:
Lady, it is to be presum'd,
Though arts hid causes are not found,
All is not sweet, all is not sound.

Give me a looke, give me a face,
That make simplicitie a grace;
Robes loosely flowing, haire as free:
Such sweet neglect more taketh me,
Then all th'adulteries of art,
They strike mine eyes, but not my heart.   (I.i.91–102)

This may be in praise of simplicity and artlessness, but it is certainly itself neither simple nor artless; nor does it pretend to be. Instead it offers a civilised and sophisticated attitude that is both cynical and moral—indeed it is a minor attack on the targets of Appearance and Opinion; in expression it is precise, pointed, graceful and musical, but at the same time direct and plain-spoken ('All is not sweet, all is not sound'). These are qualities shared in some degree by all Jonson's lyrics; even in trifles he retained the characteristics of a 'man's poet'—craftsmanship, plain language and sober meaningfulness.

II

When he spoke of the lack of a 'third dimension' to Jonson's poetry Eliot (adapting a judgment of G. G. Smith's) pointed at a quality which is common to all Jonson's work. His poems are very 'self-contained', in the sense that whatever emotion they generate is strictly kept within the bounds of the poem; there is no diffusion or spilling-over of generalised emotional force irrelevant to the meaning of the poem (as there certainly is with Swinburne). This is a quality of which Eliot could approve, but it carries with it the limitation that Jonson's poems rarely, if ever, lead the mind beyond themselves, to explore remoter areas of emotion or thought. If Jonson is never flabbily evocative in his poetry, he is not often imaginatively stimulating. *Mutatis mutandis*, this is generally true of his writing. Throughout his work Jonson's firm intellectual grasp of the principles of his art and his rigorous discipline in following them were a source of weakness as well as strength. He very often achieved what he wished to accomplish, but he very seldom achieved more. The 'grace beyond the reach

of art' is something which Jonson lacked; he is not often free from
a sense of effort, and there is very little in his writing which we can
believe is the result of some 'happy accident'. It is here that Swinburne's reference to his lack of 'natural taste' has point.

We cannot blame Jonson for being the man he was. We may
suspect that if he had dropped his guard a little and relaxed his
unvarying control he might have freed himself to write not only
differently, but better. But we cannot prove this, and it is plainly
unfair to criticise him for not writing as it would have been repug-
nant to his critical canons to write, or for failing to achieve what
he did not want to achieve. On the other hand it is not a final
defence of a writer to say that he succeeded in writing as he
intended: the reader is perfectly justified in accepting this, but
preferring something different. It has been Jonson's fate throughout
the years to find his greatest contemporary preferred to him. For a
time in the seventeenth century he held his own—indeed, was in
the ascendent—but from the time of Dryden's comparison in the
Essay of Dramatic Poesie with its final summing-up—'I admire
him, but I love Shakespeare'—the verdict has never been in doubt.
And, as Coleridge noted, because of our admiration for Shakespeare
we undervalue Jonson in comparison with others of his contemporaries as well. Jonson's uniqueness in his period cannot be
overstressed: he is the exception to almost any generalisation that
can be made about the English drama of his time. Where other
Jacobean playwrights are weak he is strong, especially in verisimilitude and constructive skill; but he is also weak where they are
strong, most obviously in the vivid imaginative expression of
dramatic emotion. Because we admire Shakespeare so highly, we
tend to elevate above Jonson those writers, like Webster, who are
stronger in these 'Shakespearean' ways; if Shakespeare had never
lived, not only would Jonson be unchallenged as the greatest
dramatist of his period, but the critical ranking of his contemporaries would be different. We obtain an even fairer view of Jonson
if we judge him outside the context altogether of Jacobean English
drama and in the perspective of European comedy; he should be
compared not with Shakespeare, but with Molière, Goldoni and
Holberg, and in this company he will not be disgraced.

In the end, however, Jonson defies any attempt to place him in
a 'tradition'. He was an original, *sui generis*. It was an originality
arrived at by conscious thought, not the originality which, like
that of a romantic poet, is the product of a unique imaginative
vision of the world. It was conditioned, therefore, to produce
works of art in a given period and answering certain critical

demands, and outside that period, when these demands are no longer made, it seems alien, even monstrous. This quality of monstrosity was noted by Coleridge:

> It was not possible, that so bold and robust an intellect as that of Ben Jonson could be devoted to any form of intellectual Power vainly or even with mediocrity of Product. He could not but be a Species of himself: tho' like the Mammoth and Megatherion fitted and destined to live only during a given Period, and then to exist a Skeleton, hard, dry, uncouth perhaps, yet massive and not to be contemplated without that mixture of Wonder and Admiration, or more accurately, that middle between both for which we want a term . . . [24]

Jonson's first drive was to glorify his art, and to justify himself as an artist. In order to do this, he needed to write correctly, and this involved him in deciding what the proper rules were for Comedy, or Tragedy, or Masque, are whatever 'kind' with which he was concerned. He would never take these rules on trust: he was ready to study the works of others, *tamquam explorator*, to find out how they solved the problems, but the final judgment was always his own. There is in him an element of singularity, and therefore for the reader a need to understand what he was attempting before a judgment can be made. The need for understanding, however, produces its own dangers, as Eliot noted:

> . . . not many people are capable of discovering for themselves the beauty which is only found after labour; and Jonson's industrious readers have been those whose interest was historical and curious, and those who have thought that in discovering the historical and curious interest they had discovered the artistic value as well. [25]

It is inevitable that Jonson should attract the attention of scholars—indeed he set out to do so. It seems that he saw himself as a Crites or Horace writing for an audience of Wellbreds and Truewits, if not of Camdens and Donnes, and that it was in default of these auditors that he had to supply his own choric commentators. Not everything that he put into his work was meant to be understood at first glance, and modern scholars labouring at their tasks may console themselves that Jonson was one author at least who would approve of their efforts. He offers less satisfaction, however, to the interpretive critic. His intentions may not always be obvious, but they are definite, and all his works are perfectly finished specimens of their kind. There is little scope for fresh interpretations, or imaginative reconstruction of what should be in his plays but is not, and in seeing his work through the press with such care he even removed the opportunity for bold textual emendation. From this point of view Jonson is a poor vaulting-horse for a critic's ambition. For the scholar the danger which Eliot saw remains—that the satisfaction of curiosity and the pleasure of acquiring understanding may be mistaken for genuine enjoyment.

Both scholarly investigation and imaginative effort are necessary, however, to enter Jonson's world. It was above all a moral world. There is no need to query the genuiness of Jonson's ethical views. No doubt he desired in theory a moral perfection which in his own life he was incapable of achieving; most people do. He certainly did not find it possible to maintain the calm, moderate Horatian pose which he desired, and he appears often ill-tempered, insensitive and uncharitable. Yet this need not invalidate his attraction towards the ideal, or make him a hypocrite. Again it is true that his attacks on the evils of Society, although they were violently, even brutally, expressed, were not as bold as they purported to be. Had he been a saint—or a revolutionary—he might have said more, and the remedies he proposed are certainly more conventional palliatives than radical specifics. In this he was hampered by the insecurity of his social position, but perhaps still more by the limitations of his own mind. His was a clear, logical and decided morality, but it was neither original nor profound. He saw no reason to challenge, at least publicly, the accepted ethical thought of his day, and he interpreted it rigidly rather than flexibly. No one would go to Jonson for the delicate probing of moral uncertainty or the subtle discrimination of confused motives; his is the world of appetite and energy, not of velleity and doubt. The firmness and clarity of his vision give his work its consistency and strength, but they shut out irony and ambiguity. Despite its apparent elaboration, his was a simple view of life, and he was simply not capable of the complex response to life evinced by greater writers, the kind of complexity we find in Chaucer and Shakespeare.

There is another dimension lacking in his world. We know that he suffered at least to some degree from the religious uncertainties of his age, passing from the English to the Roman church, and back again, and we would presume that he must have spent much thought on matters of faith and doubt. If so, nothing of it appears in his writings. The only religious comment in his comedies is contained in his attacks on the Puritans—and this could as well be motivated by professional interest as by any religious feeling; as a playwright the Puritans were his natural enemies. The religious poems give an impression of sincerity, but they are few and conventional. Perhaps he was restrained by prudential considerations, but it seems that, as a creative writer, at least, anything that might be termed religious was outside his range; he thought in terms of Right and Wrong, rather than Good and Evil (and this is one of the limitations of his tragedies). But if he fails to meet the highest demands we make of a writer, neither illuminating for us the shadowy recesses of the human personality nor enlarging the boundaries of our conception of reality, he was driven by a real desire to teach, to convey an interpretation of human existence, and his convictions seem to have been genuinely held. No one can read his comedies and tragedies without feeling the force of his horror at the manifestations of man's irrational pride and lust for power, or read the masques and poems without a sense of his reverence for the beauty and nobility of Reason and Virtue.

It is not this, however, that makes Jonson a great writer, nor was it all that drove him to write. He was committed, as a serious Renaissance writer, to instruct his public, but he was committed also, both as a popular playwright and a court poet, to entertain. As an entertainer he was sustained by two drives, an urge to record the idiosyncrasies of human character, and a desire to exploit the resources of the English language. As always with Jonson, there are limitations which we have to accept: there are aspects of character beyond his comprehension, and powers in words which he either could not, or would not, unleash. But his greatest work succeeds in spite of these limitations, or even because of them. *The Alchemist*, *Volpone*, and *Bartholomew Fair* could only have been created by a writer of Jonson's great if limited strength; the acceptance of any wider range of human activity or emotion would have weakened their outline, the play of any greater psychological subtlety would have lessened their impact. Again, the vigour and the fullness of Jonsonian comedy may be the products of a limited sensibility, but they are also the expression of a creative urge as powerful as that of any writer. Jonson's kind of interest in human character was very English. Stripped of its theoretical trappings, the Comedy of Humours is simply based on that response to humanity evinced when any Englishman says of another that 'he is a character'; it is the expression of an instinctive relish for oddity and absurdity. The English have always preferred, unlike other European peoples, to describe character rather than analyse it, and to emphasise individuality rather than to generalise; of this tradition Jonson is a part, and indeed to some degree an originator. He was certainly an intellectual, by almost any definition of the term which can be offered, but abstract concepts were for him secondary to actual experience. Of his love of the English language little further need be said: in his use of it he had a range insufficiently appreciated by the ordinary reader, whose knowledge is confined to his best-known plays, and this points up a flaw in many judgments of Jonson. His work is much more varied than is often realised, although at the same time it has an essential unity. In part this unity comes from Jonson's consistently maintained moral and critical views, in part from a less easily detached and analysable quality of personality. A knowledge of all his works— what Eliot called an 'intelligent saturation' in them—is necessary for a full understanding of any one, and a partial familiarity may be confusing. *The Sad Shepherd*, for example, is inexplicable without a previous knowledge of *The Entertainment of Althorpe* and *Pan's Anniversarie*, and a realisation that Jonson was as interested in rustic life as he was in that of the city; his aims in his non-dramatic poetry can only be understood by reference both to the ideals expounded in *Poetaster* and to the notes he made in *Discoveries*. Jonson is not a writer easily summed up on brief acquaintane.

It is the strength of his personality and his personal vision which makes him a living force in our literature. Like Chaucer, though less subtly, he capitalised on his own idiosyncrasies and made himself a character in his own work, and this, together with the unmistakeable stamp he put on all he wrote, has made him a figure more real to most readers than, say, Wordsworth or Tennyson (and it matters little in his context how close to the real man this *persona* came). It is in some ways an odd and not always attractive personality. Jonson has good claims to be called the first English 'Man of Letters', the first professional writer, that is, wholly dedicated to his craft and relying on his exercise of it to establish his place in Society. This links him with Dryden, Pope and the eighteenth century, yet he retains not only the flavour of his own age but that of even earlier times. Because of his social position, and also by reason of his twin aim to Instruct and Delight, he retains something of the air of the medieval Court poet who, like Skelton or Dunbar, combined the qualities of the learned clerk and the jester or buffoon. Despite the dignity he desired for the poet, Jonson offers himself up at times for the amusement of his patrons, and he, too, has his 'flytings' and his beggings for money.

Again, as Dryden noticed, Jonson was the first Englishman to practise criticism as we understand it. He never published a complete account of his critical views, and what we have is scattered over his plays, prefaces and notebooks, but it is possible without difficulty to distinguish the outlines of a considered theory of literature, and a not ignoble one. In his actual critical observations about others, it is true, he seems to have been sometimes actuated by personal malice. This may be the unjust result of a haphazard preservation of his views—Coleridge thought Drummond to blame for having preserved Jonson's impromptu remarks about his contemporaries, made in confidence and without forethought. Jonson wrote hard things about his rivals, however, as well as saying them. Yet he was not always unjustified. Inspired as he was to justify and ennoble his art, he was right to attack cheap and careless writing, and although he was often ungenerous in not recognising merit in writers he disliked, he was not always wrong in pointing out their faults. Marston was indeed both scurrilous and bombastic; Dekker did lack an artistic conscience; Daniel is often empty and dull, and did not deserve his inflated reputation in his own day, which placed him above Spenser. With some, to him more considerable writers, such as Chapman and Drayton, Jonson's relations were not always cordial, but were tinged with more respect; Chapman in particular he seems to have paid the courtesy of accepting as a rival for the favour of the learned. What is of most significance is that Jonson reserved his highest praise—and it is very generous, though never totally unqualified—for the three greatest writers of his age, Shakespeare, Donne and Bacon. Whatever Jonson's limitations in critical theory or personal feeling, they did not prevent him from recognising what was truly good. Envy expressed in malicious and ill-founded attack on writers was to him the progeny of Ignorance, and the greatest enemy of the Art which he tried to serve. He himself was not envious of the truly great artists that he knew: the same could not be said of all poets.

Drummond noted that Jonson was 'a great lover and praiser of himselfe, a contemner and Scorner of others', but he also jotted down that 'of all stiles he loved most to be named honest'.[26] Honesty is a quality which Jonson frequently holds up for praise. To be 'honest', to him, was not simply to be trustworthy and frank, but to be exactly what one claimed to be—the exact sense in which Iago is *not* 'honest' (and in which Jonson recorded that Shakespeare was). It implied, therefore, a bluff readiness to speak one's mind, and this can easily appear brusqueness and conceit; but it implied also a readiness to state one's principles and abide by them. There is no doubt that this, as a writer, Jonson did. He was always explicit about his aims and methods, and he tried conscientiously to provide the satisfactions that he promised. In that sense he is one of the most 'honest' writers in our literature. This openness was in some ways a restraint upon him, and there were other, graver limitations in the scope of his creative mind. Yet Dryden's remark is true: 'he managed his strength to more advantage than any who preceded him'.

He set out to write at what appeared to be a great disadvantage, with the need to satisfy a volatile and largely uneducated public in a form which was generally despised. By establishing his own standards and relentlessly observing them, he managed to satisfy both public taste and critical precept—and also, and most importantly, his own artistic conscience. His efforts to please both the 'vulgar' and the 'judicious' were not uniformly successful, but at his best he produced plays which were—and still are—eminently rewarding both on the stage and in the study. It is impossible for us to regret, however much he himself may have done so, that circumstances forced him into the public theatre. If he had found a patron to support him he might have devoted himself exclusively to poetry and criticism, and would perhaps have written only closet drama, constructed according to the most stringent neoclassical rules. The result would no doubt have been interesting to the literary historian, but to no one else. But we cannot be sure that he would have been satisfied with this. Jonson was driven on by something more than a literary theorist's desire for 'correctness' and the moralist's urge to instruct; as F. R. Leavis has said, he

was as robustly interested in men and manners and his own talk as in literatures and the poetic art.[27]

He recognised himself that when his enemies wanted to attack him they did not do so on the grounds that his art was too abstract and intellectual, but because it was too close to real life:

Alas, sir, *Horace*! hee is a meere spunge; nothing but humours, and observation; he goes up and downe sucking from every societie, and when hee comes home, squeazes himself drie again.[28]

Jonson's dedication to Art was not a matter of intellectual conviction only, but was the product of an artist's desire to express his personality through his own vision of the world. Different artists achieve this in different ways; Jonson's chosen way was through stage illusion. It is this impulse that has given us his plays. That they are still alive, and that through them we can experience a world long since dead, is the true measure of his greatness.

NOTES

ELH: *English Literary History*   M.L.R.: *Modern Language Review*
P.Q.: *Philological Quarterly*   R.E.S.: *Review of English Studies*
S.P.: *Studies in Philology*

Chapter 1

1. *Elizabethan Critical Essays*, Ed. G. G. Smith (Oxford, 1904), I, p. 300.

2. *The History of the Worthies of England* (1662), II. 243.

3. Epigram xiv (*Ben Jonson*, Ed. C. H. Herford, P. and E. Simpson (Oxford, 1925–52), VIII, p. 31; all quotations from Jonson are from this edition, which is cited hereafter as '*Works*'.

4. Chapman made his famous translation from Homer with the aid of the Latin version of Sponde.

5. Jonson visited Drummond at his home at Hawthornden, near Edinburgh, at the end of 1618, when he made his tour to Scotland. The notes which Drummond made of their conversations are a source for some details of Jonson's life, and of his critical opinions, as well as of some unimportant pieces of gossip. Unfortunately the MS has disappeared, and is represented only by a transcript, made about 1700 by Sir Robert Sibbald; this is reprinted in *Works* (I.132 ff.). Since some of the facts recorded in the *Conversations* are demonstrably incorrect the authenticity of the whole has been impugned. Most scholars think the notes are basically genuine. though there is a disturbing possibility that they may have been 'doctored' —i.e. spurious material may have been incorporated with them; for this reason they can only be fully relied on when they are corroborated by other sources. The reference in the text is to *Conversations*, lines 328–9 (*Works*, I.141).

6. From *Discoveries*, Jonson's notebook. This was first published after his death, in the Folio edition of 1640; it consists largely of quotations from other writers, mainly Latin, which Jonson translated and set down, presumably because they expressed views on life and literature with which he agreed. The result is not (as has sometimes been claimed) a coherent piece of literary theorising, but much can be learnt from it of Jonson's critical opinions; it also records a few biographical details. It is reprinted in *Works*, VIII, pp. 561–649; the reference in the text is to lines 483–7.

Drummond records Jonson reciting poems by heart, among them Donne's *The Bracelet* which he apparently greatly admired (*Conv.*, 118–20).

7. *Disc.*, 2467–9.

8. *Essays*, Ed. W. P. Ker (Oxford, 1900), I.43.

9. loc. cit.; Aubrey, in his *Brief Lives* (Ed. O. L. Dick, 1958, p. 77), tells how while he was working on the New Buildings at Lincoln's Inn, one of the Benchers heard him repeating some lines from Homer and gave him an exhibition to maintain himself at Trinity, Cambridge. There is no record of him there or at St John's Cambridge of which College Fuller says he was a member for a brief period.

10. *The Return from Parnassus* (in *The Three Parnassus Plays*, Ed. J. B. Leishman, 1949, pt. ii, I.ii.293).

11. See Dekker, *Satiromastix*, IV.i.130–2.

12. *Brief Lives*, Ed. Dick, p. 275.

13. Two advances to Jonson in respect of 'additions' to *The Spanish Tragedy* are recorded in Henslowe's *Diary*: one on 25 September 1601, and the other on 22 June 1602. The edition of *The Spanish Tragedy* published in 1602 contains five new passages, including the famous 'Painter scene' (III.xiia). If these passages are in fact by Jonson he was capable of a quite different sort of tragic poetry from anything in his acknowledged tragedies, but (partly because these additions are so different from his accepted style) critics have been very reluctant to accept them as his.

14. *Works*, I.195.

15. ibid., V.21.

16. See the Preface to *The Fawn* (1606).

17. Edmund Gayton, *Pleasant Notes upon Don Quixote* (1654) (*Works*, XI.505).

18. ibid., VIII.409.

19. See O. J. Campbell, *Comicall Satyre and Shakespeare's 'Troilus and Cressida'* (San Marino, 1938).

20. *Elizabethan Critical Essays*, I.170.

21. In the Latin these are lines 333–4; in Jonson's translation lines 477–8.

22. Lodge, 'Defence of Poetrie' (*Elizabethan Critical Essays*, I.80).

23. Samuel Rowlands, *The Letting of Humours Blood in the Head Vein* (1600), Epigram 27.

24. *Elizabethan Critical Essays*, I.176–7.

25. Dedication to *Promos and Cassandra* (ibid., I.60).

26. *Coleridge on the Seventeenth Century*, Ed. R. F. Brinkley (Durham, N.C., 1955), p. 61.

27. See E. W. Talbert, 'Classical Mythology and the Structure of *Cynthia's Revels*', *P.Q.*, xxii (1943), pp. 192–210, and A. H. Gilbert, 'The Function of the Masques in *Cynthia's Revels*', ibid, pp. 211–30.

28. Crites may just possibly have been intended to be a portrait of Donne: he is called 'Criticus' in the Quarto, and Jonson told Drummond that in

the Preface to his 'Art of Poesie' (which is not extant) 'by Criticus is understood Donne' (*Conv.*, 84–5).

29. 'Of Discourse'.

30. The fullest treatments of the *Poetomachia* are in R. A. Small, *The Stage Quarrel* (1899), and J. H. Penniman, *The War of the Theatres* (1897); see also A. Davenport, 'The Quarrel of the Satirists', *M.L.R.*, xxxvii (1942), 123–30, and R. W. Berringer, 'Jonson's *Cynthia's Revels* and the War of the Theatres', *P.Q.*, xxii (1943), 1–22.

31. Manningham, *Diary*, Ed. J. Bruce (Camden Society, 1868), p. 130. The autographed copy of *Sejanus* which Jonson presented in 1605 to Sir Robert Townshend is still extant.

Chapter 2

1. *Works*, Ed. P. P. Howe (1930–4), VI.262.

2. 'On Master William Shakespeare', prefixed to *Poems: Written by Wil. Shakespeare. Gent.*, 1604; (*Works*, XI.496).

3. George Puttenham, *Of Poets and Poesy* (1589), ch.xv (*Eliz. Critical Essays*, II.35).

4. Preface to *The Whore of Babylon* (1607).

5. See D. C. Boughner, *The Devil's Disciple* (New York, 1968), ch. 5.

6. *Selected Essays* (3rd ed., revised, 1951), p. 148.

7. Preface to *The Alchemist*.

8. In *The Masque of Augurs*, ll. 43–51.

9. *Calendar of Venetian State Papers*, Ed. A. B. Hinds (1909), XV.114 (the Italian text is printed in *Works* X.580–4).

10. *Hymenaei* 6–9; cf. *The Kings Entertainment at Welbeck*. 679–80, and *Masque of Blackness*, 90–1, and see D. Cunningham, 'The Jonsonian Masque as a Literary form', ELH, xxii (1942), 123–30. The account of *Hymenaei* which follows is based on Professor Gordon's brilliant analysis ('*Hymenaei*: Ben Jonson's Masque of Union', *Journal of the Warburg and Courtauld Institutes*, vii (1945), 107–45)

11. In his description of the staging of *The Masque of Queens* Jonson notes that the steps of the third dance were 'graphically dispos'd into *letters* . . . honoring the Name of the most sweete and ingenious *Prince, Charles, Duke of Yorke*' (*Works*, VII.315–16).

12. ibid., VII.91.

13. ibid., 314.

14. ibid., 750.

15. See D. J. Gordon, 'Poet and Architect: The intellectual setting of the Quarrel between Ben Jonson and Inigo Jones', *Journal of the Warburg and Courtauld Institutes*, xii (1949), 152–78.

16. See E. K. Chambers, Ed., *Aurelian Townshend's Poems and Masques* (Oxford, 1912), pp. 83 and 119.

17. See Cunningham, op. cit., and also W. T. Furniss, 'Ben Jonson's Masques',

in *Three Studies in the Renaissance: Sidney, Jonson, Milton* (New Haven, 1958), pp. 88–179.

18. *Conv.*, 34–6.

19. *Ben Jonson* ('English Men of Letters' series, 1919), p. 137.

Chapter 3

1. *Coleridge on the Seventeenth Century*, p. 644.

2. Nothing is known about Mrs Jonson except Jonson's description of her to Drummond: 'a shrew, yet honest'. Apparently he lived apart from her at one stage: see *Conv.*, 254–5.

3. 'Defence of the Epilogue to *The Conquest of Granda*' (*Essays*, Ed. Ker, I.174).

4. He objected to Daniel's allusion to the 'sweet silent rhetoric' of his mistress' eyes, and twice (*Staple of News*, Induction 36–7, and *Discoveries*, 662–5) refers to a line from Shakespeare's *Julius Caesar*, 'Caesar never did wrong but with just cause' (which is in fact not in the text as we have it).

5. See Edmund Wilson, 'Morose Ben Jonson', in *The Triple Thinkers* (London, 1952). Mr Wilson regards Jonson's combination of sulkiness and outpourings of words as a sublimation of infantile anal eroticism.

6. *Conv.*, 58–9.

7. *Epistle to Lady d'Aubigny*, ll. 9–10 (*Works*, VIII.116).

8. See Ian Donaldson, 'Jonson's Tortoise', *R.E.S.*, n.s., xix (1968), 162–6.

9. *Selected Essays*, p. 151.

10. See D. J. Enright, 'Crime and Punishment in Ben Jonson', *Scrutiny*, xii (1940), 231–48.

11. See J. B. Bamborough, *The Little World of Man* (1952), pp. 36 ff.

12. Theseus' speech (*M.N.D.*, V.i.2–22) is a general account of the power of the Imagination.

13. *Of Wisdom*, tr. S. Lennard (1607), pp. 67–8; qu. *Disc.*, 43–9.

14. *E.M.O.*, II.v.45–8; (cf. III.ix.6–30).

15. Chorus after Act I of *The Magnetic Lady*, ll. 54–7.

16. *Staple of News*, III.ii.241–8.

17. H. W. Baum, *The Satiric and the Didactic in Ben Jonson's Comedy* (Chapel Hill, 1947), p. 22.

18. *New Inn*, IV.iv.213–5.

19. *Epicoene*, IV.vi.64–9; this adds ironic point to Haughty's later remark to Dauphine: 'It is not the outward, but the inward man that I affect' (V.ii.17–18).

20. *Disc.*, 801–6.

21. *Staple of News*, 'The Prologue for the Court', pp. 7–8.

22. *E.M.O.*, Induction, ll. 201–3.

23. Dedication to *Volpone*, 108–9.

Chapter 4

1. *Essay of Dramatic Poesy* (*Essays*, Ed. Ker, 1.81).

2. *Works*, Ed. A. H. Thomson (1910), p. 20.

3. For Jonson's possible connection with the Shakespeare Folio see E. K. Chambers, *William Shakespeare: a Study of the Facts and Problems* (Oxford, 1930), I.135, and R. C. Rhodes, *Shakespeare's First Folio* (Oxford, 1923), pp. 36 ff.

4. *Neptune's Triumph*, 34–6.

5. To Sir Dudley Carleton, 17 November 1621 (*Works*, XI.386).

6. The proposal to knight Jonson seems to have been made after the first performance of *The Gipsies Metamorphos'd*: see G. E. Bentley, *The Jacobean and Caroline Stage* (Oxford, 1941–68), IV.610.

7. *Works*, I.14.

8. John Pory to Sir Thomas Pickering, 20 September 1632 (*Works*, IX.253).

9. This aspect of Jonson is exhaustively studied in C. R. Baskerville, *English Elements in Jonson's early Comedy* (Austin, Texas, 1911).

10. *Conv.*, 409–13.

11. *Works*, Ed. R. B. McKerrow (reprinted Oxford, 1966), I.92

12. 'Digression of Spirits', *Anatomy of Melancholy*, pt. I, sect. ii, member 1, subsection 1. In the masque *Love Restor'd* Robin Goodfellow appears as the champion of old-fashioned English mirth and jollity as against the penny-pinching of Plutus.

13. *Works*, I.275 ff. and IX.268 ff.; but cf. the ed. by F. M. Snell (1915).

14. *Conv.*, 294.

15. lines 31–7. Jonson is answering Daniel, who had maintained that Pastoral should deal exclusively with the loves of shepherds.

16. The connection between Jonson's satire and the economic basis of society is studied in Professor L. C. Knights' famous *Drama and Society in the Age of Jonson* (1937).

17. See Dryden, *Essays*, Ed. Ker, I.80.

18. See E. B. Partridge, *The Broken Compass* (1958), pp. 162 ff.

19. *Disc.*, 954–8.

20. ibid., 2031–2.

21. Richard Edwards, Prologue to *Damon and Pythias* (1571), pp. 24–32.

22. See, e.g., L. S. Champion, *Ben Jonson's Dotages* (Lexington, 1968), pp. 81 ff.

23. e.g., IV.iv.247–8, 251–3, 319–23; cf. I.iii.131–6, where the Host describes himself as watching life like a comedy being enacted in his Inn.

24. See P. R. Sellin, *Daniel Heinsius and Stuart England* (1968), esp. pp. 153 ff. There is a good deal of quotation from Heinsius in *Discoveries*.

25. See T. W. Baldwin, *Shakespeare's Five Act Structure* (Urbana, 1944), esp. pp. 325–41; and cf. Boughner, op. cit., ch. 10.

26. *Essays*, Ed. Ker, I.45.

27. *Disc.*, 2555–7; cf. *Disc.*, 129–39, and *E.M.O.*, Ind., 266–70.

28. Verses prefixed to *Catiline* (*Works*, XI.335).

29. See F. L. Townshend, *Apologie for Bartholomew Fair* (New York, 1947).

30. *A Study of Ben Jonson* p. 39.

31. 'To Ben Jonson uppon occasion of his Ode to Himself' (*Poems*, 1640; *Works*, XI.335).

32. *Disc.*, 2629–33.

33. ibid., 2675–7.

Chapter 5

1. *Disc.*, 2488–95.

2. This famous passage is *Disc.*, 647–68.

3. *Conv.*, 377–8.

4. *Disc.*, 710–18; cf. *News from the New World*, ll. 152–66 (where the same quotation is used).

5. *Disc.*, 695–700.

6. *Conv.*, 48–9; 196.

7. *Disc.*, 2068–71.

8. *Conv.*, 180–2.

9. *Disc.*, 1870–1.

10. ibid., 1938–44.

11. ibid., 772–81.

12. *Essays*, Ed. Ker, I.82. See L. C. Knights, 'Tradition and Ben Jonson', *Scrutiny* iv (1935), 140–57, and E. V. Pennanen, *Chapters on the Language of Ben Jonson's Dramatic Works* (Turku, 1951), to which I am particularly indebted.

13. There are full accounts of Jonson's language in A. C. Partridge, *Studies in the Syntax of Jonson's Plays* and *The Accidence of Ben Jonson's Plays* (both Cambridge, 1953), and a fine study of his prose by Professor J. A. Barish, *Ben Jonson and the Language of Prose Comedy* (Cambridge, Mass., 1960).

14. *Disc.*, 343–5.

15. ibid., 1806–7.

16. A. C. Partridge, op. cit., p. viii; E. B. Partridge, op. cit., p. 222.

17. Barish, op. cit., p. 97.

18. See W. Trimpi, *Ben Jonson's Poems* (Stanford, 1962), which is a study of the poetry particularly from this point of view.

19. The 'Charis' poems are connected with *The Devil is an Ass* (a version of 'Her Triumph' is sung in II.vi) and attempts have been made to read autobiographical significance into this. There is however no real evidence at all to support any of these interpretations.

20. *Selected Essays*, p. 155.

21. W. Empson, *Seven Types of Ambiguity* (3rd ed., 1953), pp. 242–3.

22. E. B. Partridge, op. cit. p. 217.
23. *A Study of Ben Jonson*, p. 114.
24. *Coleridge on the Seventeenth Century*, pp. 647–8.
25. *Selected Essays*, p. 148.
26. *Conv.*, 680–1; 631.
27. *Revaluation* (1953), p. 21.
28. *Poetaster*, IV.iii.104–7.

BIBLIOGRAPHY

BARISH, J. A., *Ben Jonson and the Language of Prose Comedy* (Cambridge, Mass., 1960)

BASKERVILLE, C. R., *English Elements in Jonson's Early Comedy* (Austin, 1911)

BAUM, H. W., *The Satiric and the Didactic in Ben Jonson's Comedy* (Chapel Hill, 1947)

BOUGHNER, D. C., *The Devil's Disciple* (N.Y., 1968)

CASTELAIN, M., *Ben Jonson, l'Homme et l'Œuvre* (Paris, 1907)

CHAMPION, L. S., *Ben Jonson's Dotages* (Lexington, 1968)

CUNNINGHAM, D., 'The Jonsonian Masque as a literary form' (*ELH*, xxii (1955), 123–30)

DONALDSON, C. I. E., 'Jonson's Tortoise' (*R.E.S.*, n.s., xix (1968), 162–6)

DUNN, E. L., *Ben Jonson's Art* (Northampton, Mass., 1925)

ELIOT T. S., 'Ben Jonson' (in *The Sacred Wood* (1920); reprinted in *Selected Essays*)

ENCK, J. J., *Jonson and the Comic Truth* (Madison, 1957)

FURNISS, W. T., *Three Studies in the Renaissance: Sidney, Jonson, Milton* (New Haven, 1958)

GILBERT, A. H., 'The Function of the Masques in *Cynthia's Revels*' (*P.Q.* xxii (1943) 211–30)

—*The Symbolic Personages in the Masques of Ben Jonson* (Durham, N.C., 1948)

GORDON, D. J., '*Hymenaei*: Ben Jonson's Masque of Union' (*Journal of the Warburg and Courtauld Institutes*, viii (1945), 107–45)

—'Poet and Architect: the intellectual setting of the quarrel between Ben Jonson and Inigo Jones' (*Journal of the Warburg and Courtauld Institutes*, xii (1949), 152–78)

JOHNSON, G. B., *Ben Jonson, Poet* (N.Y., 1945)

KNIGHTS, L. C., *Drama and Society in the Age of Jonson* (London, 1937)

—'Tradition and Ben Jonson' (*Scrutiny*, iv (1935), 140–57)

LEAVIS, F. R., *Revaluation* (London, 1953)

LEVIN, H., Introduction to *Selected Works of Ben Jonson* (N.Y., 1938)

PARTRIDGE, A. C., *Studies in the Syntax of Jonson's Plays* (Cambridge, 1953)

—*The Accidence of Ben Jonson's Plays, Masques and Entertainments* (Cambridge, 1953)

PARTRIDGE, E. B., *The Broken Compass* (London, 1958)

PENNANEN, E. V., *Chapters on the Language of Ben Jonson's Dramatic Works* (Turku, 1951)

SACKTON, A. H., *Rhetoric as a Dramatic Language in Ben Jonson* (N.Y., 1948)

SMITH, G. G., *Ben Jonson* (London, 1919)

SWINBURNE, A. C., *A Study of Ben Jonson* (London, 1889)

TALBERT, E. W., 'Classical Mythology and the Structure of *Cynthia's Revels*' (*P.Q.*, xxii (1943), 192–210)

—'The Purpose and Technique of Jonson's *Poetaster*' (*S.P.*, xliii (1943), 225–32)

TOWNSHEND, F. L., *Apologie for Bartholomew Fair: the Art of Jonson's Comedies* (N.Y., 1947)

TRIMPI, W., *Ben Jonson's Poems* (Stanford, 1962)

WILSON, E., *The Triple Thinkers* (London, 1952)

INDEX

ANEAU, BARTHÉLEMI, 152
Aristophanes, 26–7, 37, 117, 118,
  147–8
Aristotle, 25, 53, 54, 137, 142,
  147, 158
Ascham, Roger, 154
Aubrey, John, 13, 178

BACON, FRANCIS, 41, 73, 157, 175
Baldwin, T. W., 181
Bamborough, J. B., 180
Barclay, John, 115
Barish, J. A., 182
Baskerville, C. R., 181
Baum, H. W., 180
Beaumont, Francis, 124, 142
Bergson, Henri, 149
Berringer, R. W., 179
Boughner, D. C., 179
Brome, Richard, 18, 147
Burton, Robert, 97, 118, 157

CAMDEN, WILLIAM, 10, 24
Campbell, O. J., 178
Carew, Thomas, 147

Castelain, M., 19
Chambers, E. K., 181
Champion, L. S., 181
Chapman, George, 33, 175, 177
Character-writing, 39
Charron, Pierre, 108
Chaucer, Geoffrey, 90, 121, 128,
  172, 174
Cheke, Sir John, 154
Cibber, Colley, 147
Cicero, 24, 53, 139
Coleridge, Samuel Taylor, 35,
  89, 90, 170, 171, 175
'Comedy of Humours', 30–3
'Comical Satire', 23–7
Congreve, William, 95
Contest between Liberality and
  Prodigality, The, 124
Corbett, Richard, 114, 120
Corneille, Pierre, 142
Country Wife, The, 94
Coward, Noël, 22
Cunningham, D., 179

DANIEL, SAMUEL, 72, 175, 180,
  181

Davenant, Sir William, 76
Davenport, A., 179
'Decorum', 33–5, 64, 110, 140, 159
Dekker, Thomas, 13, 14, 42–3, 45–6, 55, 121, 175
Dickens, Charles, 119, 140
Digges, Leonard, 51
Doctor Faustus, 121–2
Donaldson, C. I. E., 180
Donatus, Aelius, 137
Donne, John, 23, 104, 153, 161, 175, 177, 178
Drayton, Michael, 175
Drummond, William, 11, 76, 103, 117–18, 120, 152, 153, 154, 175, 177, 180
Dryden, John, 12, 51, 63, 94, 113, 133, 138, 155, 163, 170, 174, 176
Du Bartas, Guillaume, 103
Dunbar, William, 174

EDWARDS, RICHARD, 130
Eliot, T. S., 64, 65, 100, 162, 169, 170, 172, 174
Empson, W., 162

FIELDING, HENRY, 149
Fletcher, John, 94, 115, 120
Fuller, Thomas, 10, 13
Furniss, W. T., 179

GAYTON, EDMUND, 17
Gilbert, A. H., 178, 179
Gilbert, Sir W. S., 77
Goldoni, Carlo, 170
Gordon, D. J., 179
Grim the Collier of Croydon, 121

HAZLITT, WILLIAM, 51
Heinsius, Daniel, 137, 142
Henslowe, William, 14, 178
Herford, C. H., 148
Herrick, Robert, 115
Holberg, Ludwig, 170
Horace, 9, 22, 25, 34, 44, 103, 104, 139, 151, 160

IBSEN, HENRIK, 124, 141
Isle of Dogs, The, 13

JONES, INIGO, 71, 72–3, 115, 119
Jonson, Ben
  Individual Works:
    'Entertainments': *At Althorpe*, 67, 118, 174; *At Blackfriars*, 78; *At Highgate*, 76–7; *At Welbeck*, 179; *Love's Welcome at Bolsover*, 67; *Part of the King's Entertainment on Passing to His Coronation*, 76. Masques: *Augurs*, 75; of *Beauty*, 66, 88; of *Blackness*, 66, 68, 71, 72, 152, 179; *Chloridia*, 72, 115; *Christmas his Masque*, 79; *Fortunate Isles*, 79; *Gipsies Metamorphosed*, 68, 78–9; *Golden Age Restored*, 76; *Haddington*, 74; *Hymenaei*, 69–70, 73–4, 108, 179; *Love Freed from Ignorance and Folly*, 68; *Love Restored*, 118; *Lovers Made Men*, 68; *Love's Triumph*, 73, 115; *Neptune's Triumph*, 114; *News from the New World*, 182; *Pan's*

Anniversarie, 163–4, 174;
Pleasure Reconciled to Virtue,
67, 74; *Prince Henry's
Barriers*, 76; *Queens*, 70, 71,
74, 76, 111, 128, 179; *Vision
of Delight*, 77–8. Plays:
Alchemist, 32, 82, 90, 97–101,
106, 121, 139, 141, 142,
144, 147, 152, 165, 173;
Bartholomew Fair, 31, 82,
101–4, 124, 128, 141, 143–5,
156, 173; *The Case is
Altered*, 20–1, 27, 32, 47,
131, 156; *Catiline*, 50, 51, 54,
59–61, 62, 63, 64, 65, 86,
181; *Cynthia's Revels*, 17, 31,
37–41, 44, 48, 105, 106,
109–10, 111, 125, 127, 128,
129, 134, 168–9; *The Devil
is an Ass*, 106, 113, 116, 117,
118, 121–4, 136, 139, 157;
Eastward Ho!, 15; *Epicoene*,
35, 82, 89, 91–7, 105, 110–11,
126, 130, 137–8, 140, 141,
143, 145, 147, 148–9, 156,
157, 168; *Every Man in his
Humour*, 15–16, 21–2, 23, 24,
25, 27, 32, 41, 47, 51, 92,
107, 114, 116, 130, 143;
*Every Man out of his
Humour*, 23, 24, 26, 27, 34,
35–7, 41, 47, 48, 86, 101,
109, 110, 117, 118, 143, 157,
181; *The Magnetic Lady*, 33,
107, 136–9, 145, 146–7; *The
New Inn*, 21, 105, 109, 110,
131–5, 140, 143, 145, 164;
Poetaster, 14, 27, 29, 42–5,
47, 48, 82, 91, 105, 156, 160,
174; *The Sad Shepherd*,
120–1, 167, 174; *Sejanus*, 50,
51, 52, 54, 55, 56–9, 62, 63,

64, 82, 83, 85, 86, 165; *The
Staple of News*, 105, 106,
110, 112, 116, 117, 124–31,
136, 139, 180; *A Tale of a
Tub*, 119–20, 145; *Volpone*,
16, 82–91, 97, 99, 100, 105,
121, 125, 126, 137, 138, 144,
148, 156, 157, 159, 164, 173.
Poems: *Epigrams* 10, 104, 154,
159–60, 167; *The Underwood*,
161, 162; Individual Poems:
'Drink to Me Only', 162;
'Epistle to Edward Sackville',
166; 'Epistle to Penshurst',
166–7; 'Execration upon
Vulcan', 165; 'Expostulation
with Inigo Jones', 165, 168;
'Ode to Himself', 135–6;
'Queen and Huntress, Chaste
and Fair', 168; 'Still to be Neat,
Still to be Drest', 168–9;
'That Women are but Men's
Shadows', 152, 161.
Prose Works: 'Discoveries', 129,
141, 142, 147, 148, 153, 154,
155, 159, 174; *English
Grammar*, 154
Joyce, James, 11, 145, 162
Jung, Carl, 11
Juvenal, 22, 27, 41, 91

KIPLING, RUDYARD, 97
Knights, L. C., 181, 182

LAWRENCE, SIR THOMAS, 35
Leavis, F. R., 176
Lodge, Thomas, 26
Lovelace, Richard, 115
Lyly, John, 37–8

MANNINGHAM, JOHN, 46
Marlowe, Christopher, 23, 63,
     100, 121–2
Marston, John, 17, 41, 42–3, 56
Martial, 22, 160, 175
Meres, Francis, 14
Middleton, Thomas, 104
Milton, John, 11, 162
Molière, 86, 142, 170

NASHE, THOMAS, 13–14, 118

'OPINION', 106–12, 127, 134,
     149, 169
Osborne, John, 22, 117
Ovid, 22, 42, 43–4

PARTRIDGE, A. C., 182
Partridge, E. B., 181, 182
Pennanen, E. V., 182
Penniman, J. H., 179
Persius, 22
Petrarch, 22
Plautus, 20, 25
'Poetomachia, The', 41–2
Pope, Alexander, 44, 104, 128,
     163, 174
Pound, Ezra, 23
Puttenham, George, 54

RABELAIS, FRANÇOIS, 77
Racine, Jean, 52, 142
Raleigh, Sir Walter, 11
Return from Parnassus, The, 13
Rhodes, R. C., 181
Rowlands, Samuel, 31

Satiromastix, 45–6
Scaliger, Julius Caesar, 138, 139
Scogan, Henry, 79
Selden, John, 11
Seneca, 141
Shakespeare, 34, 35, 41, 61, 65,
     90, 102–3, 124, 126, 146,
     152, 157, 158, 170, 172,
     175.
  Individual Plays:
     A Midsummer Night's
     Dream, 33, 108, 119;
     Antony and Cleopatra, 52,
     62; As You Like It, 27;
     Coriolanus, 60; Hamlet, 33,
     51, 141; Henry V, 33;
     Henry VIII, 59; Julius
     Caesar, 180; Love's Labour's
     Lost, 67; Merchant of Venice,
     20; Much Ado About Nothing,
     20; Romeo and Juliet, 44, 67;
     Twelfth Night, 26; Two
     Gentlemen of Verona, 20
She Stoops to Conquer, 92
Sheridan, R. B., 95
Shirley, James, 147
Sidney, Sir Philip, 16, 18, 29, 32,
     36, 154
Skelton, John, 79, 174
Small, R. A., 179
Smith, G. G., 76, 169
Smollett, Tobias, 149
Southwell, Robert, 154
Spanish Tragedie, The, 19, 178
Spenser, Edmund, 21, 80, 134,
     142, 157, 175
Strindberg, August, 34, 94
Suckling, Sir John, 114
Swift, Jonathan, 91, 104, 128, 132
Swinburne, A. C., 113, 140, 168,
     169, 170

TALBERT, E. W., 178
Terence, 21, 37, 137
Theophrastus, 34
Townshend, F. L., 182
Trimpi, W., 182

'UNITIES, THE', 51–2, 142–3
Urfé, Honoré D', 131

Venice Preserved, 62
'Vetus Comedia', 27, 37, 117–19

Virgil, 42, 44
Vision of the Twelve Goddesses,
    The, 71–7

WEBBE, WILLIAM, 9
Webster, John, 170
Whetstone, George, 33
Wilde, Oscar, 95, 97
Wilson, E., 180
Wordsworth, William, 179
Wycherley, William, 33, 93–4